THE DEVELOPMENT OF PAST TENSE MORPHOLOGY IN L2 SPANISH

STUDIES IN BILINGUALISM (SiBil)

Volume 22

M. Rafael Salaberry

The Development of Past Tense Morphology in L2 Spanish

THE DEVELOPMENT OF
PAST TENSE MORPHOLOGY
IN L2 SPANISH

M. RAFAEL SALABERRY
Rice University

JOHN BENJAMINS PUBLISHING COMPANY
AMSTERDAM/PHILADELPHIA

TM The paper used in this publication meets the minimum requirements of American National Standard for Information Sciences — Permanence of Paper for Printed Library Materials, ANSI Z39.48-1984.

Library of Congress Cataloging-in-Publication Data

Salaberry, M. Rafael.
 The development of past tense morphology in L2 Spanish / M. Rafael Salaberry.
  p.   cm. -- (Studies in Bilingualism, ISSN 0928-1533 ; v. 22)
 Includes bibliographical references and index.
 1. Language acquisition. 2. Grammar, Comparative and general--Aspect. 3. Grammar, Comparative and general--Tense. 4. Spanish language--Acquisition I. Title. II. Series.
P118.S17   2000
401'.93--dc21   00-042898
ISBN 90 272 4132 5 (Eur.) / 1 55619 954 6 (US) (Hb)

John Benjamins Publishing Co. • P.O.Box 75577 • 1070 AN Amsterdam • The Netherlands
John Benjamins North America • P.O.Box 27519 • Philadelphia PA 19118-0519 • USA

A quienes me inspiraron a culminar este trabajo
desde cerca, María José
desde lejos, Mamy y Papy
desde siempre, Tata y Sor Olga

Table of Contents

Acknowledgments

I am very thankful to Jim Lantolf, Linda Waugh, and Allard Jongman for their feedback and support. I am also very thankful to Yas Shirai, Roger Andersen, Kathleen Bardovi-Harlig and the two anonymous reviewers of this series who provided me with very useful suggestions on previous manuscripts of the book. Nuria López-Ortega, Howard Grabois and Anita Pavlenko were always willing to help with data collection or to discuss any facet of the research process. Finally, María José Tort helped me with all aspects of the project since the pilot study to the conclusion of the book.

I am also very grateful to all the native and nearnative speakers who helped me during the pilot and main study for their generosity with their time: Brent Bingham, Pablo Boczskowski, Steve Bonta, Sandra Comstock, Gonzalo Kmaid, Irina Konstantinovski, Pablo Landoni, David Laraway, Jordi Marí, Hugo Moreno, Julie Pelto and María José Tort. The help of the coordinators of the Spanish courses SPA112, SPA123, SPA203 and SPA311 from the Fall 1996 academic session (Mary K. Redmond, Miriam Rice, Janine Routier-Pucci and María Stycos) from Cornell University was instrumental for the collection of data. Jose Barroso, Mary K. Redmond and Elvira Sanchez-Blake were very kind to allow me to visit their classes for the colection of data. I am especially grateful to all the students from all the Spanish sections who participated in the study for their generosity and their interest in the project.

CHAPTER 1

Introduction

The general objective of this study is the investigation of some of the cognitive processes underlying adult second language acquisition (SLA) through the analysis of the development of morphological markers of temporality in the acquisition of Spanish as a second language (L2) among native English speakers. In particular, I argue that the analysis of data on the development of verbal morphology provides empirical information to address two central questions in L2 acquisition: ultimate attainment in L2 development and the relative effect of instructed settings. In effect, paradigms of verbal morphology have become an obvious research target to uncover potential differences in the development of languages among children and adults, and to analyze the potential effect of instruction. In this respect, one of the objectives of L2 empirical research is to discover whether nonnative speakers ever achieve the same type and level of knowledge that native speakers possess: ultimate attainment (Coppieters 1987; Flynn & Manuel 1991; E. Klein 1995; Schwartz 1986; Towell & Hawkins 1994).[1] On the other hand, the effect of explicitly focusing the learner's attention on specific items of the L2 grammar has practical as well as theoretical significance (e.g., Bley-Vroman 1989; Birdsong 1992; Schmidt 1995).

The theoretical argument about the lack of ultimate attainment in the use of past tense verbal morphology is substantiated by both anecdotal and empirical evidence. First, anecdotal evidence and impressionistic accounts do not reveal a high level of congruity between native and nonnative speakers' use of morphological markers of past tense in the target language (e.g., Birdsong 1992; Coppieters 1987; Towell & Hawkins 1994). For instance, it is common to find native speakers of English who — in spite of being near-native speakers of

---

1. However, even if adult nonnative speakers exhibited similar linguistic judgments as native speakers in most types of controlled experimental settings (e.g., Flynn & Manuel 1991; White 1989), we cannot ascertain that both groups are accessing the same type of linguistic system (e.g., Paradis 1994; Towell & Hawkins 1994).

Spanish by many standards — claim that they "feel insecure" about the use of the above mentioned contrasts. In particular, Schmidt (1995) argues that grammatical features such as the subjunctive, *Tu-Vous* distinctions, and aspectual contrasts are all notorious problems for both tutored and untutored learners. Furthermore, and most important, the above mentioned type of impressionistic evidence is matched by the empirical analysis of the development of tense and aspect in L2 acquisition studies. For instance, Coppieters (1987: 567) analyzed the use of *Imparfait* versus *Passé Composé* in French (see Chapter 4) and concluded that

> extracting the precise contribution of an *Imparfait* or *Passé Composé* to the meaning of a given utterance in a given context is a very difficult and complex endeavor. Typically, the context will OVER-determine the meaning of the tense; it will be unclear exactly what the tense expresses by itself.[2]

Along the same lines, and based on data from L2 Spanish, García and vanPutte (1988) claimed that nonnative speakers seem to rely on more local cues for the selection of aspectual markers of past tense in Spanish, whereas native speakers are more attentive to the overall context of the narrative. Finally, irrespective of theoretical orientation, most studies show that the development of verbal morphology is a prime candidate for non-target-like acquisition (e.g., Bley-Vroman 1989; Coppieters 1987; Flynn & Manuel 1991; Schmidt 1995; Schwartz 1993). For instance, Paradis (1994) states that the complexity of morphosyntactic rules such as the subjunctive or aspectual differences in Romance languages are affected by maturational constraints.

Another phenomenon which represents a good testing ground for understanding adult L2 acquisition is the development of morphological markers of temporality in two distinct learning settings: untutored versus tutored learning (the latter especially represented in classroom environments). Untutored learners may be defined as natural learners because language development occurs in a natural setting of communication in the target language (i.e., normal social interaction).[3] On the other hand, there are two types of tutored learners: foreign

---

2. Not surprisingly, another grammatical item considered to be as difficult as the past tense aspectual distinction is the use of the Spanish subjunctive. Schmidt claims that the subjunctive qualifies among the "notoriously difficult areas" in L2 acquisition for both tutored and untutored learners (1995: 40).

3. The distinction may not be as clear-cut as one would wish it would be the case. For instance, the access to the L2 environment is determined primarily by the region or country where the learner lives. This method, however, may be inaccurate because, as is the case for many immigrant groups, access to the target language is relatively limited or simply non-existent (e.g., Schumann 1987).

language students (access to classroom instruction only) and second language students (access to both classroom and natural setting). For classroom learners in particular, language development occurs in an environment with access to different types of interactional settings and where there is no immediate need for the functional use of the L2. A review of the L2 acquisition literature shows that the use of morphological markers of past tense aspect among untutored learners is categorically different from classroom learners. In general, untutored learners do not rely on morphological endings to mark aspect, but they prefer to use pragmatic means such as calendric reference, interlocutor scaffolding, adverbial marking, etc. (e.g., Dietrich, Klein & Noyau 1995; Perdue & Klein 1992; Schumann 1987; Trévise 1987). In contrast, classroom learners normally engage in a meticulous analysis of verbal endings and their associated nuances of aspectual, tense and mode meaning (e.g., Bardovi-Harlig 1992, 1994; Bergström 1995; Hasbún 1995; Kaplan 1987; Ramsay 1990; Salaberry 1998).[4] In sum, the analysis of L2 development in classroom versus natural settings may provide information about the effect of differences in language input, formal and functional requirements, and interactional frameworks on the sequence and rate of acquisition of the target grammatical markers of temporality as well as their eventual ultimate attainment (e.g., Buczowska & Weist 1991).

Furthermore, from a practical point of view, understanding the stages of development of markers of temporality may inform instructional sequences. In effect, recent models of task-based instruction advocate the role of explicit pedagogical intervention to influence and speed up L2 development (e.g., DeKeyser 1998; Johnson 1996; Long & Robinson 1998; Loschky & Bley-Vroman 1993; Skehan 1998). For instance, Johnson claims that pedagogical intervention through the manipulation of task design factors such as task objectives and time constraints may help learners acquire various features of the target language. Similarly, Long and Robinson advocate that pedagogical intervention should be preceded by the learner's focus on the achievement of specific task objectives. In particular, to achieve the pedagogical objectives proposed by task-based methodologies with respect to inflectional morphology,

---

Furthermore, different degrees of literacy (as reflected in formal tutoring) also have an effect on the tutored-untutored contrast. For instance, immigrant workers — compared to university students — will not normally have access to formal education other than limited on-the-job exposure to the target language (see also Birdsong 1989 for differences in grammaticality judgments among literates and illiterates).

4. This is especially true of university-level instruction where verbal paradigms constitute the sine qua non of language learning.

it is necessary to understand how semantic-discursive distinctions (i.e., tense and aspect) are represented in verbal endings throughout various stages of development. That is, the selection of the appropriate type of pedagogical intervention as well as the timing of such pedagogical manipulation must follow the stages that learners go through in their development of inflectional morphology (e.g., Bardovi-Harlig & Reynolds 1995; Pienemann 1985, 1986, 1988, 1989). For instance, Bardovi-Harlig and Reynolds (1995) claim that the design of classroom pedagogical activities should be based on three main factors: increased focus on meaning, use of positive evidence, and reliance on information about acquisitional sequences.

1.1   English-Spanish contrasts

As mentioned above, the acquisition of the Preterite–Imperfect distinction in L2 Spanish is notoriously difficult for L1 English speakers. To show why this is the case I will present a contrastive analysis of both linguistic systems. The Preterite–Imperfect contrast in Spanish is the realization of the Perfective–Imperfective aspectual distinction by means of inflectional morphology. English, on the other hand, does not make such an overt grammatical distinction of aspect in past tense (morphological affix). Instead, English uses other means to convey information about the aspectual "contour" of a specific situation: aspectual particles and the Progressive. Aspectual particles (free morphemes) shift the aspectual nature of a particular predicate: from atelic to telic (the "telos" refers to the completion point normally represented by internal arguments of the verb; see Chapter 2 for more detail). For example *to eat* (no completion point implied) differs aspectually from *to eat up* (completion point implied). Bybee and Dahl (1989: 85–6) refer to aspectual particles as "bounders" because they typically provide a limit and/or make the verb transitive. The second most common means of conveying aspectual distinctions in past tense English is the use of the Progressive. For instance, the aspectual distinction marked with Preterite (PRET) and Imperfect (IMP) in Spanish in the following sentences may possibly be conveyed with the contrast simple past tense versus Progressive past tense in English:

(1)   a.   Juan durmió
            John slept.PRET
            'John slept'
        b.   Juan dormía
            John slept.IMP
            'John was sleeping'

However, the decontextualized example presented in (1) does not account for the actual range of uses of the simple past as opposed to the Progressive. In fact, *Juan dormía* may also be translated as *John slept*, as this is the most common option (default) unless one is contrasting two co-occurring events.

On the other hand, the example in (2) presents an apparently transparent correlation of uses of the Preterite–Imperfect contrast in Spanish with the simple past-past Progressive contrast in English.

(2)   El teléfono sonó   mientras Juan dormía (IMP)
       the phone   rang.PRET while   John slept.IMP
       'The phone rang while John was sleeping'

However, the overgeneralization of the distinction Preterite–Imperfect in Spanish with the simple past-past Progressive in English beyond the case exemplified in (2) is not satisfactory on two counts. First, it is not obligatorily marked in English for the same range of semantic contrasts common in Spanish. For instance, the use of Progressive in English may not normally be used to refer to habituals as is the case in Spanish: the use of the Progressive in English in sentence (3) renders an ungrammatical sentence.

(3)   Cuando era   niño jugaba   con mis vecinos
       when   was.IMP child played.IMP with my neighbors
       'When I was a child I *was playing/played with my neighbors'

There is another periphrasis in English that may be used to convey the notion of habitual actions in the past: *used to* (it is also possible to use *would play* to convey habituality). Second, the direct correlation of the Spanish Imperfect-Preterite contrast with the English past Progressive-simple past is invalidated by the fact that the periphrastic option in English is not grammatical with stative verbs (cf. Vendler 1967):[5]

(4)   a.   *I was seeing him running
       b.   I saw him running

In contrast, in Spanish both Imperfect and Preterite are grammatical options as exemplified in (5). As a consequence, the aspectual meaning expressed by these sentences is extremely difficult to convey to an English native speaker.

(5)   a.   Lo veía correr
       b.   Lo vi correr

---

5. See Chapter 2, Section 2.3 for the use of operational tests to classify lexical aspectual classes.

It is important to mention that there are other intricacies of the aspectual system in Spanish that cannot be directly represented in English (one-to-one mapping). For instance, the combinatorial number of grammatically marked aspectual values available in Spanish far exceeds the number in English. If we consider that the use of Progressive forms in past tense is not an exclusive option of English, but of Spanish as well, we can see that Spanish offers the option of a Progressive as well as non-Progressive Imperfect (e.g., González 1995). To that we may also add the optional use of the perfective Progressive which roughly corresponds to the aorist aspect of Greek. As a consequence, we obtain a grid of four distinct options in Spanish that correlate to only two options in English.

(6)   Juan durmió (PRET)   = John slept
(7)   Juan dormía (IMP)   = John slept
                                             = John was sleeping
(8)   Juan estaba durmiendo (IMP-PROGR)   = John was sleeping
(9)   Juan estuvo durmiendo (PRET-PROGR) = ?

Perhaps the most intricate semantic nuance of aspect for the English speaker is provided by the perfective Progressive (sentence (9)). Comrie (1976: 23) argues that English may approximate the meaning of this particular aspectual value with the use of periphrases such as: *I happened one day to be sleeping*, or *It happened one day that I was sleeping*.

In essence, from a comparative perspective, English speakers are likely to mark past tense in Spanish in the following way: (a) they may overextend the use of a single marker of past tense (Preterite only), (b) they may rely on two options if they equate Preterite with simple past tense and Imperfect with the Progressive (thereby, incorrectly overextending the use of the Progressive), (c) they may fail to mark past (most likely with the use of Present), (d) or they could be successful from the start (not documented to the best of my knowledge). However, the previous contrastive analysis is an oversimplification. In fact, researchers have considered factors other than a comparative analysis of linguistic systems such as the role of lexical semantics or the cognitive saliency and frequency of verbal endings.

Finally, it is important to mention that in both English and Spanish the morphological marker of past tense is polysemous (Fleischman 1989, 1990; Taylor 1989). Three groups of meaning are associated with past tense marking in English: temporality per se, counterfactuality (*If I had enough time ...*), and pragmatic softening (*Excuse me, I wanted to ask you something*). In standard Spanish, however, counterfactuality is expressed by the subjunctive past tense instead of indicative past tense (but see Ocampo 1990 for possible disappearance of subjunctive forms among bilingual Spanish-English speakers). For example, the verb *tener* (to have) has a Preterite and Imperfect form in indicative past tense (*tuvo* and *tenía* respectively), as well as a past form subjunctive (*tuviera* or *tuviese*). In this respect, the English native speaker may transfer the use of regular past tense for counterfactuality from the L1. On the other hand, the use of pragmatic softeners should not create any mismatch in the choice of form if there is transfer from L1 to L2. Alternatively, it is open to question whether nonnative speakers will be able to identify these functions of past tense forms not directly related to temporality per se (see Chapter 7 for discussion of these issues).

1.2   Conflicting theoretical claims

Given the complexity of verbal morphological systems, it is not surprising that the analysis of the acquisition of tense and aspect has become a central topic of research in studies of classroom L2 acquisition in recent years (e.g., Andersen 1991; Andersen & Shirai 1994, 1996; Bardovi-Harlig 1992, 1994, 1995a; Bergström 1995; Buczowska & Weist 1991; Dietrich, Klein & Noyau 1995; Harley 1989; Hasbún 1995; Housen 1994; Kaplan 1987; Lafford 1996; Liskin-Gasparro 1997; Ramsay 1990; Robison 1995; Salaberry 1998, 1999, 2000; Salaberry & Shirai, forthcoming; Shirai & Kurono 1998; Slabakova 1997, 1999). The earlier studies analyzed the effect of inherent temporal features of verbal predicates on the selection and use of verbal morphology (e.g., Andersen 1991; Ramsay 1990; Robison 1995), whereas more recent studies have expanded the research perspective to include the influence of the more encompassing discursive environment in which aspect marking occurs (e.g., Bardovi-Harlig 1995a; Housen 1994), or formal syntactic frameworks (e.g., Slabakova 1997; Slabakova & Montrul, forthcoming). However, there is still conflicting evidence about the theoretical status of the system being developed by L2 learners, especially in terms of the sequence and rate of development of aspectual contrasts, the potential effect of learning setting (i.e., tutored versus untutored learners), and the potential impact of pedagogical manipulations of the input data. For instance, Andersen and Shirai (1994) propose that the inherent temporal features of verbal predicates (i.e., aspectual information) will be represented in the use of verbal morphology of L2 learners before information about tense, whereas Wiberg (1996) argues that tense will be represented in the L2 verbal morphology at the same time, or even before, aspectual contrasts are represented.

There are several factors that may account for the contradictory claims.

First, part of the discrepancy across studies can be attributed to the reliance on different theoretical perspectives that provide the theoretical framework to understand the development of L2 verbal morphology. For example, very few studies have analyzed the development of past tense aspect in classroom learners from a narrative perspective or more formal perspectives such as Government and Binding (GB) theory or the minimalist approach (e.g., Giorgi & Pianesi 1997). Second, the few available studies from any of these perspectives do not, arguably, provide enough evidence to substantiate their claims (for an analysis of the current state of studies on the acquisition of L2 Spanish see Montrul & Salaberry, forthcoming). For instance, analyses from a narrative perspective have mostly focused on languages such as English (e.g., Bardovi-Harlig 1995b) or Dutch (e.g. Housen 1994), which do not make overt grammatical aspectual distinctions as is the case in Spanish (Preterite versus Imperfect) or French (*Passé Composé* versus *Imparfait*). Second, there are substantial differences in data collection procedures and research design that make incompatible the comparison of data among studies. For instance, most studies carried out in the US have relied on the quantitative analysis of controlled production of the target language (e.g., Bardovi-Harlig 1992, 1994, 1995a; Bergström 1995; Hasbún 1995; Ramsay 1990; Robison 1995; Salaberry 1998). In contrast, most studies carried out by European researchers have relied mostly on the qualitative analysis of data of migrant workers (e.g., Dietrich, Klein & Noyau 1995; Perdue & Klein 1992; Trévise 1987).

A third potential difference across studies is related to the effect of learning setting. For instance, classroom learners receive explicit instruction on the two contrasting options available in Spanish to mark verbal endings in past tense (i.e., Preterite and Imperfect). This instructional effect may, arguably, lead learners to disregard the potential overgeneralization of the correlation of the simple past-past Progressive contrast in English with the Preterite-past Progressive contrast in Spanish. As a consequence, learners attempt to mark aspectual distinctions with the less transparent Preterite–Imperfect contrast that is exclusively marked in verbal endings. Previous research has extensively documented such constraining factors in the acquisition of inflectional morphology (e.g., Andersen 1986; Hasbún 1995; Liskin-Gasparro 1997). In fact, the comparative analysis of aspectual marking in academic and natural environments may have consequences beyond the analysis of the development of verbal morphology. For instance, Schwartz claims that learners have ready and constant access to positive evidence in a natural setting, whereas tutored learners are more likely to have access to mostly negative evidence — or at least explicit evidence — which may not be useful for language development. On the other hand, the analysis of the sequential development of past tense aspectual distinctions in tutored academic environments may have a direct impact on the implementation of pedagogical practices, especially in terms of the analysis of the relative weight of the various factors that shape morphosyntactic development (see Chapter 2). In fact, some researchers have explicitly or implicitly argued in favor of the role of instruction in SLA. For example, Birdsong (1992: 742) argues that "… expertise in the domain of L2A would imply skill in attending to and organizing target-language input, and an ability to overcome biases imposed by one's native language that may misguide decisions about and representations of target language structure." Hence, the major role of formal instruction is to make the learner aware of the less salient grammatical elements of the L2 (e.g., DeKeyser 1996; Rutherford 1987; Sato 1990; Schmidt 1990, 1995; Sharwood-Smith 1993). In contrast, Lightbown (1987) claims that, in spite of the capricious ordering of the linguistic structures presented to L2 students in the traditional form-focused class, learner internal factors guide students towards acquiring the underlying structure of the L2 in a natural way.[6]

1.3   Focus of the study

According to Comrie (1976: 3) aspect refers to the "different ways of viewing the internal temporal constituency of a situation" (aspect as the contrast of internal compositionality versus totality of the event). In terms of language acquisition Binnick (1991: 209) states that "the problem comes when we try to understand what it is that the speaker of a language with aspectual oppositions knows which a nonspeaker does not know, and consider how to model this knowledge in the grammar." Therefore, the basic assumption to be made in this study is that knowing a language includes knowing the semantic value of aspectual contrasts and how to mark them in verbal morphological endings as is the case in Spanish (e.g., Andersen 1991; Smith 1991). As a consequence, three major questions will guide the analysis of the studies to be presented in Chapters 5 through 7: (1) what is the developmental pattern of acquisition of Spanish past tense verbal morphology among tutored (academic) learners?, (2) what are the factors which may account for the particular distribution of morphological

---

6. The argument of "learner-internal factors" may refer to formal linguistic constraints as established in Government and Binding theory (e.g., Flynn & Manuel 1990; Schwartz 1986), semantic universals (e.g., Bickerton 1981), pragmatic-discursive universals (e.g., Hopper 1982; Housen 1994), or learning strategies. On the other hand, universals should not necessarily be considered "internal factors."

endings at any given stage?, and (3) how does instruction affect the movement from one stage to the next? The analysis of the data will test the theoretical claim proposed in the lexical aspect hypothesis. I argue that the analysis of the data to be described in this study in conjunction with the analysis of the data base from previous studies of untutored learners (e.g., Dietrich et al. 1995; Perdue & Klein 1992; Sato 1990; Schumann 1987; Trévise 1987) as well as tutored learners (e.g., Bardovi-Harlig 1995a; Bergström 1995; Harley 1989; Hasbún 1995; Kaplan 1987; Lafford 1996; Liskin-Gasparro 1997; Ramsay 1990; Robison 1995; Salaberry 1998) may provide some preliminary answers about the contrast in the development of tense-aspect inflectional morphology in instructed settings.

The selection of Spanish as the target language is substantiated by the fact that there are very few analyses of the development of past tense verbal morphology in L2 Spanish irrespective of mode (written versus oral), communicative goal (controlled versus open-ended) or communicative setting (natural versus classroom learners). Previous studies of Spanish academic learning have concentrated on (i) the analysis of written tasks (e.g., Hasbún 1995) or highly controlled oral tasks (e.g., Ramsay 1990), and (ii) cross-sectional studies (e.g., Hasbún 1995; Ramsay 1990). Among studies of natural learners, the acquisition of Spanish has been the subject of very few analyses (e.g., Andersen 1986). A clear sign of such lack of prominence is the fact that Spanish is not among the languages studied by one of the most ambitious projects on the acquisition of temporality in L2 learners: the European Science Foundation Project (e.g., Dietrich et al. 1995; Klein & Perdue 1992). On the other hand, the study reported in Andersen (1986) and subsequent reanalyses of the same data base (1989, 1991, 1994) have become prominent in the literature on L2 acquisition. The analysis from Andersen (1986), however, has limited generalizability because its data base is restricted to oral interviews with two adolescents. The data to be analyzed in the present volume includes (1) an oral narrative of a silent film with a specific functional goal, (2) a written cloze test and an editing task, and (3) recorded data on the discussion about the selection of morphological markers of temporality among the group of speakers who narrated the film (data across tasks). The inclusion of longitudinal data provides a more extended picture of the development of aspectual distinction among the same group of speakers: five levels of experience with L2 Spanish recorded at two different times (approximately two months apart during an academic semester). On the other hand, the analysis of cross-sectional data allows for a higher degree of generalizability of the findings from the longitudinal analysis: two levels of experience in L2 Spanish and one control group (monolingual Spanish speakers).

In sum, the present study is important for the following reasons: (1) there are few empirical studies which address the nature of aspectual development in L2 acquisition in general and Spanish in particular, (2) the present study provides both cross-sectional and longitudinal analysis of the data, (3) it provides an analysis of the development of aspect across language tasks, (4) it analyzes oral narratives instead of written narratives, and (5) it includes an analysis of the online processing of past tense morphological marking (joint problem-solving think aloud).

The organization of the chapters is the following. In Chapter 2 I outline the general problem faced by the L1 English speaker (i.e., lack of correspondence of the aspectual distinctions present in English vis-à-vis Spanish), and I describe the notion of aspect within the overall framework of temporality marking. I specifically point out the limitations in the use of operational tests for the classification of lexical aspectual classes when the overall context of discourse is not considered as the framework of analysis of such aspectual classes. In Chapter 3 I review some of the most relevant studies on the acquisition of tense and aspect in L1 acquisition, and I claim that, although the number of studies which focus on the acquisition of Romance languages is limited, it seems that the Preterite appears first in development (associated with a limited number of verbs) followed by the Imperfect at around age three (in the context of temporal and non-temporal phenomena such as mood). In Chapter 4 I review previous empirical studies on the development of past tense markers among L2 adult learners, especially with regards to Spanish and other Romance languages. I show that the reanalysis of several data sets, especially for beginning stages of development, raises some doubts about the validity of the role of lexical aspectual classes for the use of past tense markers among less experienced classroom learners. In Chapter 5 I present the analysis and discussion of the data from the pilot study that preceded the present study, I substantiate the operationalization of two sets of null and alternative hypotheses, and I describe the research design and methodology of the main study. In Chapter 6 I present the results of the main study and in Chapter 7 I discuss those results in the context of the earlier empirical investigations on the development of past tense markers in academic L2 Spanish.

CHAPTER 2

Aspect

The analysis of the development of aspectual distinctions in both L1 and L2 acquisition is inextricably linked to the theoretical characterization of aspect as a linguistic category. The conceptual understanding of aspect, however, does not appear to be as straightforward as it would seem. For instance, Olsen (1997: 3) claims that "given the variety of lexical, grammatical, semantic, and pragmatic elements contributing to the interpretation of aspect, it is not surprising that analyses — whether broadly theoretical or examinations of aspect in a particular language — differ widely." Consequently, it is necessary to address the theoretical conceptualization that underlies various definitions of aspect that have been used as the foundation for the analysis of the development of past tense verbal morphology in Spanish. In this chapter I present an overview of aspect as a linguistic phenomenon which is part of the larger notion of temporality. In Section 1 I review various definitions of aspect as a grammatical marker of temporality. In Section 2 I distinguish the notions of lexical and grammatical aspect and I elaborate on the components that make up the inherent lexical value of aspect. In Section 3 I review the various operational tests of aspectual categories originally developed for English, and later used in the analysis of data from Spanish. Finally, in Section 4 I analyze two debatable classifications of verbs into lexical aspectual classes: accomplishments versus achievements and statives versus achievements.

2.1 Definition of aspect

Time and space are two physical domains that are represented in linguistic phenomena. Time and space are also basic cognitive categories that shape our experience of the world. For example, in a cross-linguistic analysis of the development of tense and aspect systems, Bybee and Dahl (1989: 77–83) show that the Progressive morphological marker evolves from locative expressions (see also Desclés 1989; Giorgi & Pianesi 1997). Furthermore, Fleischman (1989, 1990) argues that the spatial concept of distance may be used as a semantic prime for both semantic and pragmatic phenomena: for instance temporality as well as politeness (see also Frawley 1992: 370–1). Klein (1994: 1) points out that only temporality — as opposed to space — is redundantly encoded in every finite verb. He argues further that linguistic analysis has concentrated on the inherent temporal characteristics of predicates even though temporality is also encoded in lexical semantics beyond the head of the verb phrase (adverbials, particles, etc.). Tense and aspect are the two major concepts of temporality encoded in verbal morphology.[1] Tense is a deictic category that relates the time of an event frame to a tense locus (Chung & Timberlake 1985: 203). In general, tense is defined with reference to the time of the utterance or, alternatively to the speech time (Lyons 1968: 315). When it is relative to speech time, it refers to absolute tense; when it is relative to the time of the utterance, it refers to relative tense (Comrie 1976: 2). In both definitions tense is the function of two different times: time of event and time of locus. Reichenbach (1947) proposed a third reference point (point R) in order to account for the grammaticality of certain sequences of tenses. With three points of reference instead of two it is possible to account for more temporal relations (Binnick 1991: 339–53; Klein 1994: 19). For example, in simple past tense time of the event and reference point coincide, whereas in the perfect tense they do not.

Comrie (1976) points out that there are two options to relate a situation to the time line. First, the location of the situation is related to a specific point or segment (tense). Conversely, the internal temporal contour of the situation is represented as a point or stretch on the time line (aspect). Hence, aspect is concerned with situation-internal time, whereas tense is relative to situation-external time. Comrie defines aspect as the "way of viewing the internal temporal constituency of a situation" (beginning, middle and end) (p. 5). From this perspective, aspect, unlike tense, is not a deictic category because it is not relative to the time of the utterance.[2] An alternative perspective on the characterization

---

1. Tense has been studied for over two and a half centuries, whereas the modern concept of aspect has only recently been established since the 1930s, according to Binnick (1991: ix).

2. Aspect is the product of a French translation of the Russian word *vid*, which is a cognate of vision or view. The analysis of aspect has been a traditional target of Slavic linguistics since all verbs in Russian mark aspectual distinction (Perfective versus Imperfective) in all tenses. As such, this Perfective–Imperfective dichotomy has been regarded as the archetypal representative of aspectual differences. In other languages such as Greek one finds three categories of aspectual distinction: Imperfect-pluperfect-aorist.

of aspect is provided by Chung and Timberlake (1985) who define aspect as the different relationships of a predicate to the time interval over which it occurs (event frame). Two concepts are crucial to the latter definition: (1) the notion of "change-no change" is central to aspect (states and events can remain constant or change over time), and (2) the interval of time to be related is selected by the speaker (the situation may occur within the event frame or over a larger interval of time). Klein (1994) presents a more formal approach to the deictic notion of aspect hinted at by Chung and Timberlake. In any given utterance Klein distinguishes between a non-finite component (INF) and a finite component (FIN). The former represents a selective description of a situation generally associated with a predicate and its arguments and even adverbials (lexical content). The latter refers to the time for which the claim about the situation has been made: Topic Time (TT). Klein defines the TT in the following manner:

> Although a situation that is partly described by the lexical content of an utterance has a time — the time of situation (TSit) — it is not TSit which is directly linked to the time of utterance (TU). There is an intervening link — the time for which the particular utterance makes an assertion" (p. 37). Aspect refers to the relationship between TT and TSit. That is to say, it depicts the way the situation is "hooked up to some TT"

In contrast, the relationship between TT and TU represents tense. Klein exemplifies the above mentioned contrast with a scenario where a judge asks a witness the following question "What did you notice when you entered the room?" The witness responds "A man was lying on the floor." (p. 40). In this case, TU is obviously the time at which the question and answer exchange occurs, whereas TT is represented by the time at which the witness entered the room. On the other hand, TSit refers to the information portrayed by the verbal predicate and associated arguments and adjuncts. That is to say, in this case the relationship between TT and TU (tense) represents past tense, whereas the relationship between TT and TSit (aspect) represents Imperfective aspect.

The analysis of verbal morphology representing tense and aspect has also been studied from the perspective of Government and Binding theory (e.g., de Miguel 1992; Tenny 1994) and, more recently, the minimalist approach (e.g., Giorgi & Pianesi 1997; Slabakova 1997, 1999; Slabakova & Montrul, forthcoming). For example, according to deMiguel (1992), the aspectual value of a verb will constitute a projection of its lexical value. Information about aspect is incorporated in the lexical entry of the predicate by means of a special covert argument: davidsonian argument ⟨e⟩ (event argument).[3] The projection of the eventive argument provides information that is not subsumed under the TENSE node; instead, it will project a new functional category: the aspectual phrase (AspP). The AspP is represented by a binary node: ± perfective. Most important, the aspectual nature of the event argument of the predicate will have overall syntactic consequences. Some of these syntactic manifestations of the role of the AspP have been studied extensively in Spanish: passives, absolute participles (deMiguel 1992; Hernanz 1991), impersonal *se* (deMiguel 1992; Suñer 1990; Zagona 1994), etc.

Recent theoretical accounts on the notions of tense and aspect have recognized that tense and aspect are interrelated in various ways. For instance, Comrie argues that the overt morphological marking of aspect is more commonly represented in the past tense than any other tense (pp. 71–73). This entails that a theory of aspect cannot be developed in isolation from other temporal phenomena. For example, Lyons (1968: 306) argues that the future tense is also a modal (e.g., *shall* and *will* in English). Similarly, in French (and English as well), the past tense functions as a modal when used in hypothetical clauses (e.g., *Si j'étais ...*). A similar construction in Spanish requires the subjunctive. In fact, both tense and aspect are also associated with other non-temporal phenomena such as quantification (Smith 1991; Verkuyl 1993). As we will see the [+quantized] or [–quantized] nature of an internal argument may have an impact on the classification of predicates into aspectual classes. Finally, from a broader perspective, aspect is also associated with the larger discourse in which the utterance is embedded (Binnick 1991: Ch. 8).

2.2   Covert and overt categories of aspect

Aspectual distinctions in a language can be marked overtly (grammatical aspect and Aktionsarten) or covertly (inherent lexical aspect). Table 2.1 presents a summary of the features of these categories (Binnick 1991). In spite of their inherent semantic value (Aristotelian aspect), verbs may be overtly marked by grammatical aspect. Grammatical aspect is obligatorily encoded in the form of auxiliaries plus participles (e.g., *Passé Composé* in French), inflectional

---

3.   An event argument is an extra argument also called Davidsonian after D. Davidson who proposed the existence of such an argument to account for the grammaticality of action predicates. However, ter Meulen (1995) rejects the proposal that aspectual information can be encoded in a Davidsonian event argument.

Table 2.1. Three different classifications of aspectual distinctions[a]

Grammatical aspect	Aktionsart	Aristotelian Aspect
grammaticized	lexical	lexical
systematic	unsystematic	unsystematic
obligatory	optional	obligatory
language specific	language specific	universal
overt	overt	covert

[a] Binnick labels inherent aspect as Aristotelian aspect since the notion of inherent semantic differences associated with each verb is due to Aristotle.

morphology (Imperfect-Preterite in Spanish), periphrastics (Progressive in English, French and Spanish), etc. Aktionsart is represented by secondary modifications of basic verb meanings (Klein 1994: 17) usually by the use of affixes and sometimes periphrastics. For instance, in English, verbs may be qualified in terms of aspect by means of adding prepositions which do not alter the verb form and which are not obligatory: *eat up, read through*, etc. or periphrastics such as *to resume* (Binnick 1991: 207). German offers similar examples: *erblühen* (to start flowering: inchoative aspect), *blühen* (flowering) and *verblühen* (to wither: resultative aspect).

Some researchers in the L1 acquisition literature have collapsed these two types of aspect (Aktionsart and lexical aspect) into a single category (e.g., deMiguel 1992; Shirai 1991). The conflation of these two categories does not generate any major consequences for the analysis of grammatical aspectual development in Spanish for three main reasons. First, Spanish does not use prefixes or prepositions to the extent that the Germanic languages do (but see Nishida 1994 for the analysis of aspectual *se* in Spanish). Second, there are underlying similarities between lexical aspect and Aktionsarten: they are lexical and unsystematic (see Table 2.1). Third, grammatical aspect — but not Aktionsart — is obligatorily encoded in each verb (restricted to past tense in the Romance languages). The relationship between the overt category of aspectual distinctions in Spanish (grammatical aspect) and the overt one (lexical aspect) will be addressed in the following section.

2.2.1 *Lexical aspect and viewpoint aspect*

The inherent lexical meaning of the verb is determined by the temporal features intrinsic in the semantics of the predicate in its base form. The notion of inherent semantic differences of verbs comes from Aristotle's classification of verb types:

energiai (which was later subdivided into *ékhein* — states — and *energein* — activities) and *kinesis* (accomplishments and achievements). Kenny (1963) maintained the unitary classification of accomplishments and achievements, which he labeled performances. Subsequently, Vendler (1967) classified verbs into four types: States, activities, accomplishments and achievements. The following definitions take into account some modifications introduced by Comrie (1976):

– States: no input of energy
– Activities: arbitrary beginning and end point (process)
– Accomplishments: durative and inherent end point
– Achievements: inherent end point, but no duration (punctual)

The Vendlerian classification of lexical aspectual classes is particularly important because it has been used as the framework of analysis of aspectual morphological marking in the studies of L2 Spanish by Andersen (1986, 1989, 1991) and subsequent researchers (e.g., Hasbún 1995; Ramsay 1990). The reanalysis of Comrie takes care of some inconsistencies in Vendler's original definition. For instance, Comrie (1976: 49) points out that it is not accurate to say that statives involve no change (e.g., being standing in a position may or may not involve change), nor that dynamic situations necessarily involve change (e.g., an oscilloscope emitting a pure tone at 300 Hz does not necessarily involve visible change). A more accurate representation is to say that statives do not require effort whether from inside (agentive) or from outside (non-agentive). A list of typical verbs associated with each aspectual class is presented in Table 2.2.

Table 2.2. Classification of some verbs according to lexical aspectual class (based on Andersen, 1991)

States	Activities	Accomplishments	Achievements
have	run	paint a picture	recognize (sth.)
possess	walk	make a chair	realize (sth.)
desire	swim	build a house	find (sth.)
like	breathe	write a novel	win the race
want	pull	grow up	lose (sth.)

A more formal characterization of lexical aspectual classes of predicates has been provided by Dowty (1986: 42):

– Stative: A sentence φ is a stative iff it follows from the truth of φ at an interval I that φ is true at all subintervals of I.

–   Activity: A sentence φ is an activity iff it follows from the truth of φ at an interval I that φ is true at all subintervals of I down to a certain limit in size.
–   Accomplishment/achievement: A sentence φ is an accomplishment/ achievement iff it follows from the truth of φ at an interval I that φ is false at all subintervals of I.

As we can see Dowty does not distinguish between accomplishments and achievements. Furthermore, Dowty's classification rests on the assumption of a primitive "notion of truth of a sentence with respect to an interval of time" (p. 41). I will expand on this issue in subsequent sections and Section 2.4 in particular. ter Meulen (1995: 6) has offered a more metaphorical representation of the three dynamic aspectual classes

> holes correspond to activities or processes, description of events that apply throughout their internal structure homogeneously ... filters correspond to accomplishments ... which are descriptions of change that never apply to any part of an event they describe, ... plugs are special cases of filters commonly called 'achievements,' which are in a conceptual sense instantaneous, since they do not consist of an initial and a final stage

The classification of lexical aspectual classes can also be made in terms of three basic semantic features of the verb: dynamicity, durativity and telicity. According to telicity (from Greek telos: limit, end, or goal) states and activities are atelic (no inherent end point) whereas accomplishments and achievements are telic (inherent end point).[4] Dynamicity contrasts stative versus non-stative verbs (activities, accomplishments and achievements). Finally, durativity distinguishes non-durative punctual events (achievements) from durative events. Among these components, the telic-atelic distinction has been regarded as the basic semantic feature determining lexical aspect (e.g., Dowty 1986; Hopper 1982; Maingueneau 1994; Smith 1991; Tenny 1994; Verkuyl 1993). For example, Hopper (1982: 6) argues that 'the potential or real bounding of events in (this) discourse is a significant parameter in the strategies for formulating an utterance (see Depraetere 1995 for a principled distinction between boundedness and telicity). Similarly, Smith (1991: 19) claims that the fact that 'telicity is generally not open to aspectual choice is that humans see it as an essential property. Telicity is not, therefore, a property that can be shifted for purposes of emphasis and point of

---

4. The original article published by Vendler in 1957 coincided with the appearance of Garey's proposal (1957). Both articles recognized the semantic distinction between telic and atelic events. Subsequently Kenny (1963) classified verbs into three categories: states, activities, and performances; thereby, conflating accomplishments and achievements into the single telic category of performances.

view.' For example, if we interchange the prepositional phrase in sentence (1a) (a locative PP) with the one of 1b (a directional PP), the aspectual nature of the verb constellation will be fundamentally changed (examples are from Smith 1991: 7): from an activity to an accomplishment.

(1)   a.   Mary walked [in the park]. (locative: atelic)
       b.   Mary walked [to the park]. (directional: telic)

On the other hand, durativity has been considered non-essential for the classification of verbs into semantic aspectual classes (e.g., Chung & Timberlake 1985; Dowty 1986; Kenny 1963; Klein 1994; Mourelatos 1981). A more extended discussion of the effect of semantic factors will be presented in Section 2.4.

Lexical aspect is not the only determinant of grammatical aspect. For instance, in Spanish any verb type, irrespective of its lexical aspectual class can be marked with Imperfect or Preterite. Therefore, it is necessary to make a distinction between lexical aspect and viewpoint aspect. Smith (1991) defines the selection of aspectual marking as a process incorporating two distinct levels which are independent from each other: the situation type (verb + arguments + adverbials), and viewpoint aspect. The situation type represents the way humans perceive and categorize situations (verb + arguments). It constitutes a covert category of grammar instantiated in all languages (cf., cognitive concepts such as telicity). On the other hand, viewpoint aspect refers to the partial or full view of a particular situation type as marked by an overt grammatical morpheme. Smith argues that lexical aspectual categories are not language dependent, but based on human cognitive abilities. In contrast, viewpoint aspect appears to be inherently tied to cultural language-dependent conventions. In sum, aspect may be defined as a general cognitive phenomenon (e.g., Reinhart 1984) and as a language dependent phenomenon (e.g., Smith 1983, 1986, 1991). However, not all perspectives consider the contribution of the situation type as a fundamental component of aspectual marking. For example, Lunn (1985: 51) claims that "(the Spanish) Preterite–Imperfect distinction is defined not in terms of categories of verbs or of time spans, but by the point of view which a speaker adopts with respect to a verbal situation." Lunn claims that this second component of aspect subsumes the first one, thereby making it unnecessary to keep such a convoluted characterization of aspect.

2.2.2 *Components of lexical aspectual values*

Klein (1994) and Verkuyl (1993) argue that linguistic analysis has concentrated on the inherent temporal characteristics of predicates even though temporality is also encoded in lexical semantics beyond the head of the verb phrase (adverbials, particles, etc.). By definition, the lexical aspectual class of the verb is not determined solely by the verb, but also by its subcategorization grid (internal and external arguments) and also adjuncts (see also Tenny 1994). For example, the quantized feature of the internal argument changes the basic semantic nature of the predicate in an essential way. The effect of the distinction mass-count nouns on the telic nature of the predicate is exemplified in sentences (2a) and (2b):

(2)   a.   Mary smoked [cigarettes]. (–quantized: atelic)
         b.   Mary smoked [a cigarette]. (+quantized: telic)

If we consider that the quantized nature of the internal argument of the predicate will obligatorily affect the inherent semantic value of the verb (Verkuyl 1989, 1993), one must go beyond the level of the head of the verb phrase in the analysis of lexical aspect. Along the same lines, Fleischman (1990: 21) adds that the definiteness of the internal argument has an effect on the aspectual profile of a sentence. With regard to Spanish in particular, Bull (1965: 169) claims that events and not verbs underlie the classification of cyclic and non-cyclic functional sets: *to eat* is non-cyclic, but *to eat an apple* is cyclic.

Even the nature of the subject of the utterance (the external argument) may affect the inherent semantic aspectual value of the verb (e.g., Depraetere 1995; Langacker 1982; Maingueneau 1994). For instance, Mainguenau (1994: 71) shows the effect of the external argument on the semantic value of the predicate in French:

(3)   Luc a   franchi le pont   toute la matinée
        Luc has crossed the bridge all   the morning
        'Luc crossed the bridge all morning long'

(4)   La foule a   franchi le pont   toute la matinée
        the crowd has crossed the bridge all   the morning
        'The crowd crossed the bridge all morning long'

In example (3) one surmises (based on world knowledge) that Luc traversed the bridge several times during the morning — not that it took him the whole morning to cross the bridge. In example (4), in contrast, it is reasonable to assume that it took a whole morning for the crowd to cross the same bridge (again, this is based on our knowledge about the world: see Klein 1994). The latter case represents the single crossing of many people and the former many crossings of a single person (see below for further analysis of distinctions between lexical and world knowledge). Finally, adjuncts are another basic element in the composition of the aspectual value of a predicate.

Among adjuncts, the effect of adverbial phrases on lexical aspectual classes is apparent even in treatments of aspect that rely heavily on verb-level classifications. For instance, Vendler argues that the application of the operational test of aspect modification with the Progressive of prototypical stative verbs such as *to know* renders an ungrammatical sentence: *I am knowing*. It is possible, however, to say *Now I know it*, or *And then suddenly I knew*. In the latter two examples Vendler points out that *to know* is similar to *getting married* (achievement) rather than *being married* (a stative). In essence, the inceptive point of a state — determined by adverbial phrases (adjuncts) — is to be considered as an achievement in contrast with the state itself (see also Dowty 1986; Dry 1983; Guitart 1978; Smith 1983).

Another, more formal, proposal that links lexical semantics and syntactic properties of a sentence is Tenny's (1994) Aspectual Interface Hypothesis (AIH). Traditionally, the interaction between syntax and semantics is predicated on the way thematic roles map onto syntactic positions. Tenny, however, views previous proposals that link the meaning of thematic relationships and some level of syntactic representation as inadequate (i.e., the Universal Alignment Hypothesis, or the Universal Theta Alignment Hypothesis). Tenny argues that the theory of thematic roles does not provide a rigorous set of diagnostic tools to determine theta roles. In contrast, the AIH relies on the notion of aspectual roles. Tenny argues that aspectual roles provide only linguistic information relevant to syntactic argument structure in contrast to thematic roles that encompass a variety of information. Aspectual roles represent only a subset of the lexical semantic information provided by the predicate. As a consequence, aspectual roles provide a one-to-one mapping of roles to syntactic positions. The basic proposal of the AIH is predicated on the aspectual notion of delimitedness: "the property of an event's having a distinct, definite and inherent endpoint in time" (p. 4).[5] To determine the telic or atelic nature of a verb it is necessary to analyze the subcategorization frame of the predicate. Each verb is associated with a specific argument structure: internal argument, adjuncts (i.e., indirect internal arguments), and external arguments. Direct and indirect internal arguments are subject to aspectual semantic constraints: the measuring-out constraint and the terminus constraint respectively. Internal arguments "measure out" the verb (quantification, definiteness, etc.); adjuncts specify the terminal point of an event (terminus). In contrast, external arguments do not measure out the event, nor do

---

5.   Tenny prefers not to use the term "telicity" because it implies a focus on the orientation or goal of certain events. However, this is only a matter of labels. Delimitedness is synonymous with telicity (cf. Smith 1991).

they provide a terminus for the event. It is important to point out, however, that Tenny explicitly recognizes that "much, if not most, of the aspectual phenomena to be found in natural language" is not addressed by the AIH (p. 4). For instance, Tenny acknowledges the effect of other sources of aspectual information such as adverbials and aspectual morphology (i.e., marked values of grammatical aspect).

In sum, the lexical value of aspect represents the inherent semantic value of the interaction between the verb (temporal) and its arguments (atemporal), but also other elements that are not arguments proper such as adverbials. Therefore, operational tests of lexical aspect should incorporate all of the above information in their classificatory scheme.

2.2.3   *The semantic multivalence of verbs*

There are many recurrent problems that undermine the notion that lexical aspectual classes can be determined according to verb types: (1) the classification of lexical aspectual classes is vague (undetermined effect of contextual information), and (2) there is crosslinguistic variation in the lexical aspectual values of different verbs (lack of universal categories of lexical aspect). In most cases, the difficulty with the classifications arises because the lexical semantic aspect of the predicate is highly dependent on contextual features. For instance, the predicates in sentences (5) and (6) (from Smith 1991) can be ambiguously classified as activities or accomplishments (are they telic or atelic?); whereas the predicate of sentence (7) can be ambiguously classified as accomplishment or achievement (is it punctual or non-punctual?).

(5)   Mary combed her hair

(6)   John mowed the lawn

(7)   Candace solved the problem

Dahl (1985) mentions three major problems in the use of lexical (Aristotelian) aspect: (1) the separation of inherent meaning from contextual influences (no neutral aspectual context), (2) the flexible use of verbs, and (3) the lack of an appropriate distinction between the nature of aspectual marking as a lexical (derivational morphology) and not a grammatical marker. Similarly, Mourelatos talks about the semantic multivalence of verbs. For instance, the verb *to understand* commonly classified as a state may also be categorized as an activity or as a telic event as mentioned above. In example (8) it functions as an activity verb (homogenous):

(8)   I'm understanding more about quantum mechanics as each day goes by

More dramatically, it may also become a telic event: it is punctual in example (9) and it may be used as part of an imperative construction in sentence (10) (see operational tests).

(9)   Please understand (get the point)!

(10)   Once Lisa understood (grasped) what Henry's intentions were, she lost all interest in him

Mourelatos argues that the multivalence of verbs may be the rule rather than the exception. Therefore, a bottom-up approach may help researchers analyze how verbs dynamically contribute to but not determine the build-up of temporal structure. In other words, the argumental structure of the predicate does not determine the final grammaticized form of aspectual value.

A second problem for the identification of lexical aspectual classes is the existence of variation across languages. For instance, Youssef (1988, 1990) argues that the aspectual status of perception verbs may differ in creole languages as compared to English and Japanese. Similarly, Rispoli and Bloom (1985: 472) claim that "a stative predicate in English need not be a stative predicate in Japanese." In fact, the categorization of verbs according to inherent lexical aspect varies crosslinguistically as well as within the same language. For example, Kachru (1995) claims that the stative-dynamic categorization of verbs is irrelevant in Indian English. In turn, a classification of verbs in terms of *volitionality* is more adequate as is the case in Hindi, Marathi, Kashmiri, etc. Because of this difference, the treatment of verbs such as *know, see, hear*, etc. as dynamic verbs is more conventional in South Asian varieties of English.[6]

2.3   Operational tests of inherent lexical semantics

2.3.1   *The shifting nature of lexical aspectual classes*

As mentioned in the previous section, verbs may change semantic aspectual classes depending on the contextual information that accompanies the representation of the verbal predicate (see also Olsen 1997, for a similar perspective). Chung & Timberlake (1985) argue that the shift in aspectual classes is determined by two

---

6. As reported by Youssef these types of verbs are not treated as statives in creole languages either (1988: 452).

main factors: (1) dynamicity and (2) telicity (pp. 214–8). First, any verb may be represented as dynamic or non-dynamic. To convert a process (11a) to a state (11b) one needs to remove the sense of change:

(11)   a.   John is opening the window
        b.   The window opens onto the garden,

or present the verb as a property of its arguments as in (12b):

(12)   a.   John is running a mile in six minutes
        b.   John runs a six-minute mile

On the other hand, to convert a stative verb (13a) to a process (13b), one must add a sense of actual or possible change:

(13)   a.   I understand my problems
        b.   I am understanding my problems more clearly every day,

or present the subject of the sentence as an agent as in (14b):

(14)   a.   You are obnoxious
        b.   You are being obnoxious,

or by modalizing the concept of change as in (15b):

(15)   a.   John lives with his parents
        b.   John is living with his parents until he finds a place of his own

Verbal predicates may also be presented as closed (telic event or inception and termination of state) or open (atelic event or stative). With respect to events (activities versus accomplishments and achievements) Dowty (1972: 28) mentioned that he could not find any atelic verb which could not be interpreted as a telic verb in at least some special sense of the context. With respect to statives, Comrie (1976: 48–51) mentions that the start or end of a state is dynamic, "since for a state to be started or stopped something must come about to bring about the change into or out of the state." In essence, the inception and termination of a state represent closed events. Similarly, Smith (1986) considers the inception of a state as an achievement verb. On the other hand, Robison distinguishes the inceptive value of a stative from the stative itself with the introduction of a grid of six types of lexical aspectual classes. In such classification, the inceptive value of states is considered to be a punctual stative. Finally, Guitart (1978) refers to three types of stative verbs determined by boundaries: ingressive statives and egressive statives (inceptive and terminative points of a state) as well as persistive statives. Persistive statives are events which are "the manifestation of a certain state that does not come to an end upon being manifested" (p. 153).

2.3.2   Criteria to classify lexical semantics of verb phrases

According to Klein (1994) there are two major types of evidence that determine the inherent lexical semantics of predicates and associated arguments and adjuncts: (1) the nature of the situation we are describing (the case in reality), and (2) combinatorial linguistic restrictions (operational tests of lexical content). The first line of evidence is inconclusive because it is 'methodologically difficult to separate what is the case in reality from what is the case in the lexicon' (Klein, p. 32). In fact, lexical contents refer to selective descriptions of reality. Consequently, Klein argues that we should only classify lexical contents according to 'inner-linguistic restrictions' if we are to obtain reliable and consistent classifications of predicates. Klein lists three major criteria to classify lexical contents: (1) adverb modification, (2) aspect modification, and (3) presuppositions and implications. As we will see, only the latter of these three categories appears powerful enough to distinguish lexical contents.

The first two criteria are perhaps the most extended ones in the literature on the acquisition of aspect. For instance, telic and atelic events may be discriminated by adding two different adverbial phrases: *in x time* (e.g., minutes) versus *for x time* (e.g., minutes) (Dowty 1979: 56; Vendler 1967: 100). Telic events are considered grammatical with the former, but ungrammatical with the latter. The opposite case obtains with atelic events. Klein, however, claims that the constraints exploited by tests based on adverb modification are inadequate (see also Tenny 1994 for similar criticism). For example, if we follow the rationale that underlies the use of this test, the lexical content of '*to open a window*' in (16) will be classified as a telic event (example from Klein):

(16)   a.   He opened the window in five seconds
   b.   *He opened the window for five seconds

But, the second statement may also be considered grammatical under a different interpretation. That is, *to open the window* is a combination of two different states: window not open — window open (source state and target state).[7] It is only when we refer to both source and target state at the same time that we obtain an ungrammatical reading. If, on the other hand, we focus our attention on

---

7. See Klein's (1994) classification of lexical contents into 0-state, 1-state, and 2-state.

the resulting state only, we obtain a possible reading of the statement. In this case, the use of the adverbial phrase *for five minutes* instead of *for five seconds* shifts the focus of attention from the change from source to target state, to focus only on the target state. Extending the analysis to Spanish data we can see that stative verbs in Spanish may be equivalent to telic events in terms of their behavior according to some operational tests of adverbial modification.

(17) a. Estuvo   en Montevideo en cinco días
          was.PRET in Montevideo in five   days
          '(She) was in Montevideo in five days'
      b. Estuvo   en Montevideo por cinco días
          was.PRET in Montevideo for five   days
          '(She) was in Montevideo for five days'

Both examples above are grammatical if we use a contrastive operational test of adverbial modification supposedly designed to distinguish stative versus non-stative verbs. In example (17b) the subject was in the city of Montevideo for five days (stative verb). In contrast, in example (17a), it took the subject five days to get to Montevideo (telic verb). Of course, the context one associates with each sentence will not be the same. To get the grammatical reading associated with a nonstative verb in sentence (17a) one imagines, for example, a long five-day itinerary, whereas such a context is not necessary for sentence (17b).[8] In sum, adverbial tests are not accurate because they are semantic tests 'focusing on a particular interpretation of the sentence or expression' (Tenny 1994: 7).

The second set of criteria, aspect modification, is generally tested on stative verbs. For instance, Vendler differentiated between verbs that 'possess continuous tense and verbs that do not.' Stative verbs are not expected to accept the *-ing* morphological marker of Progressive aspect. Against this prediction we find locative predicates (inherently statives) that normally accept the Progressive even in languages like English: *I am standing on the floor.*[9] Klein (1994: 34) comments that the test of aspect modification is open to the criticism of circularity if statives are defined as the verbs corresponding to the aspectual class that does not tolerate the Progressive marker; or simply false according to the example above. Finally, entailments are the most consistent of the available criteria (e.g., Dowty 1979; Hasbún 1995; Shirai 1991). Entailment tests, however, are only available to distinguish telic from atelic events because they are predicated on the

---

8. This argument is valid for the translation in English as well.

9. In fact, we may also find non-locative predicates: *I am liking that.*

notion of an end point (telicity). The test of telicity distinguishes telic versus atelic verbs by questioning the predicate in the following way:

If you stop in the middle of V-ing, have you done the act of V?

If the answer is affirmative, the verbal predicate is atelic; if the answer is negative, the verbal predicate is telic. I will elaborate further on the entailment test in Section 2.4.

2.3.3   *Operational tests in English*

One of the first sets of operational tests designed to distinguish "the time schemata presupposed by various verbs" (i.e., lexical aspectual classes) were those developed by Vendler (1967). Vendler's tests were specifically designed for English. Vendler offers sets of operational tests to distinguish statives from activities, activities from accomplishments, accomplishments from achievements, and statives from achievements. For example, to distinguish between activities and accomplishments Vendler presents an operational test based on questioning the predicate of the sentence (test of telicity): *drawing a circle* is an accomplishment, but *pushing a cart* is an activity. Hence, the question *For how long did you push the cart?*, (activity) is considered to be "grammatical," whereas *How long did it take to push the cart?* (no end point established) sounds odd. The opposite result with the same questions reveals that *drawing a circle* is an accomplishment (pp. 100–01). The verbs lacking continuous tenses (states and achievements) can be classified in a similar way. Achievements are determined by the following type of question: *At what time did you reach the top? At noon sharp*. For states the following is a more appropriate question: *For how long did you love her? For three years* (pp. 102–3).

Another set of tests used to distinguish aspectual classes in English was developed by Dowty (1979).[10] He classifies operational tests into three types that distinguish (1) statives and dynamic actions (six tests), (2) activities and accomplishments (five tests), and (3) accomplishments and achievements (six tests). For instance, to distinguish statives from activities and accomplishments, Dowty claims that only non-statives have a habitual interpretation:

John knows the answer (non habitual)
John runs (frequentative meaning possible)
John recites a poem (frequentative meaning possible)

---

10. Dowty's list, in turn, is based on George Lakoff's (1968) dissertation.

On the other hand, to distinguish activities from accomplishments Dowty
proposes the use of, for instance, a general test of entailment:

> "If V is an activity verb, then x V-ed for y time entails that at any time during
> y, x V-ed was true. If V is an accomplishment verb, then V-ed for y time does
> not entail that x V-ed was true during any time within y at all"

> If John built a house from May to October, it is false that John built a house
> in any subinterval of that time span.

> If John ran from 1 to 2 PM, it is true that John ran in any subinterval of that
> time span.

Finally, to distinguish accomplishments from achievements Dowty proposes that
the use of the adverb *almost* renders only one reading which is acceptable with
punctual events (see Section 2.4 below for extended analysis)

> *John almost noticed the painting
> John almost ran

Recent empirical studies of L1 and L2 acquisition have generally used a subset
of the above mentioned tests. For instance, in a study of L1 acquisition, Shirai
(1991) used the 3 tests presented above. Similarly, in L2 acquisition, Robison
(1995) adapted a series of tests from various sources including some from
Dowty's classification.

2.3.4 *Operational tests in Spanish*

The tests developed for Spanish are intended to account for potential differences
in semantic meaning from one language to another. The most comprehensive
battery of operational tests for Spanish was used by Hasbún (1995), who
followed the criteria from Clements (1985).[11] Clements in turn based his
criteria on the tests from Dowty reviewed above (implemented originally in
English).[12] Hasbún applied a total of eight tests: six tests distinguish stative
versus non-statives and two tests discriminate dynamic verbs according to telicity

---

11. Other studies in Spanish L2 acquisition have not reported the operational tests used to determine
aspectual classes (e.g. Andersen 1986, 1991; Ramsay 1990).

12. The avowed goal of Clements' dissertation is to identify the factors (projection rules from the
lexicon) "that trigger verb class change and feature addition." Interestingly, the conclusion reached
by Clements is the following: "What all verbs share is the fact that the semantic nature of the theme
is crucial for a grammatical reading with an aspectual change. Hence, Aktionsart (i.e. grammatical
aspect according to the label used by Clements, R. S.) is not only a phenomenon of single lexical
items ... but it is clearly a sentential and even a contextual phenomenon as well" (1985: 276–7).

(activities versus accomplishments and achievements) and punctuality (achievements versus activities and accomplishments). The following are the eight tests used by Hasbún:

1. "A stative Imperfective does not imply another Imperfective:"[13]
   Juan sabía Latín → *Juan sabe Latín
   Juan estudiaba Latín → Juan estudia Latín
2. Only dynamic verbs take Progressive:
   *Juan está sabiendo la lección
   Juan está estudiando la lección
3. Statives are incompatible as complements of *obligar/convencer*
   *Juan lo obligó a que supiera la lección
   Juan lo obligó a que estudiara la lección
4. Statives are incompatible with adverbs that describe actions as voluntary
   *Juan sabe la lección a propósito
   Juan estudia la lección a propósito
5. Statives are incompatible with imperatives
   *Sabe la lección
   Estudia la lección
6. Statives are incompatible with the phrase *acabar de*
   *Juan acaba de saber la lección
   Juan acaba de estudiar la lección
7. Only non-punctual events pass the test of durativity: *X pasó y time verbeando*
   Juan pasó la tarde escribiendo (activity)
   Juan pasó la tarde escribiendo la carta (accomplishment)
   *Juan pasó la tarde llegando (achievement)
8. Only telic events pass the test: *X tardó y tiempo en verbear*:
   Juan tardó dos años en escribir el libro (accomplishment)
   Juan tardó dos horas en llegar (achievement)
   *Juan tardó dos horas en leer (activity)

The first test used by Hasbún (test one) is not part of the criteria presented in Dowty (1979), nor was it part of the criteria used by Clements to contrast stative

---

13. According to the previous definition of the test, the sentence from Hasbún is ungrammatical although it is not marked as such in the original text. Notice that present tense is by definition Imperfective (e.g. Bybee & Dahl 1989); hence, the definition and the grammaticality of the example are not logically connected.

versus dynamic verbs (1985: 73–77). It is not clear how such a test would discriminate statives versus non-statives. At most, it is a satisfactory test to distinguish the aspectual value (grammatical) of meaning-changing Preterites (e.g., Studerus 1989). That is to say, only the marked use of a stative with the Preterite does not imply the same sentence in the present. However, the use of Imperfect grammatical marking with that same stative does not necessarily prevent it from being valid in the present:

Juan supo Latín → *Juan sabe Latín
Juan sabía Latín → Juan sabe Latín

On the other hand, tests three through five from Hasbún gauge different degrees of agentivity instead of distinguishing statives versus non-statives. Hasbún recognizes this problem in a footnote and asserts that these tests may fail to identify statives if the feature of agentivity is removed (p. 35). Because of this, Hasbún claims that the test with the Progressive (test of aspect modification: number 2 above) should be the decisive one. As we have seen in Section 2.3.2, however, tests of aspect modification are not reliable. The following examples represent counterevidence against the validity of the tests proposed by Hasbún:

Test 2: Prototypical statives in Spanish accept the progressive:
Estoy teniendo más problemas cada día
Estoy viviendo peligrosamente estos días

Test 3: Prototypical statives in Spanish function as complements of obligar:
Juan lo obligó a que tuviera cuidado
Juan lo obligó a que viviera decentemente

Test 4: Prototypical statives in Spanish co-occur with the adverb conscientemente:
Juan ama a Dios conscientemente
Juan vive en la pobreza conscientemente

Test 5: Prototypical statives in Spanish can be used in the imperative:
Ama a Dios
Vive decentemente

Finally, test six successfully disqualifies statives because it makes reference to the terminative boundary of a state. However, the inceptive boundary of the state is normally represented as a telic event. The test of durativity (punctual versus non-punctual telic events) is theoretically unnecessary and empirically invalidated as will be shown in Section 2.4. I will address the (ir)relevance of test 7 in the following section.

In sum, only two of the eight tests used by Hasbún appear to be appropriate for application to a wide variety of predicates (i.e., tests six and eight). In any case, as long as one test is able to discriminate between two aspectual classes the analysis of the data should be comparable to other studies including the present one. The set of two tests to be used in the present study will be introduced in Chapter 5: test of habitual interpretation (statives versus non-statives) and the general test of entailment (telic versus atelic events). The selection of the above mentioned operational tests was based on the fact (as mentioned in Section 3.1 above) that there are two major factors which allow verbs to shift lexical aspectual class according to context: (1) dynamicity and (2) telicity (Chung & Timberlake 1985).

2.4   Lexical, grammatical and situation aspect

The selection of a valid operational test to classify verb phrases into lexical aspectual classes is, as shown above, of substantial importance to test the lexical aspect hypothesis. The application of the semantic criteria subsumed in an operational test, however, may be difficult to tease apart. Hence, it is important to make a distinction between aspectual values (inceptive, terminative, imperfective, iterative, habitual, etc.), aspectual grammatical marking (Preterite, Imperfect, Progressive, etc.), and the temporal schemata of the situation or lexical content (lexical aspectual classes). Confusion in the use of these terms may generate misunderstandings that may, eventually, obfuscate the analysis of the development of verbal morphology in languages which mark aspectual distinctions such as inceptive-imperfective through grammatical means. In the present section I will analyze two potentially difficult classifications of lexical aspectual classes that have generated discrepancies in previous analyses of data: accomplishments versus achievements and statives versus achievements.

Given the fact that some studies have relied on the use of a single category of telic events (conflating accomplishments and achievements) it is important to show: (1) theoretical reasons for the conflation of both categories, (2) the lack of reliability of operational tests which discriminate the aforementioned distinction, and (3) empirical findings that contradict the proposed distinction. Indeed, previous researchers have rejected the separation of telic events into two distinct categories. For instance, Mourelatos (1981: 193) claims that accomplishments and achievements should be integrated because 'both are actions that involve a product, upshot, or outcome.' Klein (1994) provides further theoretical justification for such claim: time is not discrete but dense. In this respect, no situation can be 'punctual' in the sense of being instantaneous (no duration) (see also Verkuyl 1989). Some researchers, however, have argued that this is not a problem because it is not the situation per se what is at stake in the classification of lexical aspectual classes; what is important is the linguistic representation of real situations (e.g., Shirai 1991; Smith 1986: 103). But, are linguistic representations devoid of any contact with the real situation? Probably not because the linguistic realization of a situation is by definition a selective description of reality. In fact, Klein (1994: 88) argues that punctuality is part of world knowledge and not lexical content. For example, to find is a prototypical telic-punctual event:[14]

(18)   Clive found a nugget (possibly punctual)

However, if we change the internal argument associated with the predicate (singular to plural), the duration associated with the verb will change as a result of our knowledge of world events:

(19)   Clive found a bucket of nuggets (non-punctual)[15]

Similarly, Dowty (1986) argues that achievements are punctual only in the framework of a narrative in which sequenced events in a story are not interrupted, but that nothing prevents accomplishments from becoming sequenced events in the story. At most, the punctual nature of achievements may be obtained as a matter of conventional interpretation of world knowledge as argued above.

There are, however, operational tests that purport to distinguish accomplishments from achievements. For example, Shirai (personal communication, February 1997) claims that one of the most powerful tests to differentiate accomplishment from achievement verbs is the use of the adverbial test with *almost* (Dowty 1979). This adverbial qualifies the predicate under analysis and generates two possible readings with accomplishments, but only one with achievements. Shirai (1991: 64) describes the use of such test in the following way:

Is there ambiguity with "almost"?

If yes → Accomplishment (e.g., He almost painted a picture has two readings; i.e., 'he almost started to paint a picture' and 'he almost finished painting a picture')

If no → Achievement (e.g., He almost noticed the picture has only one reading.)

---

14. The following examples are from Klein (1994).

15. It is also possible that Clive found a whole bucket of nuggets at once. But that interpretation is not necessarily preferred over the other one.

I believe, however, that the above test is unreliable for the distinction of durative from non-durative telic events. First, notice that for achievements beginning and end points of the event have been collapsed (i.e., punctual), whereas for accomplishments beginning and end points are separate (i.e., durative). The task is to find counterevidence that shows that the above mentioned test fails under appropriate contextual circumstances which override the conventional value of the *almost* test with some verbs. For instance, if we take a prototypical punctual verb (achievement) such as *to break*, the *almost* test fails to distinguish punctual versus durative telic events:

(20)   Mary almost broke the stick

In this example it is possible to get both readings attributed to accomplishment verbs only: (1) she almost started to break the stick, ... but decided it was not worth her time, and (2) she almost succeeded in breaking it (finished), ... but she was not strong enough (i.e., it is reasonable to believe that she tried for some time and even caused some cracks on the stick). Many other examples also show that the *almost* test fails to distinguish achievements from accomplishments. *To kill* constitutes another prototypical punctual-telic event:

(21)   John almost killed the judge

There are two possible entailments: (1) ... but he decided not to do it because he realized he would have been sentenced to the death penalty (almost started), and (2) ... but he was stopped by the police while he was beating him/her (almost finished). The reason for the failure of this test is simple: the only distinction the test makes is one of agentivity; or, more precisely, a distinction between volitional and non-volitional states. That is to say, only when there is an involuntary state (i.e., the external argument of the predicate is not volitional) does the test distinguish accomplishments versus achievements: *He almost died*, *He almost noticed the painting*. For example, in *The cable almost snapped* we only get one reading: the cable was on the verge of breaking due to possible damage (the duration of the event collapses and durativity is not a factor). We can also imagine a cartoon in which the cable is endowed with animate faculties, in which case it is possible to obtain the interpretation that the cable almost got mad (snapped), ... but regained control of itself just in the nick of time. The lack of duration in the conventional reading of the sentence is a matter of pragmatics and not necessarily due to the semantic value of aspectual class. In fact, Robison's (1995: 350) distinction between punctual states and punctual events (non-durative by definition) is precisely based on the differentiation involuntary and voluntary states of affairs. More importantly, recent empirical data from L2 development contradict the proposed theoretical distinction between accomplishment and achievement verbs as two separate categories of telic events (e.g., Bardovi-Harlig & Bergström 1995; Hasbún 1995; Ramsay 1990; Salaberry 1998).

While the distinction between accomplishments and achievements may be unsubstantiated, as shown above, it does not seriously compromise the findings of previous studies because both categories share two important semantic features (i.e., dynamicity and telicity). A more problematic situation arises in the potential misclassification of achievements as statives. For instance, compare the following sentences:

(22)   a.   En ese momento Juan supo la verdad
              At that moment Juan found out (PRET) the truth (knew, inceptive)
        b.   Juan sabía la verdad
              Juan knew (IMP) the truth (knew, Imperfective)

The translations in English show two alternative lexical choices: *to find out* versus *to know*. According to Bull (1965: 170) 'the Spaniard's [sic] way of organizing reality is ... thoroughly disguised by the English translations.[16] The use of the appropriate operational test for stative, however, determines that the first instance of *saber* fails to qualify as a stative, whereas the second case of *saber* does represent a stative. The difference lies on the existence of the adverbial phrase *at that moment* in (22a) but not in (22b). The adverbial in (22a) marks the topic time (TT) as the inception of the state (see Klein 1994, 1995). Its absence in (22b) renders the default reading of a stative (see above). In passing, notice that the classification of lexical aspectual classes was not made in terms of morphological marking (*supo* versus *sabía*), but, rather, on the existence of the adjunct phrase that qualifies the verbal predicate (see Smith 1991).

2.5   Conclusion

In this chapter I have reviewed several characterizations of the grammatical category of aspect and I have analyzed in further detail the important distinction between lexical and grammatical aspect. Following previous research it was argued that the lexical value of aspect represents the inherent semantic value of the interaction between the verb (temporal) and its arguments (atemporal), but

---

16. Spaniards do not constitute the only national group which speaks the — originally — Castillian dialect that in its many varieties is spoken by people throughout the world.

also other elements which are not arguments proper such as adverbials. As a consequence, operational tests of lexical aspect should incorporate all of the above information into their classificatory scheme. It was further claimed that the distinction of telic events into punctual and durative events is theoretically and empirically unjustified. In the following chapter I will review empirical data on the development of past tense verbal morphology among children and I will analyze the claims of various theoretical frameworks such as the lexical aspect hypothesis.

CHAPTER 3

The development of aspect in L1

The hypothesis about the explanatory role of lexical semantics in the development of verbal morphology among adult second language learners has evolved from arguments initially made for the evolution of linguistic systems across time as well as first language acquisition studies. Of particular importance for the analysis of the acquisition of verbal endings in L2 Spanish among L1 English speakers is the claim that in emergent linguistic systems, aspect markers precede the appearance of tense markers (e.g., Bybee 1985, 1995; Bybee & Dahl 1989; Frawley 1992; Jakobson 1957). It is open to question, however, whether the same historical sequence of language development will be instantiated in second language acquisition, especially in cases like Spanish where both (past) tense and aspect markers are fused into a single morpheme (see also Shirai & Andersen 1996: 759). In contrast, the line of evidence from first language acquisition appears to offer a more compelling argument for the analysis of adult second language acquisition. In effect, the original motivation for the elaboration of the lexical aspect hypothesis in L2 acquisition can be traced back to the work done in first language acquisition during the 70s and 80s (e.g., Antinucci & Miller 1976; Bloom, Lifter & Hafitz 1980; Bronckart & Sinclair 1973; Brown 1973; Rispoli & Bloom 1985; Smith & Weist 1987). Hence, it is important to analyze the extent to which the lexical aspect hypothesis is able to account for the development of past tense verbal morphology among children. In the first section of this chapter I analyze the general characteristics of the development of temporality among children as part of an overall development of cognitive capacities, and I summarize the early empirical findings on the development of past tense aspect in L1 acquisition. In Section 2 I summarize the theoretical claims of three major hypotheses that attempt to account for the development of verbal morphology among children. Finally, in Section 3 I contrast the nature of language acquisition among children and adults insofar the marking of temporality on verbal morphology is concerned.

3.1   The development of temporality in a first language: Piagetian proposals

The analysis of the development of aspectual distinctions among children is part of the overall development of temporality. That is, there is general agreement that there is a cognitive/conceptual developmental sequence that constrains the development of aspectual differences in children's language. There is some disagreement, however, about the relative appearance of aspectual and tense distinctions in the children's grammatical system as well as on the order of stages. Weist (1989) proposed four stages to analyze the development of temporal systems: (1) speech time (ST), (2) event time (ET), (3) restricted reference time (RRT), and (4) reference time (RT). Weist claims that the use of Reichenbach's notion of reference time is not fully operational during the beginning stages of development (e.g., the child is able to use present perfect: *I have played*, but not past perfect: *I had played*). During the first stage of development (ST) there is no coding of tense, aspect or modality in the child's grammar. Notwithstanding this limitation, children are able to make reference to past experiences, if not with past tense morphology, with the use of words such as "gone" and "more" (Weist 1989: 70–1). During the second stage (ET) — approximately between ages 1;6 and 2;0 — the child signals aspect relationships such as internal and external perspective, modal distinctions, and deictic temporal relations between past (ET) and nonpast (ST). At this stage RT is formed at ST. In the third stage, between ages 2;6 and 3;0 the child starts using temporal adverbials and present perfect (RRT). The appearance of temporal adverbials is the harbinger of the concept of reference time as separate from ST. Finally, between ages 4;0 and 4;5 the child is able to mark past perfect, thereby coordinating the three temporal intervals as in the adults' grammar: event time, speech time and reference time. There are, however, some major discrepancies in the theoretical analysis of how temporality develops in L1 acquisition. For instance, according to Buczowska and Weist (1991: 536) "in L1 acquisition children code deictic relationships with morphological contrasts in an early phase of acquisition … and they use adverbs and adverbial clauses at a later phase." But, contrary to Weist's position, Clark (1985) argues that the distinction and contrast of temporal terms are first marked with adverbials which appear at around age 2;6: children distinguish present versus non-present (*yesterday, today and tomorrow*).[1] I will

---

1. It is important to mention that the data from Weist is represented mainly by Slavic languages especially Polish, whereas Clark relies on data from Romance languages.

not delve further into these issues as they are beyond the scope of analysis of this work. On the other hand, it is important for the purpose of this study to analyze previous empirical findings on the development of past tense verbal morphology in L1 acquisition.

Among one of the earliest studies on the development of L1 verbal morphology, Bronckart and Sinclair (1973) noticed that under similar conditions (after the event had taken place) children of three years or younger tend to say things like *il lave la voiture* ('he is washing the car') and *il a poussé la balle* ('he kicked the ball').[2] Bronckart and Sinclair wondered: Why would children mark past tense with some verbs and not others? Is it a systematic process tied to developmental processes? To answer these questions Bronckart and Sinclair analyzed the use of inflectional morphology by 74 French speaking children in an experimental setting. Their ages ranged from 2;11 to 8;7. The children were asked to describe eleven actions performed by an adult with toys. The actions differed in type of result, frequency, duration and the explicit or non-explicit nature of the goal of the action. The results of the experiment revealed that children used present tense forms mostly with durative verbs, and past forms with achievement and accomplishment verbs (i.e., actions with clear end results). Moreover, children tended to use past forms more often for events of shorter duration. This tendency diminished as the children grew older, thus approximating adult use. The Bronckart and Sinclair study was conducted within the Piagetian framework. As such, the results of their study were attributed to a cognitive deficit: children have no concept of tense during the pre-operational stage.

Antinucci and Miller (1976) represents another frequently cited study on the L1 acquisition of verbal morphology. Their study was also conducted within the Piagetian framework of analysis (i.e., cognitive development is at the basis of language development). Antinucci and Miller analyzed the development of past tense expressions in the conversational data of one English (age 1;6 to 2;2) and seven Italian speaking children (roughly of age 1;6 to 2;4). The past tense aspectual system of Italian is similar to the one of French: one simple tense (*Imperfetto*) and one compound tense (*Passato Prossimo*). For their study, Antinucci and Miller assumed that the grammatical marking of aspect is to be

---

2. Bronckart and Sinclair also noted that "younger children seemed to single out different features from those most frequently described by older children. Three-year olds, for example, after having been shown a red truck pushing a green car, would say 'there's a green car'; slightly older subjects were fond of announcing 'there's something wrong with the car' or 'the car is in the garage'" (p. 109). That is to say, the orientation or focus of attention of the child with reference to a similar activity is different according to maturation (i.e., age).

associated with the inherent lexical value of the predicate: "the past of a non-stative verb is expressed by means of the *Passato Prossimo*" and "the past of a stative verb is expressed by the use of the Imperfect tense" (pp. 168–9). The analysis of data from the Italian subjects revealed two important findings: (1) the past participle of transitive verbs agreed with the non pronominal object (standard Italian marks agreement with the object only when the latter is pronominal), and (2) the majority of verbs marked with past tense were the ones of change of state with clear results. Along the lines of Bronckart and Sinclair, Antinucci and Miller argued that "the child is able to make reference and encode past events only when their character is such that they result in a present end-state of some object" (p. 182). On the other hand, Antinucci and Miller claimed that state and activity verbs are marked with the Imperfect at a later stage (between 2;0 and 2;8) in the specific context of story telling. Antinucci and Miller pointed out that in the latter case "the child is not narrating a past event, and in most cases is not even narrating a story that someone previously told him" (p. 186). In other words, the Imperfect marks the distinction between pretend world versus real world: "the ability to make this distinction, as Piaget shows, is more complex and later to develop than the ability to take account of a physical transformation" (pp. 186–7).[3] In sum, Antinucci and Miller claimed that the evolution of the system of aspectual distinctions cannot be understood by the simple categorization of inflections according to the inherent lexical aspect of the verb and its arguments. Bickerton (1981: 174), however, was skeptical about the account offered by Antinucci and Miller. He argued that the claim that children grammatically mark pretend play from real events is suspicious because we should expect that the use of Imperfect should "be extended to all types of verbs, including change of state verbs."

Indeed, the late use of the Imperfect is also common in Spanish and other Romance languages. Most studies in Spanish detect the first instances of productive use of the Imperfect at around age three. For example, Morales (1989) analyzed data from informal interviews with 16 children whose ages ranged from 2;0 to 6;0. Morales detected the first use of the Imperfect with a proportion of 11% (compared to 84% of use of the Preterite) in the four children whose ages ranged from 3;0 to 4;9. She argued that the actual temporal nature of the Imperfect — in contrast with the Preterite in a narrative — appeared in the group with ages ranging from 5;0 to 6;0. On the other hand, Villamil (1983) detected the use of Imperfect (proportion of 29%) at an earlier age: between ages 2;0 to 3;2. The

---

3. Note that this distinction is similar to the contrast realis–irrealis in Bickerton (1981).

results from Villamil were corroborated by Sebastian and Slobin (1994). The latter collected experimental data — as opposed to spontaneous data as was the case for the studies of Morales and Villamil — from narratives based on the children's book "Frog Story." Their study included 12 subjects in each one of the following age groups: 3 year-olds, 4 year-olds, 5 year-olds, 9 year-olds, and adults. The use of the Imperfect was already proportional to the use of the Preterite in their first age group (3 year-olds). Further confirmatory data come from Krasinski (1995), who analyzed spontaneous data from one child raised bilingually: his mother was a native speaker of Spanish and his father was a native speaker of English. The data were based on diary entries maintained by both parents (both linguists). The first appearance of the Imperfect was detected between ages 2;6 and 2;8 with the word *estaba* (was or were) exclusively used as a locative. Finally, data from Portuguese and French also support the previous account about the use of the Imperfect: Simões and Stöel-Gammon (1979) detected the use of the Imperfect at age 2;5; deLemos (1981) recorded its use at age three; and Schylter (1996) detected the use of French *Imparfait* at age 3 as well.

3.2   Theoretical explanations and debate

3.2.1   *The lexical aspect hypothesis*[4]

The Piagetian explanation of the above mentioned data lost its impetus in the 1980s in favor of accounts based mostly on linguistic factors. Most notably, Bloom, Lifter and Hafitz (1980) investigated the development of verbal morphology to establish whether children's use of verbal inflection followed the use of rules, or whether it was based on lexical learning. Data from four first-born English speaking children of college-educated parents were analyzed. Their longitudinal data covered the following range of mean length of utterance (MLU): 1;5–2;0 to 2;5–3;0. Bloom et al. replicated the results of Bronckart & Sinclair and Antinucci & Miller: children used past marking (irregular past) more often with accomplishment/achievement verbs (telic), and the Progressive form (*-ing* inflection) mainly with activity verbs. Contrary to previous researchers, however, Bloom et al. attributed the bias in the distribution of verbal morphology to the *aspectual contour of the actions rather than their end state*. The cognitive-

---

4. Andersen and Shirai (1996: 534) present a list of the studies in L1 acquisition which have investigated the effect of the lexical inherent semantics of the verb phrase in the acquisition of verbal morphology.

deficit explanation was not upheld by Bloom et al on theoretical and method-ological grounds. The theoretical perspective of Bloom et al. follows the cognitive saliency rationale offered by Jakobson (1957), who claimed that aspect marking is closer to the stem than the shifting deictic forms of tense marking. In passing, notice that this claim does not apply to Spanish since both (past) tense and aspect markers are fused into one single morpheme (e.g., Bybee 1995; Andersen & Shirai 1994; Shirai & Andersen 1995). In terms of the methodology, Bloom et al. argued that previous studies did not pay attention to the use of present tense inflections (e.g., Antinucci & Miller 1976), even though the differential use of all inflections may be informative of the development of temporality in the child's system. It is also important to mention that Bloom et al. did not overextend their claim beyond what was evident in their data:

> although the 2-year-olds in the present study did not appear to be using the inflectional morphemes as tense markers, it is probably not true that such learning would wait until age 6 as claimed by Bronckart and Sinclair
> (pp. 234–5)

The claim of Bloom et al. generated an extended debate. Weist (1983) and Weist et al. (1984) argued that aspect and tense emerge simultaneously in Polish children as young as 2;6 years old. Notice that one major difference between Polish and English is that both tense and aspect are grammaticalized in Polish (with both prefixes and suffixes). Weist (1983) collected data from ten children with an average age of 2;6 and ten children with an average age of 3;6. The experimental procedure consisted of a sentence-and-picture-matching condition with one sentence and two pictures in each instance. The results of this study were limited as acknowledged by Weist: all of the verb phrases used in the aspect tests were result verb phrases or telic events (i.e., accomplishment and achievement verbs only). On the other hand, this study was important because it showed that — contrary to one of the operating principles of Slobin — Polish children were able to pay attention to both the beginning and the end of the words (prefixes and suffixes). In turn, Weist et al. (1984) analyzed natural data (caretaker-child interactions) collected from three younger children (1;7–1;9) and three older children (2;0–2;2). The results of their study showed that the perfec-tive versus the imperfective aspectual distinction and the deictic relationships of tense evolve simultaneously in Polish children. Weist et al. claimed that their results did not support the "defective tense hypothesis" (DTH) which they attributed to previous studies (e.g., Antinucci & Miller 1976; Bloom et al. 1980; Bronckart & Sinclair 1973). According to Weist et al., the DTH proposes that (1) only telic verbs will receive past-tense inflections, (2) tense distinctions will be redundant and only accompany aspectual distinctions, and (3) only references to immediate past situations will be made" (p. 348). Bloom and Harner (1989) and Rispoli and Bloom (1985) responded to the claim of Weist et al. For instance, Bloom and Harner reanalyzed the data from Weist et al. and concluded that development within the span of four months was highly constrained by the lexical aspect of the verb. Table 1 of Bloom and Harner shows indeed that telic verbs in the data of Weist et al. were overwhelmingly marked with perfective aspect (252 tokens) and hardly ever marked with the Imperfective (13 tokens). On the other hand, atelic verbs were mostly marked with the Imperfect (77 tokens) in comparison to the use of the perfective marker (48 tokens).

Recent empirical studies from other languages, however, have uncovered more discrepancies with the proposed lexical aspect hypothesis (i.e., relevance of aspectual contour of the verb). For instance, Cziko and Koda (1987) analyzed the morphological marking of verbs in a Japanese child from age 1;0 to age 4;11. The results showed that — consistent with the lexical aspect hypothesis — the Progressive past tense marker -tei was used with activity verbs but not with statives. On the other hand, contrary to the claim of the lexical aspect hypothesis, the frequency of use of the past tense marker -ta was similar for both punctual and nonpunctual verbs.[5] In contrast, Rispoli's (1990) data showed that Japanese children use the Imperfective marker -tei with activity verbs and stative verbs (contrary to the results of Cziko & Koda's study and the lexical aspect hypothesis as well). Along the same lines, Mapstone and Harris (1985) noticed that a high percentage of children in their study (10 out of 22) used the Progressive marker with stative verbs in English, and Shirai (1994) showed that one of the three children analyzed by Brown (1973) used the Progressive with state verbs. Similarly, Fantuzzi (1996: 207) reanalyzed the data from one of Brown's subjects (Eve, age range: 1;6 to 1;8), and claimed that the selective use of tense morphology in English may not necessarily signal a lexical aspectual distinction because "all perfected events are also past and all incomplete events are present in the above data." Furthermore, Villamil (1983) showed that in L1 Spanish development durative verbs were marked for past with the Preterite to a much higher degree than with the Imperfect. Given that the children from Villamil ranged in ages from 1;0 to 3;2, she interpreted these results as support for the hypothesis that children mark tense before aspect. Furthermore, Villamil found that Spanish-speaking children marked verbs that carry the semantic feature [+durative] with

---

5. Interestingly, Robison (1990) obtained exactly the opposite results with an adult L1 Spanish speaker learning L2 English. That is to say, Robison's data support the punctual-nonpunctual distinction as a possible innate semantic bias, but not the stative-dynamic contrast.

the Preterite from the early stages of morphological marking of verbs. Finally, some studies of L2 acquisition among young children also raise doubts about the validity of the lexical aspect hypothesis (e.g., Rohde 1996).[6]

3.2.2 *The influence of the input: distributional biases*

In order to account for the above mentioned discrepancies several studies have proposed that particular biases in the frequency distribution of input data may account for the use of verbal morphology in L1 acquisition. For instance, Stephany (1981) analyzed data from four monolingual Greek children (three boys and one girl) interacting with their mothers in normal activities (playing, eating, etc.). Their ages ranged from 20 months, 10 days to 22 months, 25 days (1;8 to 1;10 in years). The children were recorded in sessions of 60–90 minutes during a two-week period (five to eight visits). Stephany argued that child-directed mothers' speech reflects closely the distribution of children's data more than adult-directed speech. Among studies in L1 Spanish acquisition in particular, Morales (1989) found similar results in a study of 15 Puerto Rican children of ages 2 to 6 (26 hours of recorded interviews). The distribution of ages was as follows: 2;0 to 2;9 (4 children), 3;0 to 4;9 (4 children), and 5;0 to 6;0 (8 children). The data show that children used the Preterite first with a small set of verbs. The majority of verb types (77%) of all verbs first marked with the Preterite (children of ages 2;0 to 2;9) corresponded to *irse, acabarse, caerse* and *romperse* (to leave, to run out of, to fall, to break). Incidentally, Morales points out that the first verbs marked with past tense in L1 English are similar (Brown 1973): *fell, dropped, slipped, crashed and broke*. Morales concluded that children start using past tense with the most frequent verbs they find in the input and that they adapt those forms to fulfill the semantic functions they can handle at their age (p. 129).

Interestingly, Krasinski (1995) showed that the emergence of past forms in a bilingual Spanish-English child was different in the two target languages. Verbs in English emerged in their base form, whereas verbs in Spanish were marked first with third person singular (default in Spanish), but also in the form of "imperatives, infinitives and past forms. These forms were initially invariant" (p. 268). In other words, some verbs in Spanish first emerged with past tense marking only. Hence, it is not possible to claim that the child was actually

---

6. In this respect, it is important to point out that the data used by Andersen (1989, 1991) in support of the lexical aspect hypothesis comes from adolescents not young children.

marking punctuality when using verbs in past form (Preterite) because the child was not marking any contrast present-past (see also reanalysis of Brown's data in Fantuzzi 1996). Krasinski claimed that the Spanish verb form which emerged first "was the most frequent in the input" (p. 269).[7] As for English, the first instances of past marking were irregular past forms, which is consistent with the claim of input effects (item learning). The earlier appearance of past forms in Spanish and not English can be explained by the type of input available in each language. In Spanish past forms are consistently used in all environments, whereas in English the phenomenon of negatives and question formation (the auxiliary *did* with base form of the verb) create a more complicated system for the child to analyze. This is also consistent with the finding that the first verb forms in past tense in English were irregular forms.

Finally, it is important to point out that the cognitive saliency of temporality marking may also cause cross-linguistic effects. For instance, Weist et al. (1984) argue that the development of temporal marking is inherently linked to the particular language being developed: "the speed at which this conceptual breakthrough is reflected in a tensed child language will depend on how tense is coded in the morphology of the language" (Weist et al. 1984: 373). Weist (1989: 66) argued that languages may be classified along a continuum from relatively analytic (English) to relatively synthetic (Polish). In highly synthetic languages "the child is forced to deal with the morphology from the earliest phases of development." In fact, Weist, et al. (1991) showed that tense and aspect contrasts are more difficult for Finnish than for Polish or American children, because Finnish is the most synthetic language of all three. In further support of the previous analysis, Shirai (1991, 1994) claimed that the biased use of verbal morphology in the adult speech data had not been considered as a source of inherent aspectual development in previous studies. Shirai (1994) reanalyzed the data from the three children studied by Brown (1973) to investigate possible distributional biases in the speech of the children's mothers with respect to the extension of the Progressive to stative verbs. The results of Shirai's analysis are presented in Table 3.1.

As we can see, only one child received the type of input that contradicts the prototypical use of Progressive with activity verbs from her mother: Naomi. Accordingly, only Naomi used the Progressive with state verbs, in support of the claim that the distributional bias of motherese may influence the acquisition of verbal morphology — beyond the possible effect of lexical aspectual classes.

---

7. However, Krasinski acknowledges that she did not collect data about the input that the child received except for informal comments from the parents' diaries.

Table 3.1. Distribution of Progressive marking with stative verbs in mothers and children (based on Shirai, 1994)[a]

	Child	Mother
Adam	0.2%	0%
Eve	0.5%	0%
Naomi	3.1%	3.8%

[a] These data do not include the use of the verb *to be*, since the form *being* may plausibly be learned as a separate lexical item.

Despite the empirical research reviewed above, the cross-linguistic analysis of L1 acquisition of aspect along the lines of the distributional bias hypothesis has encountered some empirical problems. For example, Shirai (1995) presents the puzzle of Japanese L1 acquisition: the Imperfective marker (*-tei*) is used with both achievement (telic event) and activity verbs (atelic event), whereas the past marker (*-ta*) is used with accomplishments and achievements (telic events). That is, how could the child learning Japanese distinguish telic versus atelic events when the same marker (*-tei*) can be used to mark both? (see Shirai & Andersen 1995 and Shirai & Kurono 1998 for further analysis).

3.2.3   *Inherent lexical aspect and viewpoint aspect*

A final theoretical explanation related to the scope of analysis of aspectual distinctions is necessary in order to account for the use of viewpoint aspect among children. That is, native like use of the aspectual markers of any given language is — by definition — never restricted to the basic aspectual contour of the verb (cf., Lunn 1985; Rispoli 1990; Smith 1983, 1991). For instance, the use of Preterite or Imperfect in Spanish or the use of *Passé Composé* and *Imparfait* in French entail more than the association of stative and activity verbs with the imperfective or performance verbs with the perfective. As seen in Chapter 2, Smith argues that viewpoint aspect refers to the partial or full view of a particular situation type and that it is marked with an overt grammatical morpheme. Furthermore, as argued by Lunn (1985) with reference to Spanish Preterite–Imperfect in particular, we "have to explain all grammatical aspectual choices, both conventional and unconventional" if we are to obtain a complete characterization of aspectual choices. The unconventional perspective of the speaker on the particular situation being described may be expressed overtly when grammatical aspect contradicts the lexical aspect of the situation of events or states: e.g., Spanish Imperfect with telic verbs or Preterite with atelic verbs.

Rispoli (1990) argued that children have to learn to use the two separate systems of aspectual distinctions — standard lexical aspect and non-standard aspect (viewpoint) — in sequence because perspective (viewpoint) is a subjective choice. That is, children must necessarily learn the standard choices first (i.e., unmarked before marked choices of grammatical aspect). For instance, Rispoli points out that during the initial stages of acquisition children do not mark stative verbs with the Progressive form -ing in English (cf., the initial studies of Brown 1973 and subsequent investigations within the aspect versus tense framework of analysis). Adults, however, seem to mark state verbs in such a way quite normally: *I can't believe what I am seeing, When will you be needing your wake up call?* and *I'm loving every minute of this* (Rispoli, p. 376; see Olsen 1997 for additional examples). Hence, Rispoli argues that the adequate characterization of aspectual inflections should be primarily concerned with the transition from the use of standard choices of aspect (situation aspect) to non-standard choices (viewpoint) exemplified in the above mentioned discrepancies between child and adult data (marking of state verbs with the Progressive marker in English). Similar examples from other languages are also common (e.g., Kuczaj 1989; Li 1989; Mapstone & Harris 1985; Shirai 1994). For that reason, Rispoli and Bloom claim that it is necessary "to search in the contextual events which relate to the child's utterance for clues to the motivating categories and distinctions which comprise the child's knowledge in this domain" (p. 474).

Three consequences follow from Rispoli's assessment. First, this perspective is representative of a "grounding theory" of temporal markers, and, as such, it focuses on a wider framework of reference than the one represented by a sentence-level analysis. For instance, Hopper (1982: 6, italics added) claims that:

> the encoding of percepts in the world takes place within a discourse rather than a sentence framework, and that the *potential or real bounding of events* in this discourse is a significant parameter in the strategies for formulating an utterance

Second, the development of this subjective value of aspect can be attributed to the contact with cultural conventions (language dependent); therefore, it represents a non-universal process of acquisition.[8] For example, from a Vygotskyan approach to language acquisition Lantolf and Appel (1994: 10) claim that

---

8. The argument about the symbiotic effects of language and culture remains a central point of debate in the analysis of the development of aspect. For instance, Bybee and Dahl (1989: 52) — in defense of the value of cross-linguistic similarities of grammatical morphemes — contend that "Whorf and Sapir denied semantic universals and treated each language as expressing meanings reflecting, and perhaps even molding, a culture-specific world-view." The analysis of aspect from the perspective of situation aspect and viewpoint aspect provides plausible support to both approaches.

...the adult organizes the child's world ... by pointing out, through symbolic means, saliences and patterns, in the surroundings that would otherwise remain amorphous for the child. These saliences and patterns are determined by the norms, values and motives of the respective sociocultural milieu that the adult represents (see also the analysis of data from de Lemos 1981)[9]

Finally, with regards to the developmental nature of the acquisition of viewpoint aspect, note that differences in knowledge of standard and non-standard choices may be accounted for with Clark's (1987) principle of contrast. The principle of contrast establishes that differences in form in a language signal differences in meaning: "every two forms contrast in meaning" (p. 2). Most important, Clark argues that "children assign contrasting meanings to distinct forms, but they don't always hit on the conventional adult contrasts" (p. 11). For instance, the contrastive use of *here* and *there* in the acquisition of English is used for difffer- ent purposes among English-speaking children compared to the conventional adult contrast. Among children *here* marks possession transfer (e.g., the child says 'here' while giving a rattle to an adult), whereas *there* marks completion of an activity (e.g., the child says 'there' while adding the last block to build a tower).

3.3   Learning capacities and cognitive development

In a criticism of the Piagetian foundation of early proposals about children's use of verbal morphology, Andersen (1989) pointed out that Bronckart and Sinclair's (1973) position (defective tense hypothesis) was suspect, because empirical findings from L2 adult learners show results similar to the ones obtained by Bronckart and Sinclair. Hence, it cannot be claimed that adults are "cognitively deficient" to express past time reference. On the other hand, there are obvious differences in cognitive development between children and adults which may have an effect on the development of tense-aspect morphological marking. First, adults are able to understand the absolute and relative contrasts of the time system of the L2 through their knowledge of their L1 (see Weist 1989). Most important, adults could rely on their knowledge about lexical aspectual classes represented in their L1 to make decisions about the classification of lexical

---

9. It is important to point out, however, that this perspective does not invalidate the role of biological factors.

aspectual classes in the L2.[10] What adults lack, however, is access to the particular means available in the target language to express temporality contrasts. In this way we could account for the fact that the potential effect of lexical aspect may be stronger among children who, by the time they are using aspectual contrasts embedded in absolute time, have not yet developed the concept of relative time location.

Another potential difference between children and adults may be related to what Schmidt (1990: 145) considers the hypothesis of a *shift of conscious awareness* from child to adult: "adults ... do not deliberately attend to form, especially for redundant and communicatively less important grammatical features... Because children have less control over the spotlight of attention... (they) may acquire grammar unconsciously." That is, adults — due to their advanced cognitive development — may be less prone to focus on making connections between meaning and form (i.e., less attention available to process target grammatical properties). Newport (1990) presents a similar perspective instantiated in the so-called "less-is-more" hypothesis: children concentrate on small bits of information of the input data due to their limitations in perceptual abilities (as compared to adults). This learning constraint in children appears to be an asset and not a liability for the processing of a linguistic system: adults are assumed to be unable to benefit from a "componential analysis" of linguistic input due to the heightened linguistic awareness adults have developed while learning their L1.[11] Sinclair, Jarvella and Levelt (1978: 9) also refer to the shift from content to form and they relate it to Gestalt principles stating that "the stronger the semantic 'Gestalt,' the harder to break it down."[12] Even though the concept of the unconscious acquisition of language among children is debatable (e.g., Birdsong 1989; Karmiloff-Smith 1986), the proposal that there are differences in the cognitive processing of language among children and adults remains a possible explanation for child-adult differences in ultimate attainment. For instance, Bley-Vroman (1989) has proposed the Fundamental Difference Hypothesis to account for this contrast, and several studies have offered empirical evidence to argue against the assumption that the process of language

10. Even if this were a debatable point with regards to typologically distinct languages, it can at least be argued that it will be the case for English speakers learning Spanish due to the psychotypological proximity of these languages (e.g., Gass & Ard 1984; Kellerman 1979).

11. Goldowsky & Newport (1992) tested Newport's hypothesis with a learning mechanism whose objective is to learn a basic morphological system.

12. Gestalt psychology believes that organization is basic to all mental activity. The distinction between figure and ground is a central concept developed by Gestalt psychology.

learning among children and adults can be equated (e.g., E. Klein 1995; Patkowski 1990; Robinson 1996; Schmidt & Frota 1986; but, see Krashen (1982), Paradis (1994), Schwartz (1993) among others, for an opposing view). In connection with the development of tense-aspect systems among children and adults, Coppieters (1987: 569) states that

> basic differences between the cognitive processes of children and adults play a role in the kind of linguistic knowledge they acquire, particularly as far as the 'functional' or 'cognitive' aspects of language are concerned. In particular, this might explain why native language transfer occurs precisely in areas of basic grammatical contrasts such as tense/aspect, articles, and pronominal systems, and not in more strictly formal aspects of the language

Incidentally, all the examples of non-formal features of the L2 grammar mentioned by Coppieters are governed by discourse constraints. Finally, Shirai and Andersen (1995) try to account for possible extensions of the basic system of aspectual marking by arguing that "initially children restrict their use of tense/aspect inflections to the prototype of the category, then gradually extend the category boundary, and eventually acquire the adult norm" (p. 759). In this respect, it could be argued — along the lines of Schmidt's and Newport's claim — that adults are unable to restrict their analysis of aspectual distinctions to basic prototypes.

3.4   Conclusion

The previous review of empirical studies on the development of temporality marking in L1 acquisition reveals several lacunae in our knowledge. More importantly, it is apparent that the body of empirical evidence is not comprehensive enough to provide a clear account of the phenomena of tense and aspect marking (especially with regards to the availability of data from a variety of languages). In fact, most of the early empirical evidence on the acquisition of aspectual distinctions among children comes from studies in L1 English acquisition (e.g., Bloom, Lifter & Hafitz 1980; Brown 1973).[13] A review of most of the published data in the L1 acquisition of Romance languages shows that the majority of studies were based on French and a limited number, of mostly longitudinal data, were based on Italian data (Clark 1985). The published research in Spanish and Portuguese is limited. Beyond the scarcity of studies,

---

13. See reviews in Weist (1983).

three important factors seem to make the analysis of aspectual marking in the L1 acquisition of Romance languages particularly difficult: the data from different languages are not directly comparable in most cases, the longitudinal data (except French) focus mostly on the earlier stages of acquisition (up to three years old), and there are very limited data on the particular uses of different aspectual forms in different conversational settings.[14]

Compounding the problem of limited data, there appear to be several competing theoretical explanations to account for the different developmental trends evident in the available data: one major claim is based on the possible existence of language acquisition universals and two others are language-dependent factors. First, the lexical aspect hypothesis (as proposed by Bloom et al. 1980, inter alia) claims that the use of inflectional morphology is dependent on the inherent (lexical) aspectual contour of the verb phrase.[15] Second, there is a possible effect brought about by particular distributional biases in the input data available to the child (e.g., child-directed speech, synthetic versus analytic languages). Finally, in consonance with the previous claim, there is also a potential effect of the discursive context that may affect the use and development of temporality marking in the child's language (e.g., viewpoint aspect in contrast with lexical inherent aspect). The existence of empirical data that both support and contradict several of the above mentioned claims makes tenable the idea that not one but several factors are responsible for the L1 development of aspect and tense morphology in L1. Hence, Shirai (1995), among others has argued that all three factors may interact and concurrently play a role in the development of aspectual distinctions in L1 acquisition.

---

14. Clark argues that only by expanding the perspective of our analysis (age and discursive environment) of aspect marking "...can we arrive at a fuller picture of how children acquire the range of aspectual and temporal options available to them" (p. 764).

15. Associated with this claim there is another argument that focuses on the potential effect of innate semantic universals as argued, especially, by Derek Bickerton (Language Bioprogram Hypothesis).

CHAPTER 4

The development of aspect in L2

There are several questions that figure prominently in the agenda of SLA studies. Will adult classroom learners develop their L2 grammar in the same way as children in the natural environment? Is the contextualized use of the target language essential for the processing of the inherent aspect of each verb? Will formal instruction (classroom setting) help L2 learners notice the most important features of the aspectual system of the target language? Can classroom language instruction help learners speed up the acquisition of aspectual differences in the L2? In the present chapter I assess some possible answers for the above-mentioned questions based on the analysis of the conclusions reached by previous empirical studies on the L2 development of morphological markers of temporality among both tutored and untutored learners. In the first section I analyze the, typically pragmatic, means used by natural learners to mark temporality. In Section 2 I analyze potential differences across natural and tutored settings and I differentiate the predictions made by several theoretical accounts about the development of past tense verbal morphology among L2 learners (e.g., the lexical aspect hypothesis, the discourse hypothesis, the conventional aspect hypothesis, the unmarked past tense hypothesis). In Section 3 I summarize the findings from some empirical studies on the L2 development of tense-aspect morphology, with special reference to studies on classroom learning. Finally, in Section 4 I analyze some of the factors, brought about by instruction, that may have an effect on the development of past tense verbal morphology.

4.1 The pragmatic marking of aspect

The analysis of data from studies on natural language learners reveals that most learners mark temporality by means of linguistic and extralinguistic devices during the beginning stages of acquisition (e.g., Dietrich, Klein & Noyau 1995; Meisel 1987; Perdue & Klein 1992; Sato 1990; Schumann 1987; Trévise 1987;

Véronique 1987). Tense and aspectual contrasts, however, are generally not marked through verbal morphology. This is not unexpected since "adults ... do not deliberately attend to form, especially redundant and communicatively less important grammatical features" (Schmidt 1990: 145; see also Bley-Vroman 1991; Schmidt 1995; Zalewski 1993). In effect, Stutterheim and Klein (1987: 194) argue that the languages analyzed within the scope of the ESFP (European Science Foundation Project) — mostly IndoEuropean languages — "share a similar concept of temporality, at least on a general level." Therefore, in this case the adult second language learner — unlike the first language learner — does not have to acquire the underlying concepts of temporality, modality, locality and the like. Instead, adult L2 learners have to learn the specific ways to express temporality in the target language. This will also be the case of the source and target language analyzed in the present study: English and Spanish respectively. Furthermore, Stutterheim and Klein state that learners are constrained in their selection of specific linguistic features of temporality in the target language through: (1) selective versus obligatory marking, (2) implicit versus explicit marking (e.g., principle of contextual inference), and (3) selection of specific linguistic devices (e.g., inflectional morpheme, adverbial expression). These options are obviously interrelated. For example, the selection of the Preterite–Imperfect inflectional endings in Spanish constitute explicit and obligatory markers of temporality (aspect and tense).

When the encoding of temporal reference is not explicitly represented with morphological markers (e.g., Preterite or Imperfect in Spanish) the learner may rely on pragmatic devices of two types: (a) discourse organization principles and (b) implicit reference. The discourse organization principles are represented by the principle of chronological order (order of reported events reflects order of actual events: Labov 1972), and the bracketing principle (temporal embeddings which are not elements of the temporal discourse organization: background information). On the other hand, temporality may also be conveyed by means of implicit reference: inherent temporal reference (lexical semantics), and associative temporal reference. As explained in Chapter 2, lexical aspectual categories (inherent temporal reference represented in verbal predicates) allow the learner to convey temporal coherence without explicit linguistic devices of the target language. In contrast, the association of local expressions (e.g., name of city where one used to live and name of city of present dwelling) may help convey reference about temporality (e.g., past and present). The following two examples from the data from Stutterheim and Klein shows the use of the above mentioned pragmatic devices:

(1)   Turkey vacation come back, my husband ill

(2)   Turkey vacation, my husband ill

In example (1), the inherent telic nature of the verb *to come* helps to reconstruct the meaning of the sentence. In example (2), the spatial reference (i.e., vacation in Turkey) locates the event in time (i.e., the time when the vacation in Turkey occurred). In both cases, the reconstruction of the meaning is also helped by the overall context that surrounds those expressions.

Most studies of the ESFP show that among natural learners the development of verbal endings is a slow and gradual process which in some cases takes years, and in others merely leads to fossilization (e.g., Dietrich, et al. 1995; Klein & Perdue 1992; Meisel 1987; Perdue & Klein 1992).[1] For instance, Klein, Dietrich and Noyau (1995) show that morpho-syntactic agreement among natural learners is a marginal phenomenon: most learners do not develop their interlanguage beyond the "basic variety." Perdue & Klein (1992) argue that during the first stages of L2 acquisition learners develop a basic variety of the target language that represents an equilibrium between semantic, pragmatic and phrasal constraints. Perdue and Klein point out that some natural language learners fossilize at this stage, while others develop further their basic variety to make it conform to target language standards. The learners who continue developing their L2 system are the ones who perceive lexical and structural inadequacies between the basic variety and the L2. Meisel (1987: 222) claims that developmental sequences reveal increasing performative complexity (e.g., operating principles) and/or decreasing pragmatic usefulness. In essence, natural language learners seem to be especially affected by the particular contextual features of natural discourse: the use of verbal morphology is not necessary to establish communication in the L2 among natural learners.

In some cases the effect of communicative demands is so great that it overrides the use of morphosyntactic features which are shared by both native and target languages. For example, Trévise (1987) analyzed data obtained from several interviews with a Spanish-speaking 49-year-old who had spent three and a half years in France by the time of the interview. Trévise noticed that her subject used "a single past tense form, /e/, which is not an *Imparfait* or *Passé Composé*," and that only two verbs — *donner* (to give) and *payer* (to pay) — were used in the two forms of past tense (*Passé Composé* and *Imparfait*). The speaker avoided use of past tense morphological marking by using periphrastics

---

1. It is important to point out that non-European studies show similar trends in the analysis of natural learners (e.g. Sato 1990; Schumann 1987).

such as *venir de* — a strategic move which "does not hamper comprehension at all" (p. 235). *Venir de* is literally translated as "to arrive from (doing something)." It is quite surprising that a native speaker of Spanish, a language that shares the same aspectual distinction required by past tense French, does not capitalize on that knowledge. Instead, this subject builds a rather complex narrative with adverbials, periphrastics, sequential information, interviewer scaffolding, etc. In this way the learner avoided the use of overt grammatical markers of aspect even after a long period of exposure to the target language in the natural setting. In fact, Howard Grabois (personal communication, May 5, 1997) found a similar case with an academic L2 French student who was raised as a bilingual English-Spanish child but whose schooling was in English only; hence, illiterate in Spanish. Grabois, who was the French instructor, had to remind the above mentioned student that the distinction *Passé Composé–Imparfait* was basically the same as the Preterite–Imperfect one in Spanish.

Schumann (1987) also argues that during the first stages of acquisition (basilang stage) L2 speakers do not mark aspectual distinctions morphologically in their interlanguage. Schumann analyzed the interlanguage of five speakers of three different languages (one Chinese, one Japanese and three Spanish) who had been living in the United States for at least 10 years at the time of the study. The subjects had learnt English without formal instruction.[2] In spite of the length of residence in the United States the interlanguage of these nonnative speakers was quite marginal, if comprehensible at all (data samples from pp. 30–37). Schumann argues that basilang speech "is acquired through the pragmatic functions of the mind's general cognitive mechanisms and therefore does not attain morphosyntactic regularity" (p. 39). Basilang speech constitutes a system of communication: the formal linguistic features of the interlanguage will develop to the extent that communication does not break down. For instance, morphosyntactic aspectual markers will not be a necessary feature of this type of interlanguage insofar as other temporal markers fulfill the function of marking aspect in some other way. Schumann argues that basilang learners mark temporal reference with four basic linguistic tools: (1) adverbials, (2) serialization (sequence of utterances reflects actual temporal order of events), (3) calendric reference, and (4) implicit reference (temporal reference is inferred from context). Schumann's data show that ten or more years of residence in the United States are not enough to learn to use past tense inflectional morphology in English.

---

2. Schumann does not provide information about the linguistic environment where his informants lived (what was the language used at home or at work?), nor about the amount of time they used English (did they live in a non-English speaking community?).

In relative terms, classroom learners learn faster than natural learners do.

Further suport for the claim about the limited extent of use of morphological markers of past tense among natural learners comes from a longitudinal study carried out by Sato (1990). She examined the development of L2 English past tense inflections (among other features) of two Vietnamese-speaking brothers (ages 10 and 12) during a 10-month period in the United States. Neither subject received formal instruction in English during the observation period, but their exposure to English was intensive through their adoptive parents and the surrounding community (probably different from the adult subjects of Schumann). The analysis of Sato was based on recorded conversations (intervals of four weeks) between the researcher and the two adolescents. The boy's foster mother was present in most meetings and the interaction included diverse topics from spontaneous conversation (e.g., subjects' experiences at school and their soccer teams) to help with homework tasks (e.g., spelling and vocabulary worksheets). Sato's data show that these learners did not mark temporality with morphological means: there is no apparent developmental change from parataxis to sintacticization (within this 10-month period). In contrast, both subjects relied on other-than-morphological means to mark past tense reference (e.g., adverbs, interlocutor's marking of past tense, etc.). Sato states that conversational interaction might be a necessary but not sufficient condition to "generate acquisition of all the linguistic devices that encode PTR (past time reference)" (p. 90). On the other hand, Sato argues that discourse processes might still be useful for the incorporation of lexical markers of pastness into the interlanguage (e.g., adverbs, and irregular past tense tokens).

In sum, the analysis of data from studies based on adult natural learners do not show any extended use of verbal morphology as usually reported in the case of classroom learners (e.g., Dietrich et al. 1995; Klein & Perdue 1992; Meisel 1987; Perdue & Klein 1993; Sato 1990; Schumann 1987; Trévise 1987; Véronique 1987), or they show that verbal morphology develops very slowly (e.g., Andersen 1986; Klein et al. 1995; Schumann 1987).[3] Accordingly, Klein et al. proposed a series of three developmental stages for the acquisition of overt markers of temporality in the nonnative language: pre-basic variety, basic variety, and beyond the basic variety. The pre-basic variety is defined by the following traits: (1) there is no functional inflexion, (2) complex constructions are put together according to pragmatic principles (e.g., focus last), and (3) constructions

---

3. It is important to mention that the analysis of non-tutored learners has revealed some contradictory findings: past tense is used with background information and foreground marked with the base form (e.g., Kumpf 1984; Perdue & Klein 1992: 264).

are heavily context-dependent. The basic variety is defined by the following features: (1) utterances consist of uninflected verbs, arguments and optional adverbials, (2) lexical verbs appear in base form and there is little use of copula, (3) there is steady increase in use of adverbials, and (4) aspectual verbs (boundary markers) emerge. Klein et al. argue that development up to the basic variety reflects general properties of natural language, whereas development beyond the basic variety is less uniform and more likely to be affected by specific features of the target language. Finally, the development beyond the basic variety exhibits the following traits: (1) acquisition is not driven by functional demands (there is coexistence of various morphological forms without appropriate function), (2) further development is slow, gradual and continuous (no sharp developmental stages), (3) tense marking precedes aspect marking, and (4) irregular morphology precedes regular morphology (inductive learning). It is interesting to note that the traits that characterize the stage beyond the basic variety among naturalistic learners seem to reflect the type of language learning that takes place in classroom instruction: no functional demands, slow and gradual development, and inductive learning is essential for the incorporation of non-prototypical verbal morphology. In sum, it may be argued that communication demands (functional needs) may constitute a necessary but not sufficient condition to reach native-like mastery of the L2. On the other hand, classroom students are faced with the problem that the contextualized use of the target language may be essential for the processing of the discourse-based grammatical marking of aspect.

4.2   The morphosyntactic marking of aspect

Classroom learners also use alternative means of temporal reference instead of tense or aspect morphology. For example, second language teachers know that during the beginning stages of instruction, students use a process of relexification of their native language to communicate in the L2 (Ramsay 1990: 202). What is interesting is that classroom students eventually incorporate past tense aspectual distinctions into their interlanguage system by sheer pressure to comply with target language norms (e.g., Bardovi-Harlig 1994; Bardovi-Harlig & Reynolds 1995; Bergström 1995; Hasbún 1995; Kaplan 1987; Ramsay 1990; Salaberry 1998; 2000; Teutsch-Dwyer & Fathman 1997). In other words, it is not the pressure to communicate per se that forces learners to incorporate morphosyntactic markers of aspect in their system (see discussion in Dietrich, et al. 1995; Sato 1990; Schumann 1987). If what distinguishes basilang speakers (from two to ten years of exposure to the L2 in the studies mentioned above) from classroom learners (from two to four semesters of instruction on average) is the type of linguistic environment, we have to conclude that classroom instruction is successful in generating a high level of use of morphosyntactic (inflectional) instead of pragmatic means of marking tense and aspect. These findings raise two important questions: (1) how do classroom students learn to redundantly mark temporality (tense and aspect) on the verb? and (2) is the nature of their morphological system stable across language tasks (attention to form)? But, there is a third, more encompassing question: why do students select inflectional means — as opposed to pragmatic means as natural learners — to mark temporality?

4.2.1 *The lexical aspect hypothesis*

Several researchers have directly tied the inherent lexical aspectual value of the verb to the development of past tense verbal morphology (e.g., Andersen 1986, 1991, 1994; Andersen & Shirai 1994, 1996; Bardovi-Harlig 1994; Bardovi-Harlig & Bergström 1996; Bardovi-Harlig & Reynolds 1995; Robison 1990, 1993, 1995). The lexical aspect hypothesis claims that the learners' selection of verbal morphology will be dependent on the inherent lexical semantics of the verb phrase: completed events (achievements and accomplishments), simultaneous processes (activities), and states. More specifically, Andersen and Shirai (1994, 1996) claim that the hypothesis is composed of four basic tenets:

1. Learners use perfective past marking (e.g., Preterite) first on telic events, and they later extend its use to verbs from other lexical aspectual classes
2. The imperfective marker (e.g., Imperfect) will appear later than the Preterite in association with atelic events (states and activities), eventually extending to telic events
3. The use of the periphrastic Progressive will initially appear in association with activity verbs and then extend to telic events
4. The use of the periphrastic Progressive will not overextend to stative verbs

The last principle represents, in essence, an extention of principle (3). Furthermore, principle (4) is adduced to be operative in L1 acquisition only (Shirai & Kurono 1998). Principles (1) to (3) will be the ones relevant to the analysis to be presented in the following chapters.[4] Notice also that Shirai and Kurono claim that the sequence proposed by the lexical aspect hypothesis "arguably has the status of a universal in SLA" (p. 249).

---

4. The lexical aspect hypothesis is referred to with a variety of labels such as Primacy of Aspect hypothesis (e.g., Robison 1990, 1995), the Redundant Marking hypothesis (e.g., Shirai & Kurono 1998), and, originally, the Defective Tense hypothesis.

The lexical aspect hypothesis was originally proposed by Andersen (1986) based on data collected from adolescent natural language learners (two siblings). For example, Anthony, an English-speaking adolescent learned L2 Spanish outside of school with his friends (his schooling in Puerto Rico was in English). Two samples of Anthony's speech were collected in 1978 and 1980 respectively. In 1978 Anthony had already spent two years in Puerto Rico and was able to interact with no problems with his Spanish-speaking friends. At that time Andersen noted that 50% of the verbs used by Anthony in contexts requiring obligatory past tense/perfective aspect were marked as such. On the other hand, none of the verbs requiring imperfective carried any mark of grammatical aspect.[5] In 1980 Anthony used the Preterite in 88% of all obligatory cases which required perfective aspect, whereas the Imperfect was used in 43% of all obligatory cases. Most verbs describing punctual events were marked with perfective aspect, whereas the verbs marking states or durative events were not marked with past endings in 1978, and only to a certain extent in 1980. Andersen argued that the use of perfective aspect in Anthony's interlanguage was closely associated to the specific situations in which the verbs were used. For example, the following are examples of how Anthony marked perfectivity: *safué* = (s/he) left, *loviste* = (you) saw him, *sapartió* = (it) broke, and *roberon* = (they) stole. These are non-standard forms: the marking of person and number was usually wrong, and clitics were incorrectly incorporated as morphological inflections of the verb. These examples, however, are quite common among natural learners who are exposed to the spoken language: the parsing of the speech does not conform to the standard form of the target language (where does one "word" start or finish in the speech stream?). In effect, these "chunks of linguistic information" reflect the lack of appropriate segmentation of the stream of acoustic signals: linguistic information is inherently tied to the situational context.

Based on the previous data, Andersen (1991: 318) argued that L2 learners follow a particular sequence in the development of aspectual markers: Ø > punctual > telic > dynamic > statives. The apparent correlation of such a sequence with the Aristotelian classification of aspect led Andersen to conclude that past tense morphological marking in L2 acquisition is based on the lexical semantic value of the verb. Accordingly, Andersen proposed that the use of imperfective markers spreads from stative verbs to punctual events, and the use of perfective markers spreads from punctual events (achievement) to stative verbs.

---

5. Learners sometimes use present tense to convey imperfective aspect in contrast to the correct grammatical marking of perfectivity. The important point to note here, however, is that Anthony did not use the target-like marking of grammatical aspect.

This gradual spread of the use of grammatical aspect according to verb type is argued to occur sequentially in time in eight stages (1991: 315): Table 4.1.

Table 4.1. Development of Spanish past tense aspect (based on Andersen, 1991)[a]

	STATE	ACTIV.	ACCOMPL.	ACHIEVEM.
1	tiene	juega	enseña	se parte
2	tiene	juega	enseña	*se partió*
3	*tenía*	juega	enseña	se partió
4	tenía	jugaba	*enseñó*	se partió
5	tenía	*jugaba*	enseñó enseñaba	se partió
6	tenía	jugaba *jugó*	enseñó *enseñaba*	se partió
7	tenía	jugaba jugó	enseñó enseñaba	se partió *se partía*
8	tenía *tuvo*	jugaba jugó	enseñó enseñaba	se partió se partía

[a] The selected Spanish examples from Andersen may be translated in the following way: *tener*: to have; *jugar*: to play; *enseñar*: to teach; and *partir (se parte)*: to break.

At stage 1 learners mark neither past tense nor aspect. At stage 2 the use of the Preterite is encoded in punctual verbs only. At stage 3 prototypical stative verbs appear in Imperfect forms. At stage 4 the Preterite spreads to accomplishment verbs, and the Imperfect spreads to activity verbs: all verbs are now marked in past tense. At stage 5 the use of verbal morphology begins to overlap within each verb type: accomplishments (telic events) can now be marked by Imperfect or Preterite. At stage 6 activities can be used with perfective or imperfective aspect, and at stage 7 also punctual events can be marked by either Imperfect or Preterite. Stage 8 constitutes the end of the sequence: stative verbs can be encoded in perfective aspect. Stage 8 is the final development of the system of aspectual distinctions (near-native competence).

The proposed developmental sequence reviewed above, faces both theoretical problems (not all developmental stages are accounted for by the hypothesis), as well as empirical problems (lack of support from several studies).

First, it is important to point out that neither the Relevance Principle (aspect is more relevant to the meaning of the verb than tense, mood or agreement) nor the Congruence Principle (learners choose the morpheme whose aspectual meaning is most congruent with the aspectual meaning of the verb) can explain the use of Preterite and Imperfect after stage 5. From stage 5 to 8 the learner is marking grammatical aspect irrespective of the lexical aspectual class of the verb (i.e., viewpoint aspect: see Smith 1991). In other words, the aspect hypothesis is relevant for the development of L2 past tense marking until stage 4. Second, the relevance principle is based on Bybee's (1995: 447) claim that:

> aspect has greater relevance to the verb than tense because aspect affects the way the internal temporal contours of the situation are viewed, while tense takes the situation as a whole and places it in relative time without changing the perspective on the nature of the event described by the verb.[6]

However, there is no independent evidence to support this statement with respect to Spanish except for the fact that aspectual markers tend to occur closer to the stem of the verb in other languages (e.g., Dahl 1985). In Spanish both tense and aspect markers are fused into one single morpheme. Alternatively, Bybee (1995: 447) claims that aspect markers "tend to have a greater morphophonemic effect on the stem rather than tense markers" (Bybee 1995: 446–447). She shows that for several Spanish verbs (e.g., *poder*: to be able to, *poner*: to put, *querer*: to want, and *saber*: to know), the Imperfect is formed regularly (i.e., *podía, ponía, quería, sabía*), whereas the Preterite may generate changes on the stem of the verb (i.e., *pude, puse, quise, supe*). Notice, however, that the Imperfect and the Preterite are both tense and aspect markers; hence, the argument of Bybee works both in favor and against her claim depending on what interpretation one prefers (no independent evidence to disambiguate the claim). In other words, Bybee's explanation is non-discriminating because we must assume that the Preterite (but not the Imperfect) carries aspectual meaning (but not tense) when it affects the stem of the verb. On the other hand, we must assume that the Imperfect (but not the Preterite) carries tense meaning (but not aspectual meaning) when it does not affect the stem.[7] Finally, there are also empirical findings that appear to contradict the basic claim of the lexical aspect hypothesis. First, several studies — to be reviewed below — have failed to obtain evidence

---

6. This concept was originally proposed by Jakobson (1957).

7. In passing, notice also that most of these irregular verbs mentioned by Bybee correspond to typical stative verbs: *estar, haber, poder, querer, saber, ser, tener* (to be (locative), to exist, to be able, to want, to know, to be (existential), to have).

for several of the proposed stages of sequential development of L2 aspect according to the inherent "lexical" value of each verb (Bardovi-Harlig & Bergström 1996; Bergström 1995; Hasbún 1995; Lafford 1996; Ramsay 1990; Salaberry 1998). Most important, in some cases the semantic features which underlie the lexical value of verb types are in conflict with the expected use of overt verbal endings (e.g., Robison 1990).[8]

4.2.2 The discourse hypothesis

Shirai and Andersen (1996: 759) have stated that it is difficult to claim that *early past morphology* encodes tense or aspect only.[9] Furthermore, Andersen and Shirai offer another alternative not based on the semantics of the verb (or tense constraints for that matter, as reasoned above), but, rather, on the discourse motivations of the speaker following the reasoning of Sankoff (1990). Sankoff claims that the lack of morphological marking (or present tense for that matter) does not necessarily entail that the speaker intends to encode the opposite meaning of the explicit marker; it may only reveal implicit marking. In the case of past tense verbal morphology, Andersen and Shirai reason that stative verbs are marked with present tense (or uninflected in the case of English) because speakers "do not identify states or "stative" scenarios as something needing explicit marking." And further, on the same page they add: "the semantic attributes of verbs that appear to correlate with verb morphology are really a consequence of discourse motivation to highlight some, but not other, events and situations with newly perceived morphology." Hence, it is possible to maintain the hypothesis that classroom learners mark verbal morphology endings according to narrative structure: telic and atelic events are correlated with the foreground and background of a story. Indeed, several researchers have investigated the use of aspectual distinctions in past tense from the perspective of narrative structure as a powerful predictor of aspectual use. For instance, Reid (1980) argues that aspect can be better understood from the perspective of *high and low focus* on the particular situations that comprise the narration (textual structure). Wallace (1982) makes a similar argument based on the distinction of *figure and ground*, and claims that this psychological distinction is part of an innate,

---

8. This is not surprising because the classification of verbs according to their lexical aspectual value may be unreliable (see Chapter 2).

9. Even though Shirai and Andersen's argument refers to L1 acquisition, the dilemma concerning which factor to consider more important in the early marking of past tense verbal endings is also relevant for L2 acquisition studies.

universal, perceptual distinction. Givón (1982) states that the semantic characterization of aspectual markers may also be associated with discourse-pragmatic
functions. Vet and Vetters (1994: 1) claim that the meaning of tense and aspect
forms "strongly depends on contextual factors and probably on the type of text
as well, so that tense and aspect cannot be properly studied if their contribution
to text cohesion is not taken into account." Finally, Hopper (1982: 16) argues that
the nature of aspectual distinctions in languages like French (or Spanish for that
matter) cannot be characterized by semantics in a consistent way; the adequate
reference may only come from a *global discourse function*.

Indeed, the analysis of recent empirical data from classroom acquisition
provides support for the above mentioned theoretical position. For instance, data
from Bergström (1995) "show firm use of the *Passé Composé* not only with
accomplishments and achievements but with all three dynamic verbs (activities,
accomplishments, achievements) regardless of level" (p. 153).[10] To explain
these results, Bergström conjectures that the acquisition of *Passé Composé* may
occur rapidly because it "has several indications for the learner that it is solidly
a past tense while the Imperfect does not have any besides a weak temporal one
in a certain context that is dissociated from speech" (p. 164).[11] Interestingly,
however, the skewdness of the data from Bergström may also be explained if the
use of *Passé Composé* is associated with an aspectual distinction that originates
in the discourse organization of the text (foreground). If the learner is trying to
develop a narrative event of the type exemplified in several experimental studies
(e.g., Bergström 1995; Salaberry 1998; Wiberg 1996), it is quite likely that the
nature of the task itself will generate a fair amount of foregrounded events. As
a consequence, the explanation based on the inherent semantic value of the verb
and associated arguments may not be particularly powerful due to the "inherent"
association of aspectual marking with contextual ever-changing features of
discourse (see Chapter 2).

Similarly, in an often cited study, Kumpf (1984) investigated the use of past
tense marking in the L2 English of a Japanese speaker who had been living in
the United States for 28 years at the time of the interview. The analysis of the
narrative monologues of this subject reveals that "the base form characterizes the
foreground; the background manifests many forms, including those carrying

---

10. Since there were very few true beginners among her subjects, Bergström argues that her data
were not able to track the development of the use of the perfective aspect in L2 French.

11. However, alternative explanations for the apparent advantage of use of *Passé Composé* based on
the type of input available in classroom instruction have been offered (e.g. Kaplan 1987).

aspectual distinctions, and especially tense" (p. 140). Kumpf claims that aspect may be acquired before tense, although the specific aspectual marking of her Japanese subject stands in clear contrast with the results of other studies in which telic/punctual verbs (associated with the foreground) were the ones marked with past tense (e.g., Andersen 1986; Robison 1990; Wiberg 1996). Similarly, Lafford (1996) presents evidence that reveal a higher number of uses of atelic rather than telic verbs in the L2 Spanish oral narratives of a Disney story (see Section 4.3.7 below). In another study, Véronique (1987) showed that his low level informants (natural learners of French) were systematic in their use of verb morphology: the verb stem (V) marked foreground information, whereas V+e forms were used for background information (p. 266). However, this was not the case for his intermediate-level informants. Véronique argues that "we would rather consider foreground-background as one level, maybe the most important one, of the organization of narratives" (p. 267). Finally, among studies based on tutored learners in a natural setting (ESL students from diverse L1 backgrounds), Bardovi-Harlig (1995a) suggests that the development of tense and aspect distinctions may be related to grounding in a narrative structure. It should be noted that similar results have been obtained in the analysis of creoles. Givón (1982) shows that in creoles the Ø form (base form of the verb) marks the main plot of the narrative. The main narrative action in the past — normally associated with performance verbs which carry the [+perfective] feature — is not marked grammatically:

a.   … I go out of the way,
b.   I fix that dog up…
c.   that dog *bin* come nice'n fat,
d.   all the hair *bin* grow…
e.   I spray-im with malathion'n all,
f.   I bring-im down the beach special…

…So I went out of my way, I fixed that dog up… the dog had become nice and fat, all his hair had grown back… I sprayed him with malathion, I brought him down to the beach specially… (p. 120).

It should be pointed out, however, that there is an inherent overlap in the prediction offered by the account based on the lexical semantic value of the predicate and the discourse-based approach, since completed events and punctual events sometimes define the notion of foreground (e.g., Bardovi-Harlig 1995a; Lafford 1996; Liskin-Gasparro 1996; Reinhart 1984). Reinhart (1984) lists the temporal and textual criteria that mark the notion of foreground: narrativity (only textual/narrative units can serve as foreground), punctuality (punctual events serve more easily as foreground), and completeness (completed events serve more easily as foreground). Bardovi-Harlig (1995a) also considers the feature of "newness" (new information is more relevant for the foreground). In fact, Binnick (1991: 381) claims that in Russian, aspectual choice is "highly sensitive to focus structure": imperfective is used with old information, but if the verb is in focus the perfective is used. The similarities that underlie the criteria distinguishing foreground and background information and the classification of verbs according to inherent semantic value are remarkable (telic versus atelic). Hence, the danger of engaging in a circular argument is quite high if we consider punctual and completed events as part of the defining criteria of foregrounded events. Not surprisingly, Bardovi-Harlig claims that the distinction of the predictions of each approach "may be too fine-grained for a study of interlanguage" (p. 286).

To the best of my knowledge there is only one published study in L2 acquisition which has empirically compared the relative effect of the roles of semantic (lexical aspect) and discursive (foreground-background) factors in the development of L2 aspect.[12] Housen (1994) analyzed the data collected from one English speaking subject learning Dutch. The data consist of two 90-minute recordings of open-ended oral conversations separated one year from each other. Housen analyzed the relative weight of semantico-conceptual universals and discourse-pragmatic universals in the development of aspectual distinctions in past tense Dutch. A summary of the results of his analysis is presented in Table 4.2.

Table 4.2. Past tense marking discriminated by grounding (based on Housen, 1994).

	Verb type	Time 1	Time 2
Foreground	Dynamic	55%	85%
	Stative	50%	73%
	Punctual	58%	84%
	Durative	50%	76%
Background	Dynamic	30%	74%
	Stative	3%	26%
	Punctual	26%	73%
	Durative	7%	45%

---

12. There are two recent unpublished studies that have addressed this issue as well: Bardovi-Harlig (1997) and Lafford (1996).

When the analysis of the aspectual marking is discriminated by grounding, all types of verbs in the foreground show the same degree of past marking at time 1, and there is a similar level of improvement from time 1 to time 2 irrespective of the lexical aspect value of the verb. On the other hand, the analysis of background information shows that state verbs are not marked with past tense at time 1 (3%), and that they are sometimes marked with past tense at time 2 (26%). Dynamic verbs jump from a substantial 30% past tense marking at time 1 to 74% at time 2. The advantage for punctual versus durative verbs is more apparent at time 1 (26% versus 7%). Past tense marking for both punctual and durative verbs increases at time 2 (73% versus 45%). In sum, the verbs in high focus (Reid 1980) will be marked first, regardless of the inherent lexical value of the verb. In this respect, Bardovi-Harlig (1995a: 285) explains that the foreground is functionally simple (it moves the narrative forward), whereas the background is functionally complex (it may even recount sequential events on a time line distinct from the one used for the main event in focus). The results from Housen, however, should be analyzed with caution for two main reasons. First, the number of tokens from the background cells was quite low; hence, the results according to grounding are unreliable. Second, Dutch does not grammaticize the perfective-imperfective distinction, as is the case in the Romance languages. Consequently the results of Housen — as recognized in his footnote 13 — are tentative at best. The analyses of Bardovi-Harlig (1997) and Lafford (1996) were also inconclusive on that matter.

4.2.3 Distributional biases: The role of conventional aspect

The recent account offered by Andersen and Shirai (1994) of the development of aspectual distinctions in L2 learning points in the direction of discursive-pragmatic factors (as opposed to discursive structure only) as the ultimate determinant of the acquisition of aspect in the L2. Andersen and Shirai argue that the Relevance Principle (aspect is more relevant to the meaning of the verb than tense, mood or agreement) and the Congruence Principle (learners choose the morpheme whose aspectual meaning is most congruent with the aspectual meaning of the verb) "are especially sensitive to discourse-pragmatic function. Verbs and inflections are chosen to fulfill the needs of the speaker in ongoing discourse..." (p. 147). According to the Distributional Bias Hypothesis (DBH) native speakers and learners have a "communicative need to distinguish reference to the main point/goal of talk from supporting information" (p. 152). The nature of communication, however, is inherently tied to cultural conventions — and so is the choice of the marked values of aspect (e.g., Smith 1991). In essence, we want to find out how the native speaker conventionally prefers certain marked choices of verbal morphology over unmarked ones. In this respect, it is important to distinguish the effect of three separate forces in the development of nonnative verbal morphology: (1) semantic (cognitive predisposition to distinguish semantic classes of verbs), (2) discursive (foreground-background contrast), and (3) input effects (native speakers' model) (p. 153). It appears, then, that the problem faced by classroom learners is not necessarily whether they will distinguish foreground from background information, or whether they will pick up the semantic nuances that distinguish lexical aspectual classes, but rather, whether they will be able to acquire the conventional values associated with morphological marking in the target language (i.e., the origin of the distributional bias). Wallace (1982: 217, italics added) had originally identified this problem in the following way:

> Gestalt theory makes strong claims about universal innate perceptual mechanisms, while *acquired individual, social, and cultural dispositions clearly play a role in determining, among other things, perceived figures and grounds.* The implications of such factors for the organization of language are profound, as in, for example, the difference in viewpoint or orientation...

In this respect, Jakobson argues that *shifters* are indexical symbols: they are both *symbols* (association with a represented object by conventional rules) and *indexes* (existential relation with object they represent). Pronouns are a typical example of a shifter because they change their reference according to the roles of speaker and addressee. In spite of the multiplicity of meanings that shifters may acquire by virtue of their indexical nature, they also possess a general meaning: *I* represents the addresser and *You* the addressee. On the other hand, it remains true that the assignment of the *I* and *You* to specific individuals may constantly shift during a conversational exchange.

Mainguenau (1994) claims that aspect is also an "embrayeur" (shifter) following the original distinction made by Jakobson: the meaning of certain linguistic elements (*énoncé*) is predicated on the context of the utterance (*contexte énonciatif*). As such, aspect falls within a theory of "énonciation" which pays attention to the individual act of language use as much as to the linguistic object (*énoncé*). For Mainguenau it is not possible to consider language as an objective instrument used to transfer information; language is an "activity" between two individuals where the speaker selects linguistic means capable to isolate and identify a certain object or groups of objects to the exclusion of others. In fact, the latter may be an alternative definition of viewpoint aspect (see Smith 1983, 1991). Indeed, Smith (1991: 12, italics added) argues that the speaker expresses a given aspectual meaning according to the grammar of the language and the conventions of use for that language. The grammar of a language relates linguistic forms to meanings. *The conventions involve standard and marked choices, shared information between speaker and receiver, and other pragmatic considerations.* The conventions are principles for language use rather than rules. They have the flexibility characteristic of rules of text and conversation, unlike the relatively firm rules of sentence grammar"

Similarly, from the perspective of L2 teaching, Kramsch (1986) states that discourse coherence is achieved by "entering temporarily someone else's frame of reference and following the cultural logic of their conversation." In sum, the conventions of use represent the type of information that the native speaker may not share with the nonnative speaker and where the discrepancies between them may surface.

The lexical aspect hypothesis (e.g., Andersen 1986, 1991; Robison 1990) and the discourse hypothesis (Andersen & Shirai 1994, 1996; Bardovi-Harlig 1995a) were developed from data collected in the natural setting.[13] Hence, it is not clear why classroom learners would follow the same developmental sequences of natural learners given (1) that the sequential development of aspect among the latter is determined by natural discourse (contextualized), and (2) that classroom discourse does not incorporate the features normally attributed to non-academic discourse. Even if classroom interaction incorporated more "free conversation" tasks and less grammar instruction, it is doubtful that the functional needs of true communicative interaction (i.e., natural settings) would be successfully recreated. For instance, Frawley and Lantolf (1984, 1985) argue that simple "dialogue practice" is not conducive to learning: classroom "dialogues" should be regarded as script reading, or merely as a form of practice in formulaic speech. Indeed, the true interactive nature of a spontaneous dialogue is rarely present in classroom-based dialogues because students merely perform a carefully guided academic task based on linguistic exchanges. On the other hand, if we were to consider classroom instruction discourse as "authentic academic discourse" (vanLier 1996), classroom and everyday discourse still represent different kinds of contextualizations. Notice also that immersion in a community of native speakers is not the same as remaining in a closed community of nonnative speakers meeting several times a week for academic purposes — no matter how authentic the academic environment is. In sum, classroom discourse tends to efface the normal characteristics of everyday discourse. Therefore, if

---

13. Bardovi-Harlig's subjects were ESL learners from various L1 backgrounds studying at a university in the United States.

students do not have access to natural pieces of discourse, it is unlikely that the normal distribution of aspectual markers in the target language will guide learners in their use of aspectual distinction in the target language.

Several studies of L2 development have analyzed potential differences in the interpreation of what constitutes a marked choice of aspect (e.g., Coppieters 1987; Salaberry 1998). Specific evidence for the role of conventional aspect comes from Coppieters (1987), whose study presented native and nonnative speakers of French with decontextualized sentences of the following type:

(16)   *J'ai très souvent mangé/Je mangeais très souvent.*
         I ate very often/I would eat very often

(17)   *Quand j'étais chez ma tante, {je racontais/j'ai raconté} plusieurs fois mes aventures.*
         When I was at my aunt's I would tell/I told my adventures many times

(19)   *En 1885, Victor Hugo {mourait/est mort}.*
         In 1885 Victor Hugo was dying/died

Coppieters judged the results of his test sentences on the basis of homogeneity of responses only, because any one of the possible answers for the sentences above (*Passé Composé* or *Imparfait*) was grammatically valid. Native speakers used mostly *Passé Composé* with sentences (16) and (17), and *Imparfait* with sentence (19). Coppieters stated that "all NS's indicated that they felt a strong and marked contrast between the *Imparfait* and the *Passé Composé* in the sentences included in this section" (p. 559). Therefore, the judgments of the native speakers were homogeneous. In contrast, the judgments of the nonnative speakers were heterogeneous; hence, ambivalent (nonnative-like). Undoubtedly, native speakers were accessing a huge data base which provided a context for the adequate interpretation of the — apparently — decontextualized sentences. I believe that the heterogeneous nature of the nonnative speakers' judgments is not a reflection of lack of access to the inherent semantic value of the verb constellation of the sample sentences, but the outcome of a distinct discursive data base. That is, nonnative speakers lacked access to the same discursive environment that guided the homogeneous responses of native speakers.

There are also previous reports that confirm the observed differences between native and nonnative speakers in the use of non-prototypical marking of verbal morphology (e.g., García & vanPutte 1988; Salaberry 1998). For instance, García and vanPutte compared the selection of past tense aspectual morphology between 15 Spanish native speakers and 20 L1 Dutch teachers of Spanish. The task was implemented as a written retelling in past tense from a narrative shown in present tense. The narrative was based on the story *El Muerto* (The Corpse) from the Argentinean author J. L. Borges. The results show that the responses of both groups were polarized due to the effect of the semantic opposition perfective-imperfective, although the effect was stronger for native speakers. Of the 185 verbs in context all native speakers marked 30% of the items with Imperfect and 33% with Preterite, whereas all nonnative speakers marked 24% of the items with Imperfect and 26% with the Preterite. In other words, native speakers as a group agreed more often than nonnative speakers on the aspectual marking of a given verb. García and vanPutte also analyzed the items where native and nonnative speakers disagreed. Their analysis shows that nonnative speakers seem to rely on more local cues, whereas native speakers are more attentive to the overall context of the narrative. For example, in the following use of the verb *ser* (to be) the nonnative speakers were compelled to use the Imperfect by the lexical aspectual value of the verb, and the misleading background nature of a predicative proposition (i.e., descriptive):

> Otálora se embarca, la travesía es tormentosa y crujiente; al otro día vaga por las calles de Montevideo.

> Otálora embarks, the crossing is stormy and creaky; the next day he drifts along the streets of Montevideo.

In this example, only 7% of the responses from native speakers showed preference for the Imperfect (*era*), compared to 45% among nonnative speakers. In other words, the majority of native speakers preferred the use of the non-prototypical Preterite (*fue*): foregrounded situation. Since we may assume that the verb *ser* is normally marked with Imperfect according to the distributional bias that obtains in both native and nonnative speakers (see Andersen 1994; Andersen & Shirai 1994; Ramsay 1989), it follows that the use of the Preterite is used to move it to the foreground of the narrative. In sum, native speakers are more willing to accept the non-prototypical use of tense-aspect morphology (i.e., Preterite with the verb *ser*) — rather than the inherent lexical aspectual value of the verbal predicate — due to the effect of the larger piece of discourse evidenced in the text (see also Andersen 1994; Andersen & Shirai 1994; Lunn 1985; Silva-Corvalán 1983; Wiberg 1996). García and vanPutte's results are even more compelling if we consider that their subjects should probably be considered near-native speakers (based on their background profiles).

Finally, Salaberry (1998) compared data from a cloze-test on the selection of *Imparfait–Passé Composé* among 39 native English speakers enrolled in a second semester course of college French, and 30 native speakers of French. The responses from nonnative speakers differed from the ones from native speakers with respect to the selection of the *marked choices* (i.e., viewpoint aspect) in L2

French (only data from stative verbs available in marked choices). On the other hand, the nonnative speakers were able to select the unmarked setting (i.e., congruence of inherent lexical semantics and grammatical aspect) in ways that paralleled the results from native speakers. These findings are in line with the assumption that learners may be "stretching" a simple system (potentially relying on the lexical semantic value of predicate) to a more complex one that must incorporate discursive-pragmatic factors that are language-dependent. In sum, the system of aspectual distinctions developed by classroom students may not comply with the developmental stages representative of natural language learners (e.g., Andersen 1986, 1991), especially in terms of the expected development of the marked forms of grammatical aspect (stages 5 to 8 of Table 4.1). The discrepancies between native and nonnative speakers' preferences may be reasonably attributed to the combined effect of both universal (semantico-conceptual) and language-specific (pragmatic) aspectual choices.

4.2.4   A prototype account: a default marker of past tense

Andersen and Shirai (1994, 1996) have proposed that the acquisition of past tense verbal morphology in L2 may be based on the existence of prototype categories.[14] Their proposal is based on Taylor (1989: 149–154), who claims that the past tense is a polysemous category comprising three major functional components: past tense proper, unreality or counterfactuality, and pragmatic softener (see also Fleischman 1989, 1990; McCarthy 1991; inter alia). Taylor argues that the prototype of the category is the referential meaning of temporality, and draws on the work of Brown (1973) on L1 acquisition to propose that the central meaning of temporal past tense is "completion in the immediate past of a punctual event, the consequences of which are perceptually salient at the moment of speaking" (p. 243).[15] To this, Andersen and Shirai (1996: 556) add that the category perfective appears to have a prototype similar to the one of past tense: single event (mostly punctual), seen as a transition from one source state to a target state and with defined end-result (see Dahl 1985). Thus, Andersen and Shirai propose that there is a transition from more prototypical to less prototypical

---

14. A similar proposal has been offered for L1 acquisition (e.g., Shirai 1991; Shirai & Andersen 1995).

15. It is not clear whether Taylor is quoting Brown, or whether he is simply enclosing the above mentioned phrase in single quotation marks (the above statement appears in quotation marks in Taylor). If this is a quote from Brown, the definition of the prototype category of past tense may be circular: it is based on the acquisition data from Brown at the same time that it determines the theoretical analysis of Taylor.

members of a category that renders the following sequence of acquisition of the grammatical category of past tense:

Deictic past (achievement → accomplishments → activity → state → habitual or iterative past) → counterfactual or pragmatic softener

Andersen and Shirai (1994: 152) argue that "learners are much more heavily constrained by the One to One Principle and the restriction of form: meaning relations to the least marked member of a prototype hierarchy." Andersen and Shirai (1996: 557) acknowledge, however, two potential problems with this account. First, the account of a prototype theory may be circular if the prototype is determined by the order of acquisition at the same time that the order of acquisition is based on the prototype (see previous footnote for possible source of definition of the prototype in Taylor 1989). Second, it is possible that children's prototypes differ from adults'. In fact, it is reasonable to assume that adults come to the process of L2 acquisition with clearly established prototypes (although they need not coincide with the ones shared by target language speakers), whereas children may be in the process of developing them. Most important, notice that prototype theory may also be used as the underlying theoretical account for the argument that L1 English speakers will use the Preterite as a default marker of past tense across lexical aspectual classes in L2 Spanish. This may happen if the Preterite in Spanish is equated with the prototype of simple past tense in English (i.e., transfer). That is, the L1 English speaker may rely on the One to One Principle (Andersen 1989) and use the Preterite to convey past tense reference across lexical aspectual classes, whereas the Imperfect may be used for other functions such as making excuses (see Schmidt & Frota 1986).[16] Alternatively, the learner may rely on the use of Imperfect in association with particular lexical items present in the input. In sum, the prototype account may constitute theoretical support for the contention that tense *or* aspect marking are preferentially used in the marking of past tense verbal morphology in L2 Spanish. The analysis of these two potential alternatives will be investigated in the context of the discusion of the findings to be presented in the following chapter.

---

16. In this respect, it would be interesting to investigate the extent to which native English speakers transfer the use of past tense in counterfactual statements to similar constructions in Spanish.

4.2.5 Perceptual saliency

According to Klein et al. (1995: 271) the lexical aspect hypothesis "has to be weighted against competing strategies for mimicking the input, such as frequency (see also Meisel 1987), or the perception of irregular verbal morphology (see also Sato 1990), whatever the verb class." In effect, the analysis of data from the development of past tense verbal morphology among adult learners shows that perceptual saliency represents an important factor in the development of past tense morphology (e.g., Andersen 1986; Perdue & Klein 1992; Schmidt & Frota 1986; Salaberry 2000; Wolfram 1985). Furthermore, it seems that the effect of perceptual saliency is equally valid for natural as well as classroom settings. For instance, Perdue and Klein (1992: 264) show that one Italian native speaker learning English in England marked past tense only with irregular verbs.[17] Similarly, Salaberry (2000) claimed that Spanish speakers learning English in Uruguay were likely to rely on the use of irregular and frequent past tense morphology to mark past tense endings.

Considering the above-mentioned data, one wonders whether there is a possible interaction between the information provided by lexical aspectual classes, on the one hand, and irregular frequent morphology, on the other hand, that may possibly guide learners in their development of past tense inflectional morphology. Wolfram (1985) claimed that both tense and lexical aspect may be considered to be *higher order factors* (related to discourse level) in contrast with *surface constraints*. Surface constraints are represented by (a) regular versus irregular morphology, (b) type of irregular formation (e.g., suppletive form, internal vowel changes, internal vowel changes plus suffix, final consonant replacement), (c) frequency of the verb (usually irregulars such as *be, have, do, come, go*), (d) phonetic shape of the suffix on the regular verb (/t/, /d/ and /id/), and (e) the phonological environment that follows the verb (e.g., cluster reduction — with subsequent deletion of the past tense suffix — is favored when following vowel is preceded by a consonant). Based on Wolfram's claim, then, one would expect that, irrespective of the lexical semantic value of the verb phrase (e.g., statives versus telic events), the more frequent and irregular verb morphology is, the more likely it will appear first in the development of past marking of adult L2 learners. Most important, the prediction of the role of the lexical semantics or the cognitive saliency of frequent-irregular verbs should be

---

17. See Ellis (1987) for the argument that past tense irregular morphology in English may be associated with item or lexical learning as opposed to regular past tense morphology that may be associated with rule learning, and Ellis (1997) for a more general argument.

empirically distinguishable because "the regular-irregular distinction does not correlate with any feature of verb meaning" (Pinker 1991:531).

The above mentioned contrast in the use of irregular versus regular past tense morphology may be the consequence of the operation of two distinct cognitive processes in the development of inflectional endings in a second language: lexical (item) learning versus rule-based learning (see Pinker 1991 for L1 acquisition and Skehan 1998 for L2 acquisition). Indeed, the role of lexical learning in the development of verbal morphology has been proposed by several researchers working in diverse acquisition settings. For instance, Pinker (1991) argues that the use of inflectional endings to mark past tense (in languages like English) may be dependent on a hybrid cognitive process that combines rule-like behavior as well as memory-based associations. As such, the learning of irregular forms will be strongly affected by frequency and similarity (memorized items). Pinker points out that "the 13 most frequent verbs in English — *be, have, do, say, make, go, take, come, see, get, know, give, find* — are all irregular" (p.532). Similarly, in second language acquisition Giacalone-Ramat (1992:304) claims that "a production strategy at the [L2] learner's disposal is to use a sort of lexical unit with no morphological variation, gradually developing the necessary morphological devices for word class assignments." Hence, the use of irregular past tense morphology should precede the appearance of regularized morphology (i.e., *-ed* endings in English) in L2 development. Along the same lines, Lafford (1996:16) proposed the "saliency-foregrounding hypothesis" based on the analysis of data on the development of L2 Spanish verbal endings among L1 English speakers. Lafford claims that "phonologically salient verb forms are used to reflect salient (foregrounded) actions in L2 narrative discourse."[18] Finally, recent work in neurolinguistics provides additional support for the claim that the first morphological markers of past may represent a case of item (lexical) learning instead of rule learning. For instance, Paradis (1994) has advanced the claim that the cognitive processes that underlie lexicon and morphosyntactic development are subserved by neurofunctionally distinct systems. He argues further that "morphosyntax, but not vocabulary, appears to be affected by maturational constraints" (p.398).

Among the studies that provided support for the relevance of perceptual saliency among classroom learners, Salaberry (2000) analyzed the development of English past tense verbal morphology among monolingual Spanish speakers

---

18. In terms of phonological saliency, both Spanish past tense regular preterites with final stress and irregular preterites with internal vowel changes stand out phonologically in comparison with verbs that carry penultimate stress and that have only three irregular forms (i.e., the Imperfect).

who had access to classroom instruction only. The analysis of data collected from oral and written narratives of two excerpts from the film *Modern Times* revealed three major findings. First, there was an effect brought about by planning time (i.e., more extended use of past tense in written narratives than in the oral narratives). Second, all learners relied heavily on the use of irregular morphology to mark past tense in both written and oral narratives. In contrast, the use of regularized forms of past tense lagged behind in the production of most learners. Third, the potential effect of lexical aspectual classes was not significant in the selection of past tense verbal endings (as reflected in the differential marking of verbal morphology according to lexical semantic categories) or it reflected the opposite trend of development predicted by previous hypotheses. In sum, the analysis of data from this study provided evidence that irregular morphology (e.g., extended past tense marking of stative *be* as irregular *was*) correlated more strongly than lexical aspect with morphological past tense marking. In essence, one could claim that the effect of inherent lexical aspect (classes of verb phrases) may be independent of the effect of the cognitive saliency of irregular morphology in languages such as English or Spanish. Arguably, it is possible that data previously analyzed as evidence for the effect of lexical aspect may be alternatively explained with reference to the cognitive saliency of irregular and frequent verbal morphology.[19]

4.3   Selected previous studies

The potential influence of lexical aspectual classes on the explicit marking of temporality markers in L2 development has been tested in various L2 experimental studies. In this section I will briefly summarize the findings from some of the most prominent studies that used Spanish (or a related Romance language) as the source or target language. In so doing, I will assess the degree of support they offer to the lexical aspect hypothesis. The studies are presented in chronological

---

19. There is, however, an important caveat on this point: the category statives was represented by a limited number of verb types. This is not surprising, because in general, movie narratives rely mostly on the main plot of the story. That is to say, movie narratives are based on recounting the main events that represent the "complicating action" (with "action" verbs) while there is little orientation and evaluation of the events happening in the story (cf. Labov 1972; Silva-Corvalán 1983, etc.). Previous studies have also shown the lopsided distribution of statives in favor of a few verb types (e.g., Bergström 1995; Kaplan 1987; Salaberry 1998). For instance, Bergström stated that approximately 81% of all statives in the written narratives of her L2 French students corresponded to two statives: *be* and *have*.

order. For the sake of brevity, the studies which have been analyzed in previous sections for the purpose of outlining the major theoretical perspectives relevant for the analysis of data of this volume will not be presented again: Andersen (1986, 1991), García and vanPutte (1988), Housen (1994), Kumpf (1984), Salaberry (2000), Sato (1990), and Schumann (1987).

4.3.1 *Schmidt and Frota 1986*

Schmidt and Frota is a descriptive study of the acquisition of L2 Portuguese by Schmidt (native English speaker) during a five-month stay in Brazil based on learning diaries as well as four tape-recorded conversations (from 30 to 60 minutes per session) between Schmidt and Frota (native speaker of Portuguese). The conversations were recorded during weeks 7, 11, 18 and 22 (Schmidt did not have instruction nor interaction in the target language during the first three weeks in Brazil). The study included the analysis of several features of the target language, but the choice of tense "caused more problems ... than person, number or conjugation class" (p. 257). Their data show that Schmidt's strategy to select past tense marking in Portuguese was lexical: out of 29 verb types that Schmidt used in all four recorded conversations, 24 occurred consistently in either Imperfect or Preterite. Schmidt and Frota considered two alternative explanations for these data: the lexical aspectual class of the verbs, or the input frequency (distributional bias).

It is difficult to reach a definitive answer concerning the potential impact of one or both of these factors because the analysis of the input available to the learner was indirect and incomplete. The assessment of the available input in the L2 was based solely on the data provided by the native speaker who acted as the interlocutor of Schmidt (the co-author) during the taped conversations. In spite of the assumption made by Schmidt and Frota that the selection of past tense marking of the native speaker of Portuguese was not "bizarrely atypical," it is doubtful that it may be representative of the input available to this learner in the natural environment. In fact, in one of the diary entries (week 6) Schmidt comments that he noticed the extended use of the Imperfect in one native speaker, "which I never heard (or understood) before, and during the evening I managed to produce quite a few myself, without hesitating much. Very satisfying!" (p. 279). It is doubtful that this type of use of the Imperfect was also instantiated in the interview format of the taped conversation. In fact, Schmidt (1990: 147) argues that it is difficult to decide which one of the above mentioned options was more likely to have generated the specific selection of past tense verbal morphology made by Schmidt during the oral interviews.

4.3.2 Kaplan 1987

Among the earlier studies, Kaplan (1987) used a semi-structured oral interview procedure with 16 learners of L2 French to study the use of *Passé Composé–Imparfait* among beginning and intermediate university students. In her study, *Passé Composé* was attempted more often, and it was relatively more accurately used among third and four semester students, but not among first or second semester students. In fact, the first year students did not overtly mark aspectual differences in past tense to a noticeable level. Kaplan did not analyze her data according to lexical aspectual classes. Instead, she claims that a combination of several factors could account for the higher use and accuracy of perfective aspect: semantic complexity, sequence of instruction, saliency, pre-fabricated chunks and frequency of use. First, Kaplan argues that the semantic complexity of the *Imparfait* (it represents more than one aspect: durative, iterative, habitual, etc.) increases the demands on cognitive processing. Second, Kaplan states that the order of presentation of aspectual differences in the pedagogical syllabus favors the appearance of *Passé Composé* first (at least for her subjects). Third, the perfective aspect is more salient in form when represented in French *Passé Composé* (compound verb). Fourth, many instances of the use of *Passé Composé* occur in holistic phrases learned as "chunks" (e.g., *je suis allé, comment ça s'est passé?*, etc.). Fifth, *Passé Composé* is used more often than *Imparfait* in classroom discourse. Kaplan computed the number of instances that the teachers participating in her study used *Passé Composé* versus *Imparfait* in all contexts requiring past tense marking: 84% of the time the instructors used *Passé Composé* (data computed from a single class session). The use of *Passé Composé* is more difficult than *Imparfait* only in terms of its morphological complexity: the *Imparfait* forms are regular, whereas the *Passé Composé* requires the use of two different auxiliaries and many irregular past participles (the same is true of the contrast Imperfect-Preterite in Spanish: see Bybee 1995). In sum, it appears as if the cognitive processing of *Passé Composé* is easier than the processing of *Imparfait* in overall terms.

4.3.3 Robison 1990, 1995

Robison (1990) conducted an empirical study based on one Spanish speaker learning English (natural setting) to investigate the prediction of the Primacy of Aspect hypothesis (POA), which is another variant of the lexical aspect hypothesis. According to Robison the theory of POA holds that *in the initial stages of language acquisition*, verbal morphemes are used redundantly to encode lexical aspect — the temporal features inherent in the lexical meaning of the predicate — and not grammatical aspect or tense (p. 316, italics added)

Robison analyzed two aspectual contrasts: the stative-dynamic distinction and the punctual-durative distinction. The analysis was based on a series of oral interviews conducted by the researcher. As predicted by the POA, the distribution of Progressive morphological markers was not equal for all types of verbs. The results, however, were not unequivocal: the data show support for POA for the punctual-durative distinction but not for the stative-dynamic distinction. That is, the L1 Spanish subject marked a higher proportion of stative verbs — instead of dynamic verbs as predicted by POA — with the Progressive marker (-*ing* inflection). As we have seen in Chapter 2 the Progressive does not match the situation type of statives because the latter have no endpoints. In contrast, the Progressive is normally associated with processes. We should bear in mind that this restriction of the Progressive with statives is also valid in Spanish (the native language of Robison's subject). In consideration of the distribution of Progressive morphology in standard written English, it is reasonable to assume that the distribution of morphological marking exhibited by the L1 Spanish subject (high rate of association with stative verbs) was not present in the input from native speakers. It is an open question whether the subject picked up this idiosyncratic use of the Progressive from other nonnative speakers (or even native speakers), or whether this idiosyncratic behavior is part of a creative process of hypothesis testing of the target language system (MacLaughlin 1990). Interestingly, Gass and Ard (1984) offer an answer to this phenomenon based on their analysis of grammaticality judgments of uses of the Progressive form in English made by Spanish speakers.[20] Gass and Ard claim that learners — irrespective of L1 — will normally transfer the prototypical meaning of the Progressive (ongoing action), rather than non-prototypical meanings (e.g., Progressive with future expressions such as *tomorrow* or with habitual or generic events normally marked with present tense). Their results, however, show that Spanish speakers accepted both prototypical (e.g., *John is smoking American cigarettes now*) and non-prototypical sentences (e.g., *Dan is seeing better now*). Gass and Ard adduce that because the Progressive is not normally used in Spanish with state verbs "Spanish speakers consider this an idiosyncratic fact about Spanish and therefore assume that this lexical restriction does not hold in English" (p. 63).

---

20. Their study also includes data from Japanese speakers.

As mentioned above, Robison obtained comfirmatory evidence for the prediction of POA from the distribution of verbal endings associated with the punctual-durative distinction only. He claimed that his study

> furnished confirmation from one person's interlanguage that *when L2 verb morphemes enter the interlanguage* of an adult language learner, they are not uniformly distributed across all verbs, but rather as in L1 acquisition, may be distributed according to the lexical aspectual classes of the verbs (p. 329, italics added)

However, two paragraphs later, Robison's position changes: "the prediction supported by this study is that ... verbal morphology correlates with lexical aspect at least *during some stage during the development of an interlanguage*" (pp. 329–330, italics added). The change in Robison's perspective is substantial because the sequence and timing of appearance of morphological markers of temporality are central for the analysis of the development of aspectual distinctions in L2 acquisition. In fact, the above mentioned ambivalent position has generated some confusion among other researchers who have followed one or the other of the two conclusions reached by Robison. For example, Hasbún (1995) refers to the latter position, whereas Housen (1994) mentions the first. It is possible to interpret Robison's ambivalence as the consequence of two separate findings from his analysis. First, along the lines of Gass and Ard's argument, there is potentially idiosyncratic marking of verbal morphology at the beginning stages of L2 development. Second, the use of past tense verbal endings will eventually follow the prediction of the POA at "some stage" during development (but not necessarily the beginning stages).

In a different study, Robison (1995) analyzed data from 30 to 60-minute oral interviews with 26 college-level L1 Spanish speakers (data collected by R. Andersen in Puerto Rico). The subjects were divided into four levels of proficiency based on the appropriate marking of morphological endings from written data. A summary of Robinson's data in terms of verb tokens is presented in Table 4.3. Robison concluded that "for lower level learners, lexical aspect exerts more control over inflection than does tense," but added the caveat that the study was limited to (1) a specific source language-target language comparison (L1 Spanish, L2 English), (2) the analysis of oral interviews among young adults, and (3) the analysis of lexical aspect irrespective of narrative grounding (pp. 365–6).

Indeed, Robison's data provide strong confirmatory evidence to support the lexical aspect hypothesis. Without denying the essence of Robison's findings, however, it is important to note a few methodological caveats for the purpose of the generalization of findings to other contexts and languages. First, notice that

Table 4.3. Distribution of verbal morphology (tokens) per group and lexical aspectual class (based on Robison, 1995)

	State	Activity	Accomplish.	Achievement
Group I				
Base form	138	179	79	61
-ing	1	32	4	18
Past	2	6	4	8
TOTAL	141	217	87	87
Group II				
Base form	367	210	81	105
-ing	12	69	10	5
Past	15	13	12	53
TOTAL	394	292	103	163
Group III				
Base form	418	279	117	134
-ing	5	107	11	10
Past	4	13	17	32
TOTAL	427	399	145	176
Group IV				
Base form	274	169	63	81
-ing	5	67	9	1
Past	3	8	17	26
TOTAL	282	244	89	108

the lexical aspectual classes of statives and activities (both atelic) dominate the distribution of verb tokens in groups II through IV in a 2-to-1 ratio. In contrast, in the data based on movie narratives (e.g., Bardovi-Harlig & Bergström 1996; Hasbún 1995; Ramsay 1990; and studies described in Chapters 5 and 6 of this volume), the use of telic events (both accomplishments and achievements) is always higher than the use of atelic events (especially statives). Unfortunately, no discrimination of the effect of narrative type can be made in the data analyzed by Robison, because his data were elicited in a variety of ways. His informants were requested (1) to respond to questions based on a series of pictures taken from the Bilingual Syntax Measure, (2) to narrate a show, movie or story they had seen or read, (3) to describe various family members and friends, the last two years of their lives, their future plans and desires, what various people do in their work, and a special memory about a person place or event, and (4) to describe their neighborhood and/or hometown.[21] The variety of contexts may provide some support for Robison's conclusions with regard to the generalizability of his findings across narrative contexts, but it may also compromise his findings with respect to the validity of the elicitation task (see analysis of statistical tests below).

Second, notice that the use of past tense across lexical aspectual classes is rare (Table 4.4 presents the data in percentages). The highest percentage of past tense marking occurred with achievements in group II (32.1%), but this high percentage dropped dramatically in group III to 17.2%. Concomitantly, there is a noticeable — albeit small — increase in past marking of stative and activity verbs from group I to group II and a subsequent regression of this trend — for statives only — in the transition from group II to group III:

Table 4.4. Distribution of *past tense* morphological marking by aspectual class (based on Table 2, Robison, 1995)[a]

	State	Activity	Accomplish.	Achievement
Group I ($n = 6$)	1.4%	2.7%	4.5%	9.2%
Group II ($n = 7$)	3.7%	4.3%	10.9%	32.1%
Group III ($n = 8$)	0.9%	3.2%	11.6%	17.2%
Group IV ($n = 5$)	1.0%	3.1%	18.1%	22.6%
Natives ($n = 3$)	20.4%	15.3%	25.6%	31.2%

[a] Robison (1995) does not list the number of subjects per level. That information has been taken from his unpublished dissertation.

Table 4.4 includes the data from the group of native speakers (the native speakers' data data were summarized from Robison's unpublished dissertation).[22] Notice also, that even native speakers used past tense to a very limited extent. It is important to point out that the native speakers' data were collected by Robison in 1990, whereas the data from all students groups were collected in 1975 in Puerto Rico by Roger Andersen. Although Robison does not explicitly say so, it is apparent that these native speakers of English were probably not in contact with the Puerto Rican environment where the nonnative speakers learned English: all three native speakers grew up in the Midwest and had graduated

---

21. Robison (1995) does not provide information about the tasks nor the background of the subjects. The previous information was gathered from Robison's (1993) unpublished dissertation.

22. The native speakers received the same instructions, except for the picture narration from the Bilingual Syntax Measure.

from a middle class suburban high school. In this respect, it is doubtful that the control group of native speakers could provide a reliable assessment of the type of input that the nonnative speakers received in Puerto Rico.

Finally, both the descriptive data and the statistical significance of the analysis of the data from Robison are compromised by the fact that the Chi-square tests were performed on the combined data from each group of subjects (violation of the assumption of independence of data within each cell). In this respect, Robison does not report whether each subject contributed unequally within each group to the combined selection of morphological marking reflected in the summary of these data (Hatch & Lazaraton 1991: 409). This may be particularly problematic considering the type of elicitation procedure used to collect data as described in the previous paragraph.

4.3.4 *Ramsay 1990*

Ramsay's study was based on the analysis of guided oral production of L2 Spanish students (all L1 English speakers). The subjects were volunteers from diverse backgrounds and levels of experience with the language (including graduate students). The elicitation procedure used by Ramsay was based on a series of pictures from a children's book (Disney's "The Magic Stick"). The story was presented to the students as a series of ten episodes (ten pictures) with captions. The text associated with each picture included blank spaces that students had to complete with text. The inclusion of text with each picture was used to prevent students and native speakers from using the "historical present" in their narratives (e.g., Klein 1994: 133–41; Silva-Corvalán 1984).[23] The first episode of the story did not have any blank spaces; it was all text. The amount of text in the remaining nine episodes decreased gradually. For example, episode 3 had the following text cue:

> Esa noche llegó a un mesón para pasar la noche. "Pero no hay comida" le contestó el mesonero. "No importa," dijo Hugo, "Tengo una mesa mágica." El mesonero tenía curiosidad y siguió a Hugo a su cuarto. Hugo pensó en comida y dijo "Mesa dame comida." Cuando el mesonero vio aquello pensó: "Me gustaría tener esa mesa mágica." Cuando Hugo se durmió el mesonero llegó a su cuarto con una mesa bajo el brazo.

---

23. The implementation of the procedure was so successful that native speakers never used present tense. However, as we will see in other studies and in the data from the present study, native speakers rarely use past tense to narrate sequenced events of the type exemplified in the Disney story.

That night (he) arrived (PRE) at an inn to spend the night. "But there is no food" answered (PRE) the inn-keeper. "It doesn't matter," said (PRE) Hugo, "I have a magic table." The inn-keeper was (IMP) curious and followed (PRE) Hugo to his room. Hugo thought (PRE) in food and said (PRE) "Table, give me food." When the inn-keeper saw (PRE) that, (he) thought (PRE) "I would like to have that magic table." When Hugo fell asleep (PRE) the inn-keeper arrived (PRE) to his room with a magic table under his arm.

As is evident from the analysis of the extract, the text provided students with a series of cues about the appropriate marking of past tense morphology. Among native speakers, this procedure may help prevent the switch to the normal use of historical present. Among nonnative speakers, however, it may help them pay attention to the morphological marking of verbs in past tense Spanish (therefore, providing cues about a distributional bias that favors past tense marking according to lexical aspectual classes). It is not clear how this feature of the elicitation technique may have affected the results of the study. In spite of the above mentioned conditions of the study, Ramsay argued that her data should not be considered as "monitored data." I would claim, however, that it would be more accurate to state that Ramsay's data were less monitored than written data, but more monitored than the free oral narration of a movie as is the case in other studies. A summary of the results from Ramsay is presented in Table 4.5.

Two significant features of the distribution of the data are that (1) neither native speakers nor nonnative speakers used verbs of the activity type to a large extent and (2) the distribution of verbal endings was similar for accomplishments and achievements. This particular distribution of aspectual classes may be a result of the type of elicitation procedure used in the study: telic events provide the story line and states provide the background of the story. In essence, Ramsay's data show the distribution of verbal morphology according to two lexical aspectual classes only: statives and telic events. As a consequence it is difficult to test the proposed spreading of aspectual marking from both ends of the continuum of verb types as determined by inherent aspect (e.g., Andersen 1991).

The analysis of Ramsay's data has been interpreted in support of the lexical aspect hypothesis (e.g., Andersen & Shirai 1994: 143; Hasbún 1995: 143). For example, Hasbún claims that "Ramsay's ... cross-sectional studies of classroom Spanish learners also showed the same tendency as those of Andersen, *clearly following the general developmental pattern as predicted by the aspect hypothesis*" (p. 143, italics added). In fact, Ramsay claimed that tense develops before aspect and that her data do not show any signs of the sequential development adduced by Hasbún. The alternative interpretation of Ramsay's data provided by Andersen

Table 4.5. Distribution of verb morphology: *average number of tokens per level* (based on Table 5 in Ramsay, 1990)

	Morphology	State	Activity	Telic	Totals
Group 1	PRET	0	0	3	3
	IMP	0	0	0	0
	NON-PAST	7	2	31	39
Group 2	PRET	0	1	10	11
	IMP	0	0	0	0
	NON-PAST	12	3	28	43
Group 3	PRET	1	0	23	24
	IMP	3	2	0	5
	NON-PAST	9	2	15	26
Group 4	PRET	2	1	28	31
	IMP	13	3	3	19
	NON-PAST	3	1	4	8
Group 5	PRET	4	3	43	50
	IMP	14	3	3	20
	NON-PAST	0.3	0.5	0.3	1
Natives	PRET	4	0	55	59
	IMP	13	2	5	20

and Shirai and Hasbún, however, may be justified by making a distinction between grammatical and lexical aspect. To facilitate the interpretation of the data, the use of past tense marking according to lexical aspectual class in percentages is presented in Table 4.6.

In effect, the following features of the distribution of verbal morphology of Ramsay's data supports the lexical aspect hypothesis: (1) in general students do not mark statives with past tense markers until stage 3, but some telic events are marked with past tense since stage 1, (2) learners mark statives (mostly) with the Imperfect at stage 3, (3) in contrast, approximately 25% of all telic verbs at stage 2 (average of 10 tokens) and about 60% of telic verbs at stage 3 (average of 23 tokens) are marked with the Preterite, and (4) no telic verb is marked with the Imperfect during stages 2 or 3.

It is important to point out that Ramsay claimed that students do not mark aspectual distinctions before tense distinctions: "although the inflections of the

Table 4.6. Distribution of past tense marking in Ramsay's data in percentages across lexical aspectual classes

Level	Stative	Activity	Telic
Group 1	0%	0%	10%
Group 2	0%	25%	25%
Group 3	30%	50%	60%
Group 4	84%	80%	86%
Group 5	98%	92%	99%

perfective and the imperfective appear in approximately 50% of the verbs, they are not used to encode aspectual distinctions. It is likely that they function to encode past tense" (p. 249). She presents two types of evidence to support the above mentioned position: (1) students do not produce any errors using aspectual inflections until stage 4, and (2) the data do not show that students have two different types of past tense for one single verb until stage 4 (prototypical versus non-prototypical markers). Ramsay argues that the acquisition of the perfective-imperfective aspectual distinction implies that students recognize that the inflectional endings fulfill a function other than past tense marking. Accordingly, the appropriate use of the Preterite–Imperfect endings is only evident at stage 4 because: (1) students produce a series of systematic errors (e.g., use of Imperfect with telic verbs), and (2) students mark some verbs with both prototypical and nonprototypical markers of aspect (i.e., point-of-view aspect). In other words, at stage 4 students seem to reanalyze the functions of the Preterite–Imperfect inflections to accommodate both tense and aspect information with each grammatical morpheme.

4.3.5 Bardovi-Harlig and Bergström 1996

Bardovi-Harlig and Bergström present a contrastive analysis based on data from L2 French and L2 English. Their study is important, not only due to the incorporation of a contrast between two languages which are normally used as both source and target language, but also because it provides a detailed and cogent analysis of developmental trends in the use of verbal morphology among adult L2 learners. I will analyze the data from each language separately. The analysis of the L2 French data (based on a subset of the data from Bergström 1995) reveals one important finding: The proposed sequential transition in the use of past tense marking according to lexical aspectual classes is not corroborated.

First, as pointed out by Bardovi-Harlig and Bergström, the proposed theoretical distinction between achievement and accomplishment verbs as separate lexical aspectual classes is not empirically validated: "early strong use of achievements (63.4%) followed *closely* by accomplishments (50.0%)" (p. 318, italics added).[24] The strong use of *Passé Composé* with both types of verbs is also maintained in subsequent stages of development. As we can see, the percentages for accomplishments and achievements (presented in that order) seem to pair up from stage to stage: 66% and 72% at stage 2, 87.9% and 87.2% at stage 3, and 79.3% and 61.3% at stage 4. In passing, notice that, at stage 4 and contrary to the prediction of the lexical aspect hypothesis, achievements were marked less often with *Passé Composé* than accomplishments (61.3% versus 79.3% respectively).

A summary of the distribution of verb morphology (raw scores) of the French data by lexical aspectual class and by level is presented in Table 4.7.[25]

Table 4.7. Distribution of verb morphology (raw scores) according to inherent aspect: French data (based on Table 5 in Bardovi-Harlig & Bergström, 1996: 317)[a]

	Morphology	State	Activity	Accompl.	Achievem.
Group 1	PC	0	6	5	26
(n = 4)	IMP	5	10	0	0
	Pres	14	16	4	14
Group 2	PC	3	13	13	62
(n = 7)	IMP	6	1	1	4
	Pres	7	6	2	24
Group 3	PC	10	29	34	80
(n = 7)	IMP	14	3	2	1
	Pres	23	4	2	7
Group 4	PC	5	16	19	69
(n = 5)	IMP	23	9	9	10
	Pres	7	3	1	6

[a] The use of the progressive is not included in Table 4.7 due to the low count of tokens in that category.

24. In fact, the slight difference in percentages may also be accounted for by the huge difference in number of tokens corresponding to each category at this level: 9 tokens for accomplishment and 40 tokens for achievement verbs.

25. The use of raw scores is better because the potential low counts of tokens may generate meaningless percentages.

As was the case for the transition from achievements to accomplishments, the data from Table 4.7 show no evidence for the gradual spread of *Passé Composé* from accomplishment to activity verbs either (p. 318). Indeed, the use of *Passé Composé* with activities and accomplishments are as follows (raw scores): 6 and 5 (group 1), 13 and 13 (group 2), 29 and 34 (group 3), and 16 and 19 (group 4). In essence, the analysis of the non-stative categories — atelic events (activities) and telic events (accomplishments and achievements) — reveals that the evolution of French past tense grammatical markers is representative of tense rather than aspectual distinctions. The transition from stage 1 to stage 2 among these L2 French learners reveals a dramatic shift in the use of verbal morphology represented in the proportion of use of present tense-past tense markers across all three non-stative categories. Past tense is mostly represented by *Passé Composé*. The proportional use of *Passé Composé*-Present from stage 1 to stage 2 according to verb category is as follows: for activity verbs from 6:16 at stage 1 to 13:6 at stage 2; for accomplishment verbs, from 5:4 at stage 1 to 13:2 at stage 2, and for achievement verbs, from 26:14 at stage 1 to 62:24 at stage 2 (see Table 4.5). In fact, the shift of present tense marking to *Passé Composé* marking is also representative of the state verb category: proportional use of *Passé Composé*-Present from 0:14 at stage 1 to 3:7 at stage 2. This provides further evidence that the shift from present to past morphological marking signals tense distinctions across the whole inventory of verb types. Notice also that for state verbs, the number of uses of *Imparfait* for the state verbs remains unchanged from stage 1 to stage 2. In spite of this tendency, learners decrease the use of present tense and increase the use of *Passé Composé* within this verb category. This is even more compelling evidence since the state category is heavily represented by two single lexical items.

Furthermore, when we analyze the overall distribution of past tense use, the use of grammatical markers across all four aspectual categories is compromised by the unequal distribution of types and tokens for the category stative relative to the other categories (and especially achievement verbs). In fact, 81% of all state verbs (tokens) correspond to only two verb types: *être* and *avoir* (*to be* and *to have*). In essence, the category stative is not representative of a particular aspectual category; it more accurately reflects the evolution of two specific (basic) lexical items (an example of lexical learning) in the L2 French of these subjects. The early use of *Imparfait* with state verbs (compare with 0 counts of *Imparfait* in non-state categories at stage 1) is accounted for by the fact that language input normally favors the past tense marking of *être* and *avoir* with *Imparfait* instead of *Passé Composé* (see analysis of classroom talk from Swain 1992 and analysis of textbook explanations in Salaberry 1998). At stage 4 the use of *Imparfait* has become heavily associated with the state verbs, although a few uses of *Passé Composé* remain (marked value of aspect). Finally, the data from the three non-state verb categories show that the transition from the use of unmarked to marked values of past tense occurs in the shift from stage 3 to stage 4. It is at this stage that these learners have begun to use *Imparfait* with all non-stative categories (marked value). With regards to the proposed spread of the *Imparfait* from state to non-state verbs (Bardovi-Harlig & Bergström: 319), it is clear that the use of *Imparfait* with non-state verbs is almost non-existent until stage 4. In turn, there is a sudden jump in the use of *Imparfait* from stage 3 to stage 4 for non-state verbs.

The L2 English data reported in Bardovi-Harlig and Bergström are more difficult to analyze for three main reasons. First, the native language of the participating subjects varies widely (six L1 backgrounds). Of the total of 23 L2 English students who participated in the study 8 spoke Arabic, 4 Korean, 4 Japanese, 2 Spanish, 1 Amharic and 1 Thai (p. 326) (the L1 of the other three learners was not reported). Note also that most of these languages are not typologically related. Second, English does not provide as clear a test case of tense-aspect distinctions as determinants of verb morphology as is the case in French or Spanish (obligatory marking of both aspect and tense in past tense). Third, the L2 English students from this study cannot be considered strictly classroom learners as is the case with the L2 French students reported in the same study. Despite these major contrasts between the two groups of learners reported by Bardovi-Harlig and Bergström, the L2 English data are also revelatory of tense distinctions occurring in the target language development of these learners. The L2 English data are summarized in Table 4.8.

As with the French data, the analysis of the English data shows no signs of the proposed spread of morphological markers according to lexical aspectual classes (from telic to state verbs). As Bardovi-Harlig and Bergström put it "in English for Group 1, achievements and accomplishments show the same level of past marking, with 46.4% and 47.1%..." and "the use of simple past with states increases noticeably from Group 1 (15.0%) to Group 2 (56.9%) ..." (pp. 317–8). Second, the most interesting results of the L2 English data are associated with the use of the Progressive with activity verbs. Notice that the heavy use of present Progressive or tenseless Progressive (no auxiliary) at stage 1 shifts towards past Progressive at stage 2 (p. 320). Hence, the shift from non-past to past tense marking with activity verbs occurs at the same time that it happens with state verbs. In sum, the spread of past tense marking in association with aspectual class of verb is not evident in the English data either.

Table 4.8. Distribution of verb morphology (raw scores) according to inherent aspect: English data (based on Table 5 in Bardovi-Harlig & Bergström, 1996: 316)

	Morphology	State	Activity	Accompl.	Achievem.
Group 1	Past	3	5	16	39
(n = 4)	Progressive	0	5	1	2
	Present	10	1	1	0
	Base form	4	17	16	35
Group 2	Past	29	8	25	89
(n = 7)	Progressive	0	16	2	1
	Present	11	1	1	0
	Base form	11	13	14	34
Group 3	Past	21	19	19	118
(n = 7)	Progressive	0	12	0	0
	Present	14	0	0	1
	Base form	3	9	7	11
Group 4	Past	22	14	25	97
(n = 5)	Progressive	1	12	8	2
	Present	5	1	0	0
	Base form	1	1	1	9

4.3.6 Hasbún 1995[26]

Hasbún (1995) analyzed written data from 80 L1 English speakers enrolled in four different levels of Spanish instruction: first to fourth year. The analysis of a written task was selected because it was assumed it would generate longer narratives (p. 98). The written narrative was based on an 8-minute silent video that was an excerpt from the film *Modern Times*. The same excerpt has been used in previous studies based on data from tutored learners in the natural environment (Bardovi-Harlig 1995a), classroom students (Bergström 1995), and natural learners (Klein & Perdue 1992). After the students watched the film twice they were asked to narrate it in writing. They were allotted 40 minutes to complete the task. The students were asked to start the story with the phrase "*Había una vez ...*" (Once upon a time ...) to prevent "advanced learners and

---

26. Even though Hasbún's study appeared before the one of Bardovi-Harlig and Bergström, I decided to reverse the order of presentation because Hasbún makes reference to Bardovi-Harlig's study to substantiate her claim.

native speakers of Spanish from shifting to the historical present."[27] As a consequence of this experimental constraint, advanced native speakers rarely used present tense. Native speakers, however, were less affected by the instructions and used the historical present to a larger extent than nonnative speakers (see also Chapter 6 for even stronger findings confirming a distinct behavior among native and nonnative speakers).[28]

Table 4.9. Distribution of verb morphology (average of raw scores) according to inherent aspect

		Gram	State	Activity	Accompl.	Achiev.
Group 1	PRET	10	3	8	0
	IMP	1	0	0	0
	Present	149	105	85	96
Group 2	PRET	23	25	41	66
	IMP	39	5	3	3
	Present	52	44	59	52
Group 3	PRET	19	64	110	238
	IMP	79	27	2	6
	Present	11	6	15	13
Group 4	PRET	37	64	140	304
	IMP	126	61	9	12
	Present	26	9	4	4
Group NS	PRET	46	39	112	305
	IMP	107	55	13	20
	Present	40	54	58	143

A summary of the data from Hasbún's study is presented in Table 4.9. Arguably, these data do not present clear evidence in support of the lexical aspect hypothesis. First, the data from native speakers provide empirical evidence

---

27. There is an underlying assumption — supported by empirical data — that beginning and intermediate academic learners will not resort to the "historical present" when cued to use past tense, whereas advanced learners and native speakers will use historical present even when asked to narrate the story in the past tense. Why experienced and non-experienced speakers react differently to experimental instructions raises interesting questions to be addressed in Chapter 7.

28. Sebastian & Slobin (1994: 244) also show that adults favor the use of historical present in narratives, whereas children until age five favor the use of past tense.

against a theoretical distinction between punctual and non-punctual telic events (performances). The distribution of Preterite–Imperfect in the categories accomplishment and achievement remains proportional in contrast with the distribution of grammatical marking of statives and activities. Hence, the similarity in the use of Preterite–Imperfect with telic events does not substantiate the classification of these verbs into two different aspectual classes. More importantly, the past tense morphological marking of telic events (i.e., accomplishments and achievements) is similar across different levels of proficiency of nonnative speakers as well. Table 4.9 shows that from period 1 to period 2 there is a shift from non-past to past marking for both telic events. In periods 3 and 4 all accomplishment and achievement verbs are marked with the Preterite except for a few exceptions. In other words, the hypothesized spread of use of Preterite marking from achievement to accomplishment verbs in L2 Spanish is not evident in Hasbún's data (as was the case for the English and French data from Bardovi-Harlig & Bergstrom 1996).

Second, Hasbún's data do not show a spread of past tense marking (Preterite) from telic to atelic events (activity verbs) and later to stative verbs. In contrast, the marking of tense distinction occurs in period 2 across all categories of aspectual class. The first uses of past tense marking did not occur with achievements, but mostly with statives (followed by accomplishments and activities). The overall use of the Preterite in period 1 (10 instances) corresponds to four "frequently used verbs": *ser* (to be), *tener* (to have), *hablar* (to speak) and *ir* (to go). Interestingly, the first two are typically classified as stative verbs. The only instance of an Imperfect corresponds to another stative verb *estar* (to be). In period 2 all events (atelic and telic) are marked with Preterite in roughly proportionally similar ways. On the other hand, statives in period 2 were mainly marked with the Imperfect. The data shown in Table 4.9 do not present raw scores from other markers of temporality. For instance, in period 1 all three activity verbs classified as atelic events were marked with present Progressive, but, in period 2, of a total of seven atelic events, three were marked with present Progressive, and four with past Progressive. This change may signal the beginning of a shift from nonpast to past marking.

Third, it is reasonable to assume that the number of verb types corresponding to statives is quite limited as is the case in other studies with data from Romance languages (e.g., Bardovi-Harlig & Bergström 1996; Bergström 1995; Salaberry 1998). The low number of verb types in this category — or any category for that matter — represents an ideal scenario for item-based learning (e.g., N. Ellis 1996; R. Ellis 1997).[29] Fourth, the profile of past tense marking among advanced students is similar to the native speakers. Hasbún argues that the choice of verb morphology by native and advanced nonnative speakers is different; but this is true only to the extent that nonnative speakers used the present tense less often than native speakers did. That is to say, nonnative speakers' behavior conformed to the expectations of the researcher: the use of the phrase *"Había una vez ..."* prevented them — to a relative extent — from using the historical present. Native speakers' behavior, on the other hand, was less affected by the instructions. In sum, it can be argued that both native and advanced nonnative speakers (group 4) show a similar profile of use of the contrast Preterite–Imperfect with verbs from all aspectual classes. Hasbún concluded that the students from her study were still in the process of learning the functions of the aspectual distinction Preterite–Imperfect in Spanish. In other words, the data from her learners should be amenable to an analysis of development of past tense verbal morphology according to the proposed stages of spread of aspectual morphology predicted by the lexical aspect hypothesis. Contrary to that expectation, however, Hasbún concluded that

> it was *impossible to unequivocally place (the students) in any of the 8 stages posited by Andersen*. The distribution of emergent past tense forms was similar to the distribution in English and French reported by Bardovi-Harlig and Bergström (1995) (pp. 84–5, italics added)

In sum, the empirical evidence from Hasbún's study does not support the spread of aspectual morphology any more than the data from the study from Bardovi-Harlig and Bergström analyzed above.

4.3.7 *Lafford 1996*

Lafford (1996) constitutes another innovative study in the investigation of the development of verbal morphology in adult L2 acquisition by way of introducing a standardized method of language assessment (the ACTFL-OPI) to determine the evolution of past tense verbal morphology. Lafford asked thirteen L2 Spanish students from three different levels of intermediate proficiency (based on the ACTFL-OPI scale) to do an oral retell of a 10-minute silent video (*The Sorcerer's Apprentice* from Disney). She analyzed the data from two different perspectives: telicity (atelic versus telic verbs) and grounding (foreground versus

---

29. This assumption may only be speculative because there is no information about the number of verb types in this category.

background). A summary of the distribution of morphological markers in the data from that study is presented in Table 4.10.

Table 4.10. Distribution of morphological marking of verbs by level (atelic/telic) (based on Lafford, 1996)

	Interm. low	Interm. mid	Interm. high
Preterite	6/5	19/11	32/35
Imperfect	0/0	0/0	46/0
Progressive	1/0	1/0	9/0
Present	34/1	63/12	67/7
Total	41/6	83/23	154/42

Table 4.11. Distribution of verb selection according to telicity and grounding by level (based on Lafford, 1996)

	Atelic/Telic	% atelic	Backg./For.	% Backg.
Intermediate low	41/6	87%	33/14	70%
Intermediate mid	83/23	78%	65/41	61%
Intermediate high	154/42	79%	135/61	69%

The analysis of these data show the following: (1) the majority of verbs used by the subjects were atelic verbs (across all levels), (2) among the subjects from the intermediate-low and intermediate-mid levels the use of past tense was represented largely by the Preterite, (3) the only uses of the Imperfect among the students in the intermediate-high level were associated with atelic verbs conveying background information, and (4) the proportion of past tense-present tense was higher for telic verbs across all levels. In essence, among intermediate-low or intermediate-mid learners (the two lowest levels in Lafford's data) the Imperfect is nonexistent, whereas the Preterite is the first past tense form used irrespective of verb type. That is, the Preterite may be acting as a default marker of past across lexical aspectual classes to the exclusion of the Imperfect. On the other hand, the use of the Preterite seems to be associated with telic verbs in proportional terms: for the intermediate low level 83% of telic verbs are marked with Preterite versus 15% for atelic verbs and for the intermediate mid level 48% of telic verbs are marked with Preterite versus 23% for atelic verbs.

The data from Lafford's study show that the predictions of the lexical aspect hypothesis or the discourse hypothesis (as previously argued by Bardovi-Harlig

1995a: 286) may be indistinguishable. Table 4.11 presents the same data discriminated by telicity and grounding (both number tokens and percentages) by level. The analysis of the data presented in Table 4.11 shows that there may be a certain degree of overlap between the claims made by the discourse hypothesis (e.g., Bardovi-Harlig 1995a) versus the lexical aspect hypothesis (e.g., Andersen 1991; Robison 1990). That is to say, the ratio of atelic verbs to telic verbs is similar to the ratio of verbs that convey background information to verbs that convey foreground information (approximately 15 percentage points of difference between each classification). It should be pointed out, however, that the results of Lafford's study — even though suggestive — must be taken with caution due to the low number of tokens per cell (both within and across levels).

4.3.8 Liskin-Gasparro 1997

Another original study which expanded the purview of analysis of the development of past tense verbal morphology in L2 acquisition was the one carried out by Liskin-Gasparro. Her study is based on the analysis of oral data from both movie and personal narratives of eight advanced nonnative speakers of Spanish. More importantly, Liskin-Gasparro incorporated the use of immediate retrospective protocols to analyze the learners' judgments and their decision-making process during the selection of verbal endings. The introspections based on the speakers' personal and movie narratives were used "to analyze the conscious processing strategies of learners ..." (p. 3). Based on the data from the retrospective protocols Liskin-Gasparro argued that the choice of verbal morphology is influenced by various factors: lexical semantics, discursive constraints, instructional effects, type of narrative task, use of individual processing strategies, and, most important, *the use of the Preterite as a default marker of past tense.* In effect, the role of a default marker of past tense (prototype) in association with the frequency of particular verbs with specific endings (especially use of Imperfect) may represent an alternative explanation for the empirical data on the acquisition of L2 Spanish by native English speakers. For instance, Liskin-Gasparro mentions the case of one learner who, whenever "past tense is called for he first selected the Preterite, and then, if time and cognitive load allow, he might do some additional mental tinkering to see if the Imperfect would be more syntactically appropriate" (pp. 12–3): the Preterite appears to be used as a default past tense form. On the other hand, the influence of lexical semantics in the selection of verbal morphology for some of these advanced students appears to be categorical. Liskin-Gasparro mentions the case of Rick's 'safety things': "certain verbs are always to be encoded in the Imperfect, and others in the

Preterite," and Jason's 'default settings': "for state verbs — he opted for the Imperfect" (p. 6). In other words, for these learners it is unlikely that temporality markers are in the process of "spreading" from one lexical aspectual class to another as predicted by the lexical aspect hypothesis. In sum, Liskin-Gasparro's unique study provides us with more evidence that the role of lexical aspectual categories may be more limited than previously argued by the lexical aspect hypothesis (see also Wiberg 1996 for data from Italian for the proposal of the unmarked past tense hypothesis).

4.3.9 *Summary*

The previous review of empirical data on the development of tense and aspect morphology in classroom learning (mostly data from L2 Spanish) provides preliminary support for the argument that L2 learning may rely on the use of a default marker of past tense during the beginning stages of acquisition (e.g., Bergström 1995; Hasbún 1995; Lafford 1996; Leeman, Arteagoitia, Fridman, & Doughty 1995; Ramsay 1990; Salaberry 1998, 2000). In some cases, the results of those studies are tenuous but indicative of the stronger findings to be reported in Chapter 6. For example, the data from Bergström (1995) on the acquisition of classroom French revealed that second semester students used *Passé Composé* with all dynamic verbs irrespective of lexical aspectual class (i.e., activities, accomplishments and achievements together). Concomitantly, the data from Bergström showed (1) that the emergence of the Imperfect with stative verbs was in competition with *Passé Composé* and (2) that the Imperfect was associated with a limited number of stative verbs. In sum, Bergström concluded that her data showed support only for a "restrictive version of the aspect hypothesis" (p. 183). Similarly, Hasbún reported "no significant association" between past tense morphological marking and lexical aspectual classes at beginning stages of acquisition (second semester, first year of instruction) of L2 Spanish among English native speakers. Hasbún (1995: 204) claimed that

> beginning at Level 2, the learners in this study are most likely using verbal morphology to establish tense differences. There is no definitive evidence to prove that they are only redundantly marking lexical aspect since the grammatical markers are also tense aspects [sic]

In essence, the data from the studies of Bergström and Hasbún show that the transition from tense to aspectual marking appears to be so rapid and transient that it may conceal the effect of tense constraints during the first stages of the development of verbal morphology. In fact, the lack of support for the hypothesis that lexical aspectual classes play a role in the marking of past tense verbal morphology during the beginning stages of acquisition has led previous researchers (e.g., Bergström 1995; Hasbún 1995) to suggest that future studies should collect more data of the transition from first to third semester of academic instruction. Interestingly, the learners who participated in the studies described in Chapter 6 provided evidence for the beginning stages of such change even though the students may be considered advanced beginners. Additional evidence comes from studies that have analyzed the effects of pedagogical manipulations on the use of past tense verbal morphology in Spanish. For instance, Leeman et al. (1995: 246) point out that in their data "the Focus on Form group appears to have overgeneralized the Imperfect form, thus producing it consistently in obligatory contexts, *and often in contexts requiring the preterit*" (italics added). This finding is consistent with the idea that the Preterite is used as a default tense marker during the beginning stages of acquisition among academic learners. That is to say, initially, the Imperfect is used with a limited number of verbs (e.g., *to be, to have, to want*), whereas the rule-governed application of past tense marking is predicated on the use of Preterite. Eventually, the use of the Imperfect will overgeneralize beyond previous prototypical markers.[30]

4.4   The role of instruction

The results from the previously reviewed empirical studies on the morphosyntactic marking of temporality among natural (untutored) learners versus classroom learners show that, apart from factors such as lexical semantics and discourse grounding, instruction may have a significant effect on language development. Indeed, the data from most studies on classroom learning show that instruction on verbal morphology — not surprisingly — is associated with the extended use of verbal morphology. For example, Hasbún claims that as soon as her students were introduced to the grammatical rules that guide past tense use in Spanish, they started using those forms. Indeed, some researchers have explicitly argued in favor of the role of instruction in SLA. Buczowska and Weist (1991: 548) phrase it succinctly in the following way: "Adults are capable of processing the morphology, and given typical pedagogical practices, tutored L2 learners are not permitted to avoid doing so." As previously identified by

---

30. Incidentally, the subjects from Leeman et al. were enrolled in a sixth semester academic course probably similar to the level represented by the advanced students from the present study.

Kaplan (1987), the major role of formal instruction on the development of past tense verbal morphology in the L2 can be assessed along the lines of three major factors: frequency, saliency, and sequence of instruction. All three factors are intricately related to the notion of noticing (Schmidt & Frota 1986). Schmidt (1990: 143) lists the factors that he claims influence noticing grammatical features of the target language: (1) task demands, (2) frequency, (3) saliency of the feature, (4) individual skills and strategies, and (5) expectations created by the native language. Along the same lines, Harley (1989) suggests that the pedagogical conditions that may have a key role in acquisition are: (1) the increased frequency and saliency in the input (2) the appeal to students' metalinguistic awareness, (3) greater and more focused opportunities for output, and (4) goal-directed interaction in small group contexts. The first two factors mentioned by Harley reflect the relevance of the focus on language form, whereas the other two components highlight the importance of the functional uses of verbal morphology. In general, the two sets of conditions identified by Harley suggest that successful second language learning of past tense aspectual distinctions may be dependent on the defining features of both academic and natural settings: hypothesis testing of the target grammar structure and functional communicative demands of linguistic interaction.

As mentioned above, previous data on the effect of instruction on the development of Preterite–Imperfect in Spanish do support the claims advanced by Harley and Schmidt. For instance, Stokes (1985) reported on a pretest-posttest experimental study that shows that high levels of focus on form (monitoring) resulted in higher gains in accuracy (measurement on cloze test) for Spanish tense-aspect phenomena in comparison with other grammatical features of verbal morphology such as mode, person and number. The subjects who participated in Stoke's experiment were second semester students of Spanish (end of semester) and there was no instruction provided between tests except for the explicit mention of what feature was tested according to treatment group. Students were told that the purpose of the test was "to measure how well they could perform with regard to tense and aspect suffixes on verb forms" (p. 381).[31] In sum, the data from Stokes shows that merely requesting students to focus their attention on a target item was enough to generate an improvement from pre to posttest. Along the same lines, Jourdenais, Ota, Stauffer, Boyson and Doughty (1995)

---

31. Similarly, Sato (1988, 1990) argues that conversational interaction is not sufficient "to ensure the acquisition of *particular complex syntactic structures* in English, while encounters with written language, and the more complex syntactic structures this contains, may well turn out to be crucial" (1988: 393, italics added).

investigated the effect of input enhancement on the production of past tense morphology among five second semester students of Spanish. Five other students acted as a control group. The study was based on the analysis of (1) the production of Preterite–Imperfect in a written narrative following the presentation of a text narrating the same story, and (2) think-aloud protocols performed concurrently with the writing task (number of language related episodes containing reference to past tense verbal morphology). The treatment group received an enhanced text (Preterite shadowed and Imperfect in bold), whereas the control group received the same text with no typographical enhancement. The results of the experiment show that (1) the treatment group attempted more past tense forms than the control group, and (2) the treatment group made more explicit mentions about aspect than the control group. In essence, the type of experimental treatment exemplified in Jourdenais et al. was successful as measured by number of attempted past tense forms in written narration and explicit mention of rules during the think-alouds. There are, however, two important constraints. Firstly, the study did not attempt to control for possible long term effects of the treatment (cf., Harley 1989). Notice, for instance, that Harley (1989) discovered that after three months of a combined form-meaning instructional approach on aspectual differences in L2 French short term gains were not maintained. Secondly, it is possible that differences in production of target forms do not necessarily represent knowledge or more control of those grammatical features, but rather more attempts at past tense use. In other words, we should ask ourselves: What have students learned?, and, how long will that effect be maintained in the production of these students?

Despite impressive contrasts in the use of inflectional morphology among classroom and natural learners, researchers have been reluctant to posit any major effect for formal instruction. This is because data from longitudinal studies reveal that the beneficial effects of instruction may be short-lived. For instance, Harley (1989) found mixed results with reference to instruction in a communication-based syllabus. The students who participated in her study — grade 6 immersion students — received 8 weeks of instruction on the use of *Passé Composé–Imparfait* and were tested twice after the end of the instructional period: immediately after instruction and 3 months later. To measure past tense aspectual distinctions in L2 French, Harley used the following tasks: a free composition, a cloze test, and an oral interview. Harley's results show a positive effect for the productive distinction of *Passé Composé–Imparfait* in the tests administered immediately after instruction. However, no effect was found in the delayed post-test. This is an interesting finding for two reasons. First, these data come from a relatively free production task (at least two out of three tasks). If learners vary in their production of the target language across tasks (from controlled to free production) it is particularly important to know which tasks provide the true measurement of the nonnative grammatical system. Second, it seems that pedagogical manipulations of the input data cannot affect the natural sequence of acquisition of the L2 grammar. In this respect, Lightbown (1987) claims that, in spite of the capricious ordering of the linguistic structures presented to L2 students in the traditional form-focused class, learner internal factors guide students towards acquiring the underlying structure of the L2 in a natural way. Therefore, the existence and potential use of guided instruction raises two important questions. First, can developmental sequences be affected by instructional treatment? Second, can instruction accelerate the development of tense-aspect marking without necessarily altering the sequence of acquisition? The available empirical data appear to show that only the second question may receive a positive answer: formal instruction may only accelerate the transition through established stages of development (e.g., Bardovi-Harlig & Reynolds 1995; Bergström 1995; Salaberry 1998).

4.4.1 Pedagogy of past tense verbal morphology

With respect to the role of the input available to classroom learners, it is necessary to recognize that — as pointed out by Hasbún (1995: 192) — the data from native speakers typically used as controls do not necessarily reflect the type of input that learners receive during academic instruction. Very few studies of classroom learning of tense and aspect have reported on the nature of the language input accessible to learners. Among the few studies which have analyzed teacher input, Swain (1992: 243) reports the following on the use of *Passé Composé* and *Imparfait* among grade 6 immersion teachers: (1) only 15% of all verbs used by these teachers are in the past tense, (2) two thirds of the verbs correspond to the *Passé Composé* and one-third to the *Imparfait*, and (3) the *Imparfait* is "almost completely limited to the verbs *avoir, être, faire* and *vouloir*," *(To have, to be, to do*, and *to want)*. Similarly, Kaplan (1987) reports on data obtained from a "small sample of classroom talk" that 84% of all forms of past tense in classroom French are in the *Passé Composé*. In sum, the use of the perfective is more extended than the use of the imperfective in classroom talk. Alternatively, the effect of language input may be assessed through analysis of the language used in textbooks. For instance, Hasbún (1995) conducted a small survey of the type of input available from the textbook used by the level 1 learners from her study: *Arriba* by Zayas-Bazán, Bacon & Fernández. The Preterite was introduced in lesson 7, and the Imperfect was introduced in lesson

8 along with a comparison of both past tense markers. Hasbún estimates that the 50 verbs used in lesson 7 are distributed in the following way according to lexical class: stative verbs: 10%, activities: 38%, and telic events: 52%. In lesson 8 there are 38 verbs distributed in the following way: statives: 7.9%, activities: 81.5%, and telic events: 10.6%. The high number of activity verbs, especially in lesson 8, may be attributed to the fact that they were used in decontextualized sentences. That is to say, the lack of a telos (see measuring-out constraint in Tenny 1994) did not allow for the interpretation of the event as a closed one. Also, the actual number of stative verbs presented in lessons 7 and 8 were five and three respectively.[32] Similarly, the analysis of the type of pedagogical presentation of the contrast *Passé Composé–Imparfait* in the textbook "Deux Mondes" (Terrell, Rogers, Barnes, & Wolff-Hessini 1993: 242) shows an even stronger bias: "To describe a state of being in the past, French usually uses the Imperfect tense." The type of pedagogical recommendation of Terrell et al. (such as the one cited above) represent an explicit lesson on semantic aspectual classes (see Salaberry 1998). This provides further support for the assumption that statives probably constitute a very restricted set of verbs which learners can incorporate into their nonnative system in a non-algorithmic fashion (i.e., associative learning) (cf., DeKeyser 1994; N. Ellis 1996; R. Ellis 1987).

The dissatisfaction with textbook rules on the use of past tense aspectual distinctions is clear from a review of recent articles on the pedagogical value of grammatical presentations of the Preterite–Imperfect contrast in Spanish (e.g., Blyth 1997; Delgado-Jenkins 1990; Frantzen 1995; Hernán 1994; Ozete 1988; Westfall & Foerster 1996). For instance, Frantzen (1995: 145) argues that "textbook explanations ... often provide confusing, unreliable and even inaccurate explanations," whereas Westfall and Foerster (1996: 550) claim that textbook presentations do not address how the Preterite and the Imperfect "interact to determine discourse dynamics."[33] Some researchers have described the nature

---

32. However, it is not clear whether Hasbún counted the verbs used in the introduction to the grammatical target in each chapter, or whether she counted the number of verb types in the entire chapter. I counted the number of typical stative verbs in two pages of the presentation of the contrast Preterite–Imperfect in Chapter 8 (Zayas-Bazán, Bacon & Fernández 1997: 270–1) and there were at least five stative verbs used in the Imperfect (stative verbs in Preterite not counted): *saber, gustar, ser, tener, conocer* (to know, to like, to be, to have, to know a person).

33. Frantzen provides examples of what she considers to be the types of inaccurate rules from a survey of textbooks of college Spanish: (1) the Imperfect describes emotional or mental activity, (2) the Imperfect is used to express repeated or habitual past action, (3) *would + infinitive* signals use of the Imperfect, (4) certain words and expressions are frequently associated with the Preterite and others with the Imperfect, (5) some verbs take on a special meaning in the Preterite tense, and (6)

of general rules for the teaching of Preterite and Imperfect. Among the earliest proposals, Bull (1965: 166–71) recommends that the pedagogical presentation of the Preterite–Imperfect contrast be based on the discrimination of the three aspectual values (i.e., inceptive, imperfective and terminative) through English examples. He points out that the student does not need to distinguish between inceptive and terminative values, only to discriminate whether an event is imperfective or not (i.e., a dichotomous contrast). That is to say, Bull's approach does without the need for positing special rules (see below). Guitart (1978) expands the perspective offered by Bull offering a more encompassing approach, whereas Guitart (1995) suggested the use of a movie analogy to teach the Preterite–Imperfect contrast: the frame showing the event one is talking about is the key frame and the situation prior to the main event represents the previous frame (see Hernán 1994 for the use of movie narratives to present the distinction Preterite–Imperfect in terms of narrative foreground and background). Interestingly, key and previous frame may correspond to what Klein (1994) refers to as target and source state respectively.

In contrast with the above mentioned rules, Frantzen proposes a small set of principles to guide the pedagogical presentation of the use of the Preterite–Imperfect contrast in Spanish past tense. The Imperfect should be used for "(a) actions and states in progress at some focused point in the past, (b) habitual past actions, (c) repetitious past actions, and (d) anticipated/planned past actions," whereas the Preterite should be used to focus on "(a) the completion of past actions or states, and (b) the beginning of past actions or states" (p. 147). Notice that the use of the Preterite is straightforward: Preterite is used for inception or completion of any type of situation. In contrast, the Imperfect presents a more complex picture including various aspectual features (i.e., iterativity, habituality, etc.), a sense of modality (i.e., anticipated — not real — events) and even pragmatic connotations (i.e., the use of Imperfect for planning and requests). This complexity has been addressed as a possible reason for the late acquisition of the imperfective marker by the majority of researchers working in L2 acquisition (e.g., Andersen & Shirai 1994; Bardovi-Harlig 1995a; Bergström 1995; Kaplan 1987; Schmidt & Frota 1986). A second major pedagogical approach for the use of past tense verbal morphology is based on the concept proposed by Discourse Representation Theory (e.g., Dowty 1986; Dry 1983, 1986; Fleischmann 1995;

---

when two actions occur simultaneously in the past, the Imperfect is used. Frantzen also mentions the use of two common translations offered by textbooks to help students understand the contrast in Spanish: the progressive (*to be* + verb-*ing*), and *used to* + *infinitive*. Frantzen claims that the latter are reliable predictors of the use of the Imperfect in Spanish.

Kamp & Rohrer 1983; Smith 1983). For instance, Westfall and Foerster argue that pedagogical instruction should be based on the identification of new reference times on a narrative timeline. In this respect, only the Preterite introduces a new reference time. The sample pedagogical tasks presented by Westfall and Foerster, however, tend to rely, to a large extent, on examples that carry only prototypical marking of verbal morphology according to lexical aspectual classes. For instance, the presentation of the following text with typographical enhancement to distinguish background (in italics) versus foreground information does not incorporate any non-prototypical marking of verbal morphology (i.e., Imperfect, in italics, is associated with statives and Preterite with telic events):

El año pasado fui a Andalucía
Last year I went (PRET) to Andalucía
Hacía muy buen tiempo
The weather was (IMP) good
Visité la Alhambra en Granada
I visited (PRET) the Alhambra
Era lindísima. Tenía una fuente con estatuas de leones
It was (IMP) beautiful. It had (IMP) a fountain with statues of lions
Fui también a Sevilla durante Semana Santa
I also went (PRET) to Seville for Holy Week
Había flores por todos lados. Y las calles estaban llenas de gente de todas partes del mundo.
There were (IMP) flowers everywhere. And the streets were (IMP) crowded with people from all over the world.

In essence, Westfall and Foerster's proposal falls back on the use of lexical aspectual classes at the verb (phrase) level to convey the contrast between perfective-imperfective in past tense Spanish.

In another variation on proposed sequences of instruction, García and vanPutte (1988) state that pedagogical treatments should start with the most prototypical uses of past tense aspectual distinctions with texts which reflect a clear narrative line and where the overall context of the text does not override the inherent lexical aspectual value of the verb (see also Bergström 1995 for similar proposal with respect to French). Subsequently, the presentation of texts with reduced contextual redundancy may gradually be introduced to sensitize the students to the nuances of meaning of the context beyond the sentence level: "how to chunk discourse and, particularly, how to fore-and back-ground information" (p. 278). Finally, Blyth (1997) argues for a process-oriented conceptualization of grammatical concepts (including aspectual contrasts). In particular, Blyth addresses how a constructivist approach can help teachers "understand the learning and teaching of aspect, a core grammatical concept" (p. 50). According to Blyth, non-native speakers must learn to pay attention to foreground/background contrasts in narratives. Pedagogically speaking, he argues that first person narratives, more so than traditional cloze-type tests, give learners the opportunity to bypass the tendency to follow the Defective Tense Hypothesis (i.e., the lexical aspect hypothesis).

4.5   Conclusion

The analysis of findings from the studies reviewed in this chapter reveals some general features of the L2 developmental process of past tense morphological marking. In essence, the following phenomena appear to affect the choice of past tense marking: (1) adult L2 learners are cognitively capable of narrating stories set in past tense contexts (e.g., Dietrich et al. 1995; Klein & Perdue 1992; Schumann 1987; Trévise 1987); (2) narratives among both native and nonnative speakers are structured along the lines of figure and ground (prototypical aspectual value) (e.g., Bardovi-Harlig 1995a; Kumpf 1984; Meisel 1987; Reinhart 1984); (3) untutored learners mark figure and ground (mostly) with pragmatic devices and tutored learners (mostly) with morphosyntactic means (e.g., Sato 1990; Schumann 1987; Trévise 1987 for untutored learners; Bergström 1995; Hasbún 1995; Ramsay 1990 for tutored learners); (4) non-prototypical aspectual values reflect conventional choices made by speakers who share a common background (be it determined by linguistic or cognitive-linguistic factors) (e.g., Andersen 1994; Coppieters 1987; Ramsay 1989); (5) classroom learners do not have direct access to the distributional bias of aspectual oppositions (cf. marked values) present in native speakers' discourse (e.g., Andersen 1994; Andersen & Shirai 1994; Wiberg 1996); and (6) instructional factors (e.g., frequency and saliency) may help classroom learners speed up the process of marking temporality on verbal morphology (e.g., Bardovi-Harlig & Reynolds 1995; Bergström 1995; Salaberry 1998). Based on principles (1) and (2) we can predict that classroom learners will be able to mark temporality (e.g., tense contrasts) and distinguish foreground versus background in their narratives. Based on principle (3) we can predict that tutored learners will focus on the morphological means to mark temporality in the L2. Principles (4) and (5) address the difficulties faced by nonnative speakers with the selection of marked choices of aspect. Finally, principle (6) helps us identify the potential effect of instruction to focus the learner on the appropriate use of morphosyntactic marking of temporality. In the following chapter I will rely on the above mentioned findings in order to substantiate the research design and methodology to be used for the analysis of data of the studies to be presented in Chapter 6 and the subsequent discussion to be presented in Chapter 7.

CHAPTER 5

Research methodology in the analysis of past tense morphology

As shown in the previous chapter, there is still conflicting evidence about the theoretical status of the system being developed by L2 learners, especially in terms of the sequence and rate of development of aspectual contrasts, and the potential effect of learning setting (i.e., tutored versus untutored learners). The latter effect is primarily represented by pedagogical manipulations of the input data and task demands. Moreover, there appear to be substantial differences in the research design, data collection and data analysis procedures used across studies. For that reason, in this chapter I will describe and justify the selection of tasks and research procedures to be used in the analysis of data to be presented in the following chapter. In the first section of this chapter I present the research design, methodology and results of a pilot study (five classroom learners of Spanish) which preceded the collection of data for the main set of studies. The analysis and discussion of those findings provide a necessary background to understand the results of the other studies. In the second part I present the research design of the main studies: hypotheses, materials, testing procedure and operational tests of lexical aspect.

5.1   Pilot study

The objective of the pilot study was to analyze the use of past tense verbal morphology of five academic learners of Spanish across a variety of tasks: (i) written data (grammar tests), (ii) cued oral production (movie narratives), and (iii) spontaneous oral production (interviews).

5.1.1 *Subjects, materials and procedure*

Five English-speaking students learning Spanish as a second language in an academic setting participated in the study as volunteers. All students were paid for their participation. Four of those students (all undergraduates) were enrolled in regular academic courses offered during the summer session (intensive) at Cornell University. Three of them were enrolled in an advanced third semester course, whereas the fourth one was enrolled in a lower level third semester course.[1] All students attended three hours of daily instruction five days a week. The remaining participant was a graduate student who was studying on her own who participated in the narrative tasks only. In addition, three Spanish native speakers who participated voluntarily acted as a control group. The control group was necessary to ascertain that the selection of past tense verbal morphology in the written tasks (especially in the editing task) was appropriate (use of aspectual distinctions in Spanish is not categorical but context-based).

The four students completed three different tasks. The two written grammar tests were represented by a 41-item test based on a contextualized series of propositional clusters, and a 26-item cloze test based on three original passages from two Spanish-speaking literary authors.[2] The 41-item test was contextualized with eight cartoons depicting the events of one of the scenes of the Hitchcock movie "Psycho."[3] The 26-item cloze test was divided into two parts: a first test with blank options and a second test with underlined selections of verbal morphology to be edited by the subjects (acceptance or rejection of selected choice). The passages used in the editing task were the same ones used in the cloze test. The options provided in the second part were the original selection of past tense verb forms used by the authors of the selected texts. These examples represented non-prototypical uses of verbal morphology according to the lexical semantics of the selected verbs (i.e., viewpoint aspect). The second and third tasks were represented by oral personal and movie narratives. The length of the personal interviews ranged from approximately 30 to 45 minutes. The shortest time corresponds to the student interviewed alone. The movie narratives were

---

1. Lower level and upper level third semester courses are offered to accommodate students with diverse academic backgrounds (e.g., Spanish taken in high school or college). To be accepted in the upper level third semester, students must (i) obtain a high grade in their second semester of instruction at college, or (ii) obtain a minimum grade in one of two standardized tests: SPT (Spanish Placement Test), or LPS (Language Placement in Spanish).

2. The grammar tests used in the main study were adaptations of those used in the pilot study. Descriptions of the tests used in the main study are provided in Appendix B and C. The test based on the Psycho movie was shorter in the main study (28 items instead of 41), and the cloze and editing task from the main study contained a fourth passage which included prototypical as well as non-prototypical uses of non-stative verbs (41 items instead of 26).

3. The "Psycho" story was based on a similar passage from the intermediate Spanish textbook "Pasajes."

based on two silent films: the excerpt "Alone and hungry" from the film *Modern Times* by Charlie Chaplin (5 minutes, 20 seconds) and the complete film *The Pear Story* (6 minutes). Both films depicted a range of scenes representing background as well as foreground information. To generate a narration in the past tense students were asked to play the role of a witness who had seen all the events depicted in the specific movie they saw. The witness was requested to narrate the story to another student who played the role of a detective in charge of taking the report from the witness.

5.1.2 *Analysis of results and discussion*

The data from both written tasks were coded for past tense morphology. All verbs were also classified into three categories of lexical aspect: statives, atelic events and telic events. Section 5.3.5 presents the list of operational tests used in both the pilot and main study. The results from the first grammar test (Psycho) are displayed in percentages of use of Imperfect of total use of past tense across lexical aspectual class in Table 5.1 (i.e., the difference between 100% and the percentage for Imperfect corresponds to the use of Preterite):

Table 5.1. Use of imperfect as percentage of total use of past tense (test 1)

Verb type (41 items)	NN1	NN2	NN3	NN4
Stative (18)	78%	83%	94%	100%
Activity (8)	88%	38%	75%	88%
Telic (15)	20%	13%	20%	7%

As shown in Table 5.1, the change in morphological marking from telic events (mostly Preterite) to stative verbs (mostly Imperfect) is closely associated with lexical aspectual classes in the data from NN4: a difference of 93 percentage points. The effect of lexical aspect is less categorical in the data from the other speakers, because the range of differences decreases gradually: NN3 (74%), NN2 (70%), and NN1 (58%). The results of the second grammar test (both cloze and editing task) are displayed in Tables 5.2 and 5.3 respectively. Table 5.2 presents the results by individual student and Table 5.3 presents the contrast between students and native speakers' groups. The results from the second test are similar to the ones from the previous task. That is to say, the effect of lexical aspect is noticeable in the transition from telic to atelic events, even though the latter effect is normally weaker than the effect between stative and telic verbs.

Table 5.2. Use of imperfect as percentage of total use of past tense (test 2)

Verb type (26 items)	NN1	NN2	NN3	NN4
Statives (3)	100%	67%	100%	100%
Activity (10)	60%	50%	50%	40%
Telic (13)	38%	31%	38%	15%

Note: NN refers to non-native speaker

Table 5.3. Use of imperfect as percentage of total use of past tense for both native and nonnative speakers (cloze & editing task)

Verb type (26)	Cloze task		Editing task	
	L2 Spanish	L1 Spanish	L2 Spanish	L1 Spanish
Statives (3)	92%	100%	100%	100%
Activ. (10)	50%	40%	65%	100%
Telic (13)	31%	28%	42%	82%

Most important, the results from the *cloze test* reveal that both native and nonnative speakers preferred the prototypical value of morphological marking associated with each lexical aspectual class: 69% and 72% use of Preterite with telic events for nonnative and native speakers respectively and 92% and 100% use of Imperfect with stative verbs for nonnative and native speakers respectively. On the other hand, the results of the *editing task* show the degree of acceptance of the non-prototypical uses of past tense morphological markers with respect to lexical aspectual class. In general, all participants changed their selection of verbal ending towards the non-prototypical choices in the editing task. However, the analysis of the range of the differential scores (change from cloze to editing task) across groups — especially activities and telic events — reveals that native speakers were more willing than nonnative speakers to accept the non-prototypical marking of past tense aspect (cf. Coppieters 1987). All the verbs from the editing task were presented in the Imperfect form. If the students were oblivious to the requirements of this task, or if the task were too difficult, the most likely response would be for the students to accept the option presented in the test. However, this was not the case. In fact, the rejection of the answers from the editing task reveals that these students were opinionated about the selection of aspectual morphology and rejected (to a larger extent than native speakers) the non-prototypical marker of non-stative verbs (compared with responses associated with stative verbs).

The data from the oral tasks provided a different outcome than the one revealed in the analysis of the written data. The analysis of the movie narratives shows that (1) all students except NN4 marked some verbs with Present tense (although the narrative was set in a past tense context), (2) the data from NN4 show a close correspondence of morphological marking and lexical aspectual classes (prototypical marking), (3) only NN1 and NN2 marked a substantial number of stative verbs with Preterite, and (4) the use of Preterite was prevalent in all narratives (narration of a sequential plot). In contrast, the results of the personal narrative show that three learners (i.e., NN3, NN4 and NN5) relied extensively on the use of Imperfect and that the other two (i.e., NN1 and NN2) used mostly Preterite (or Present tense) to mark verbal endings in past tense contexts. A methodological constraint of this particular task was that the frequency of short question-answer sequences limited the use of the background-foreground contrast normally present in extended narratives such as the film retell task (see above). The question and answer sequences were more evident among the less proficient learners (i.e., NN1 and NN2). Nevertheless, one of the most advanced students (i.e., NN4) generated extended pieces of discourse where the background-foreground contrast was more evident, although her use of the Imperfect was related to the description of situations (instead of narration of sequences of events). In sum, the analysis of the oral data from all four learners shows that the use of Preterite was the preferred morphological ending to mark telic events among all learners (cf. Bergström 1995; Hasbún 1995). In contrast, the Imperfect was not categorically used with stative verbs across all learners (as predicted by the lexical aspect hypothesis): two of the five learners (i.e., NN1 and NN2) marked statives mostly with the Preterite. For NN1, out of a total of 31 tokens, 10 were marked with Present, 20 with Preterite, and 1 with Imperfect, whereas for NN2, out of a total of 21 tokens, no verb was marked with Present, 12 were marked with Preterite and 9 with Imperfect. The strongest evidence about the overreliance on the use of the Preterite as a potential default marker of past tense is provided by the data from NN1, not only due to the quantitative analysis of the data, but also due to the lack of effect of feedback provided by the interlocutor on the use of the Imperfect.

5.2   Summary and projection of results for main study

The data from the first written task (41-item propositional cluster) revealed that the selection of morphological markers of past tense was related to lexical aspectual classes as predicted by the lexical aspect hypothesis: the use of Preterite was more prevalent with telic events and the use of Imperfect was more common with statives. The results from the second written test (26-item cloze and editing tasks) showed that, relative to the selections of native speakers, nonnative speakers preferred to use prototypical markers of past tense (variation in choices from cloze to editing task). In contrast, the analysis of the data from the movie narrative was inconclusive as to the effect of lexical aspect or a default tense marker. Although the preferred marker of past tense in the movie narrative was the Preterite, the latter was used mostly with telic events. These results are compatible with the claim of the lexical aspect hypothesis: Preterite appears first with telic events and spreads towards other lexical aspectual classes. On the other hand, the use of the Preterite with a substantial number of statives in the movie narratives of NN1 and NN2 is also compatible with the claim of a preliminary stage of development when the Preterite may act as a default marker of past tense. Incidentally, the use of the Imperfect was more prevalent in the movie narrative — relative to the data from the personal narrative — to the extent that the learners were able to mark more distinctly the foreground-background contrast of the movie plot. Finally, the results from the personal narrative, the least monitored task, are more compatible with the proposal of a default marker of past tense for the beginning stages of development of verbal morphology. Following Tarone (1988) we may plausibly conclude that the variation in the data across tasks may be representative of a continuum of attention to form (monitoring operationalized as planning time: Ellis 1987; Ochs 1979). Under the assumptions (1) that the least monitored data are the most representative of the underlying linguistic competence of the learner and (2) that style shifting mirrors developmental sequences, we obtain empirical support for the unmarked past tense hypothesis (cf., Wiberg 1996). For instance, the variation in past tense marking of statives — mostly with Preterite — in the personal narrative and Imperfect or Present in the movie narrative and written tasks is clear in the comparison of the data from NN1, to NN2 to NN3.

5.3   Main study

5.3.1 *Hypotheses*

The analysis of the findings from the pilot study presented above and the data from earlier studies on L2 acquisition presented in the previous chapter suggest the potential use of tense distinctions, rather than aspectual distinctions, during the beginning stages of development of verbal morphology. The notion of a default marker of past tense is supported by both theoretical perspectives (e.g., Comrie 1976; Guitart 1978) as well as empirical analyses of acquisition data (e.g., Liskin-Gasparro 1996; Wiberg 1996). With respect to theoretical analyses, for example, Comrie argues that in the past tense, the perfective aspect is the unmarked member of the dichotomy (p. 121). More specifically, Guitart (1978: 142) claims that the Preterite in Spanish "states that an occurrence took place before the moment of speaking," whereas the Imperfect tells about an occurrence which happened before the time of speaking "in which some other situation took place or was taking place." That is to say, the Preterite acts as a default marker of past tense, whereas the Imperfect fulfills an ancillary role. With respect to empirical data, Wiberg (1996: 1100) proposed the "unmarked past tense hypothesis" as an alternative to the lexical aspect hypothesis following the analysis of Italian data from twenty-four bilingual Swedish-Italian adolescents. Furthermore, the data from Buczowska and Weist (1991) on the comprehension of tense and aspectual contrasts show that adult tutored learners were significantly better at the selection of the contrast past versus non-past rather than the contrast Progressive versus simple past. The results from the studies to be discussed in the following chapter support the findings from Buczowska and Weist with production instead of comprehension data.

Based on the above-mentioned argument, the following null and alternative hypotheses were operationalized for the analysis of data to be presented in the following chapter:

H_0: The early appearance of past tense morphological marking in L2 Spanish of adult tutored learners is independent of the effect of inherent lexical aspectual value of verbal predicates.

H_1: The early appearance of past tense morphological marking in L2 Spanish of adult tutored learners is correlated to the effect of inherent lexical aspectual value of verbal predicates (the Imperfect spreads from statives to atelic events and finally to telic events, whereas the Preterite spreads from telic events to activities to statives).

To further analyze the use of morphological markers of temporality among experienced Spanish learners (advanced students and near-native speakers), a second set of null and alternative hypotheses were operationalized:

H_0: The selection of Spanish past tense morphological marking among advanced tutored learners is independent of the effect of inherent lexical aspectual value of verbal predicates.

H_1: The selection of Spanish past tense morphological marking among advanced tutored learners is correlated with the effect of inherent lexical aspectual value of verbal predicates (the Imperfect spreads from statives to atelic events and finally to telic events, whereas the Preterite spreads from telic events to activities to statives).

It is important to point out that he existence of distributional biases (e.g., Andersen 1994; Wiberg 1996) does not preclude the use of non-prototypical markers of past tense morphology. That is to say, the target-like use of Spanish past tense markers entails that learners will be able to mark all verbal predicates with both the Imperfect and the Preterite irrespective of lexical aspectual classes.

5.3.2 *Subjects*

There were two different groups of subjects who participated in each study: one group was part of the longitudinal study ($n = 20$) and the other one was part of the cross-sectional study ($n = 47$). In addition, each section of the study used a control group of native speakers ($n = 4$ and $n = 32$ respectively). The participants in the longitudinal study were 20 college-level adult native speakers of English and four native speakers of Spanish. Sixteen of the twenty L1 English students were enrolled in regular Spanish courses taught at Cornell University. The students were enrolled in four different levels of academic instruction (four students from each level): second semester (beginners), third semester (intermediate), advanced third semester (intermediate-high) and an introductory literature course at the level of fifth/sixth semester (advanced). The students from the less advanced courses (beginners and intermediate) met five times a day (one hour of lecture and four hours of section). The students from the advanced courses (intermediate-high and advanced) met three times a week. These volunteers were offered a monetary retribution in exchange for their participation in the experimental tasks. There was also a group of four near native speakers of Spanish comprised of four graduate students representing the following areas: linguistics, literature (two) and rural sociology. Finally, a group of four native speakers of Spanish acted as a control group. The native speakers were also graduate students representing the following academic areas of expertise: Industrial and Labor Relations, International Law and Business, Rural Sociology and Science and Technology. The areas of expertise of these students ensured less influence of metalinguistic knowledge on the experimental tasks. Table 5.4 presents a summary of the academic experience of the main group of L2 Spanish students.

There are some interesting features of the academic background of the

Table 5.4. Summary of academic background from main group of subjects[a]

	HS	College	Study	Extrac.	Travel	Self-rate
beginners ($n = 4$)	1.75	1.00	4.75	2/4	0/4	2.25
intermediate ($n = 4$)	2.25	1.50	3.25	1/4	0/4	3.00
intermediate-high ($n = 4$)	3.75	1.00	5.50	1/4	0/4	2.25
advanced ($n = 4$)	2.25	4.25	6.25	3/4	2/4	4.00

[a] See Appendix D for further details on the instrument. High school study was measured in years, college study in semesters, and study time was measured in hours per week. Travel was included as a factor in their background when students had spent a minimum of two weeks in a Spanish speaking country using the target language daily. The self-rating procedure is intended to be as a rough measure of the students' perception of their abilities in the target language. As such it is very dependent on what the students perceive as the gap between what they can do and the types of models and interactions they have (most likely academic interactions only).

volunteer students. First, the high number of hours devoted to weekly study among intermediate-high students reflects the bias generated by a single subject who dedicates 10 hours per week to study Spanish. On the other hand, the number of study hours for the advanced students are more balanced across subjects. Second, notice that the self-perception of the students' ability with the target language (highest of 4 for advanced) is associated with a significant amount of travel experience and extracurricular activities. In other words, it is possible that the contact with natural environments gives these students a better idea of how good they may be. In contrast, the other students (although confident in their abilities in the classroom) are more tentative in their self-assessment (but see data from large group of subjects below). Finally, notice that the academic experience of one of the more advanced groups (intermediate-high) is based mostly on high school instruction, whereas the other group (advanced) draws mostly on experience at the college level.

In addition to the participants in the longitudinal section mentioned above a larger group of students from two of the four language courses represented by the volunteers who participated in the longitudinal part of the study (23 students from the intermediate course and 24 students from the advanced course) and a group of 32 monolingual native speakers of Spanish residing in their native country completed one of the written grammar tasks (cloze test and associated editing test). Two out of a total of six sections that comprised the intermediate course represented the intermediate level, and all three sections comprising the advanced course represented the advanced level. The number of years in high school and semesters in college are the average among all subjects. In general, the students who had had a large amount of experience with Spanish in high

Table 5.5. Summary of biographical information from nonnative speakers (large pool of subjects)

	HS	College	Study	Extrac.	Travel	Self-rate
intermediate ($n = 23$)	1.72	1.31	3.31	9/25	4/25	1.81
advanced ($n = 24$)	2.50	2.34	3.38	15/24	9/24	2.58

school did not take several of the preliminary college courses before taking intermediate or advanced ones. It is important to point out that the self-assessment average score of the large group of intermediate students is significantly lower than the same average among the four volunteers: averages of 1.81 and 3.00 respectively.[4] The same is true of the advanced students: average self-assessment score of 2.58 for the large group compared to 4.00 for the volunteer students. This is probably related to the fact that the more motivated students are also the ones who are willing to participate in an experimental study on the acquisition of Spanish. On the other hand, it appears that a large number of intermediate students traveled to Spanish speaking countries (and used Spanish), and participated in extracurricular activities as well. Table 5.6 presents the data from the background questionnaire from native speakers.

Table 5.6. Summary of biographical information from native speakers (extended study)[a]

	Knowledge English	Academic Setting	Spanish Writing	Spanish Reading
Native Speakers	2.64	30/32	4.72	4.76

[a] See Appendix F for further details. Knowledge of English was rated on a scale from 1 to 5 (highest). The instruction in English was conducted in an academic setting except for two speakers who mentioned travel and friends. Writing and reading were a measurement of literacy on a scale of 1 to 5 (highest).

The majority of native speakers were college-level students who were studying English in an academic setting (Spain). Their knowledge of English was quite limited; perhaps similar to a second or third semester of college-level Spanish in the United States. Most of them did not have any contact with

---

4. In this respect it is important to remember that all volunteers from the intermediate and advanced sections came from the same sections that comprise the larger group of subjects, although their data were not included in the large pool of candidates.

English except through classroom instruction. The native speakers also provided information about their contact with written Spanish through reading and writing to obtain a broad assessment of their level of literacy in Spanish.

5.3.3 *Materials*

There were three experimental tasks performed by the main group of subjects: (1) two movie narratives (an elicited narrative based on one of the Chaplin films and a retelling of a narrative performed by another student), (2) an individual test (aspectual choices) based on a text describing one of the scenes of the film Psycho, and (3) a second grammar task composed of a cloze test and an editing task which was done in pairs (two students from the same level). The oral task was audio recorded and later transcribed for analysis of verbal morphological marking in past tense. The joint-grammar test was also recorded for subsequent analysis of the types of strategies used by the students while performing that type of task. The larger group of subjects from the intermediate and advanced groups as well as the native speakers completed the third task individually. The latter type of data was used for an extended quantitative analysis. A description of each one of the tasks will be presented in the following sections.

5.3.3.1 *Movie narratives*
Two short excerpts from the silent film *Modern Times* by Charlie Chaplin were selected for this study: *Alone and Hungry* (5 minutes and 20 seconds), and *An Accident Occurred at the Store* (6 minutes). A summary of the events depicted by each one of the Chaplin stories is presented in Appendix G. The selected films were chosen for three main reasons. First, both films show a series of discrete sequenced actions (foreground) as well as simultaneous actions that constitute the background of the story. Second, the use of a story whose content is known to both the researcher and the students makes the task of analyzing interlanguage data easier and more reliable (Bardovi-Harlig 1995a). Third, the use of films analyzed in previous studies allows for the replication of findings from other languages or hypotheses on the analysis of the development of aspect. Excerpts from the film *Modern Times* have been used in previous empirical studies such as the ESFP (e.g., Klein & Perdue 1992), and specific studies on the L2 acquisition of French (Bergström 1995), English (Bardovi-Harlig 1995a), and

Spanish (Hasbún 1995).[5]

In previous studies (e.g., Bardovi-Harlig 1994; Bergström 1995) the Chaplin films were shown twice. However, in this study the films were shown only once to minimize the effect of planning and monitoring (Ellis 1987; Ochs 1979; Tarone 1983, 1988). Furthermore, to generate a narration in the past tense students were asked to play the role of a witness who had seen all the events depicted in the specific movie. Subsequently, the witness was requested to narrate the story to another student who played the role of a detective in charge of taking the report from the witness. Finally the student who played the role of the detective was requested to narrate what happened (as narrated by the witness) to the chief of detectives. A native speaker or near native speaker of Spanish played the role of chief. During the retelling of the film to the chief of detectives the researcher left the room and waited outside until the detective had finished the narration of the events as they were reported by the witness. The students received help with vocabulary during the narration task whenever they requested it. Help was provided by the researcher during the first narrative and by the native speaker who played the role of the chief of detectives during the retelling of the film narrated by another student. All requests for help were included in the transcription of the protocols. This elaborate procedure from the movie narrative was important to maintain the highest possible degree of communicative relevance and meaningfulness of task (cf. Tarone 1983, 1995). This procedure is comparable to the one implemented in Klein and Perdue (1992) where the researcher watched the first episode of a longer excerpt of the same Chaplin movie with the subject, then left the room before the second episode and later requested the subject to retell the end of the movie.

To the best of my knowledge Hasbún (1995) is the only study to date which has used the film *Modern Times* to collect movie narratives on the acquisition of L2 classroom Spanish. It is important to point out, however, that the methodology used by Hasbún differs from the present study: (1) number of film excerpts used, (2) length of movie excerpts, (3) type of experimental instruction, and (4) control of planning time. First, Hasbún asked her students to narrate the excerpt (*Alone and Hungry*), but not the second one used in the present study (*An*

---

5. The replacement of the film *The Pear Story* (used in the pilot study) for another one of the Chaplin films was based on two criteria: engagement of the subject and replicability. First, the pilot study showed that the students were more eager to narrate a film that was entertaining and fun (Chaplin film) instead of the less interesting film specifically created for research purposes (The Pear Story). Second, the selection of two excerpts from the same film made the comparison of the two excerpts more valid as far as content and style of the evoked narratives.

Accident Occurred at the Store). Second, the movie excerpt used by Hasbún was longer than the one used in this study (approximately two extra minutes). The extra footage used by Hasbún was considered unnecessary for the present study since both film clips include a variety of situations depicting all lexical aspectual classes. The previous assumption was confirmed by the variety of verb types used by the subjects. Third, the students in Hasbún's study were asked to start the narrative with the phrase *"Había una vez ..."* to prevent "advanced learners and native speakers of Spanish from shifting to the historical present." Hasbún reports that in previous studies this technique was successful in avoiding the use of present tense marking (see Chapter 7 for a discussion of this factor). Finally, in Hasbún's study students narrated the stoy in writing, and were provided with ample time to plan their narratives (45 minutes). Even though Bardovi-Harlig (1995a) reports that there were no effects between written and oral narratives in a study on L2 English acquisition of past tense among L1 speakers of diverse languages, other studies do not show such a correlation (e.g., Ellis 1987; Salaberry 2000).[6] In consideration of the fact that in Bardovi-Harlig's study students were shown the movie twice, the selection of oral narratives and the single exposure to the movie clip in the present study are likely to generate less monitoring of language form. Indeed, Ellis (1987) analyzed the use of English past tense verbs (regular, irregular, and copula) among 17 subjects learning EFL and detected a significant effect for planning time. Ellis asked his subjects to narrate a story depicted in a series of still pictures. In the first part of the task, subjects looked at the series of pictures corresponding to story 1, and they wrote their narration of that story (writing task). Subsequently, they were asked to narrate the same story orally (in a language lab). Finally, they were asked to perform an oral narration of a second story (story number 2). For this last task, the subjects were given two minutes to look at the pictures, but they were not allowed to do the written narration before the oral one. The "planning time" variable was determined by the possibility of doing a written narration of the story before the corresponding oral narration.[7] The results of Ellis' study

---

6. Furthermore, it is important to point out that some authors claim that there are substantial differences between oral and written narratives: in literate traditions the meaning is in the text, whereas in oral traditions the meaning is in the context (Fleischman 1990: 9).

7. Ellis (1987) argued that attention and planning can be considered as equivalent on methodological grounds, and that there is no objective means of determining how much attention a subject is paying to form in various tasks. Moreover, Ochs (1979) argues for an alternative means (an indirect way) of determining the degree of attention to form: the control of planning time. Ellis claims that "(t)he planned/unplanned distinction is clearly much the same as the careful/vernacular distinction discussed by Labov and Tarone."

showed that style-shifting across the different tasks occurred most commonly for regular past tense forms, less so for past copula, and hardly at all with irregular past tense forms. In other words, attention to forms reflected in the different amounts of planning time of the oral narrations directly affects some forms, but not others.[8]

5.3.3.2 Written tasks

There were two types of written tests used in this study. Both tests were adaptations of the ones used in the pilot study. The first written task is based on a series of cartoons depicting the main events of the Hitchcock movie "Psycho" (see Appendix B). As in the pilot study, all participants received both the text and the cartoons depicting the story to provide adequate contextualization for the story. In contrast with the pilot study the students had to perform a fill-in-the-blanks test instead of creating sentences out of a propositional cluster (see Section 5.1.1). The change was necessary because it was found that the complex nature of the propositional cluster format was confusing, and it took longer to complete it. In the modified format the students filled in the spaces in the text with the appropriate past tense conjugation of the verbs set in parentheses (infinitive). Furthermore, the test was reduced to 28 items (instead of 41) to increase the length of the second written test.

The second written test consisted of two parts: the fill-in-the-blanks section and the editing part. Both parts had the same number of target items (41). The text consisted of four different short passages (Appendix C). There were three original excerpts from two famous Spanish-speaking novelists: Juan Rulfo (passage one) and Benito Pérez-Galdós (passages two and four). These passages were cited by Lunn (1985: 58–9) as the types of narratives that contain examples of non-prototypical marking of aspect (viewpoint aspect). A fourth passage was developed by the researcher to incorporate examples of the non-prototypical use of non-stative verbs (passage three).[9] The passages were presented in the order

---

8. It is possible to argue that the forms that require the use of rules (regular forms) demand more attention, whereas the forms that may be stored as lexical elements (more or less) will be less affected by processing time. Ellis claims that at least one previous study (Hulstijn & Hulstijn 1984) supports his finding: the greatest positive difference in accuracy occurs when subjects are not under time pressure and when they are focusing on form (as opposed to content). This difference is also the greatest in Ellis' study: task 1 (written task) allowed the subject to pay attention to form under no time pressure.

9. Texts developed specifically for experimental research in the acquisition of tense and aspect have been used in previous studies. For example, the 14-item passage used by Bardovi-Harlig (1992) was modified from an original piece written by a student during a previous examination.

shown in the Appendix (both cloze and editing task). The main group of subjects (16 volunteers) received the same passages during Time 2 but in a different order. The use of a controlled written task procedure was useful because it provided for the analysis of a balanced set of verbs across lexical aspectual classes unlike the free production from the narrative. The analysis of the data from the cloze test was based on the semantic contrast between perfective and imperfective markers of past tense. As such, the violation of orthographic conventions (e.g., *reprodució instead of reprodujo) or spelling mistakes including accent markers (e.g., supó instead of supo) were not taken into account for the analysis. These types of mistakes have no bearing on the type of discursive-semantic contrast exemplified by past tense inflectional suffixes. Furthermore, the use of forms other than past tense indicative (e.g., subjunctive or conditional) were not included in the analysis of the data although those forms were quite rare. One of the notable exceptions was item (31) which was sometimes marked with the conditional by the native speakers. This item was not counted in the analysis since the aspectual contrast is not conveyed by morphological means with the conditional suffix.

5.3.3.3 On-line processing of cloze test

The results of the narratives and the written tests from the pilot study raised an interesting question about the specific decisions that the learners were making (explicit and implicit) while processing verbal morphology. Even though these data provided important information about the behavior of the learners, it was also relevant to gain access to the on-line decision-making process followed by the participants while carrying out those tasks (on-line in the context of this analysis refers to the fact that subjects did not have the option of discontinuing the task once it started). Recently, think-aloud and speak-aloud procedures of data collection have received some attention in L2 research (e.g., Ellis 1991; Davies & Kaplan 1998; Goss, Ying-Hua & Lantolf 1994; Jourdenais 1996). Due to the apparent problems of think aloud procedures (Ericsson & Simon 1983; Goss, Ying-Hua & Lantolf 1994; Jourdenais 1996) the use of the joint speak-aloud procedure as implemented in Goss et al was preferred. Given that this protocol has not yet received widespread attention in the L2 literature I will first outline the nature of this methodology as implemented in previous studies, and the particular procedure to be followed in this study. The relative length of this methodology section will be in direct correlation to the number of concerns raised in L2 experimental research about the type of qualitative nature of this type of analysis. However, the qualitative analysis will also be supplemented by quantitative data as in previous studies (e.g., Davies & Kaplan 1998).

Ellis (1991) analyzed think-aloud protocols of 8 advanced students of English performing a grammaticality judgment test in English. The subjects were L1 Chinese speakers who had been studying English for an extended period of time (between 4 and 15 years of study) and who were also residents in England (between 6 months and 4 years). The subjects were asked to complete a grammaticality judgment test twice (one week delay between tests). The second test was a subset of the first one (10 out of 40 sentences). During the second test the participants were asked to perform a think-aloud while they were engaged in the task. Ellis found that 22.5% of the responses (18 out of 80 sentences) were judged differently from the first time (low degree of reliability). The protocols from the think-alouds reveal that some subjects did not provide explicit reports of their thoughts. Among the ones who did provide explicit information, many participants were not sure of how to judge a sentence. Based on the analysis of the protocols Ellis made a list of seven main strategies used by his subjects in the process of making grammaticality judgments:[10]

1. feel (it seems, it sounds, etc.)
2. rehearsal (reading, repetition)
3. rehearsal of alternative version (rephrasing)
4. use of explicit knowledge
5. analogy (comparison with previous sentence)
6. evaluation of sentence (comparison with alternative)
7. guess (explicit reference to not being sure)

Ellis concluded that his subjects (1) were inconsistent in their judgments, (2) they relied extensively on feel, (3) they were unsuccessful in using explicit rules, and (4) they did not use the "not sure" option even when not sure. In view of these findings Ellis claimed that grammaticality judgment tests are a *valid* instrument to investigate competence: students relied on implicit instead of explicit knowledge (feel versus explicit mention of grammar rules). On the other hand, the reliability of grammaticality judgment tasks may be low: inconsistency in responses from time 1 to time 2 and reluctance to use "not sure" option. Interestingly, Christie and Lantolf (1992) argue that grammaticality judgment tasks may not be a valid instrument to test language competence, while Gass (1994) argued that grammaticality judgment tasks are reliable. It is open to question whether advanced learners (such as the ones analyzed by Ellis 1991) base their judgments on a more stable system than the one assumed to underlie

---

10. Ellis provides no quantitative data on the use of the seven strategies utilized by his subjects.

native speakers' decisions. However, even native speakers' decisions are not always reliable due to various factors such as context and order of presentation of test items (e.g., Nagata 1987), sentence complexity, and literacy level of subjects (e.g., Birdsong 1989), etc.

Goss, et al. (1994) analyzed the processing of L2 grammaticality judgments with a methodology different from think-alouds: speak-aloud protocols from students solving a grammaticality judgment task in groups (dyads and triads). Goss et al. argue that the joint problem-solving methodology is better than the traditional think-aloud technique for the following three reasons: (1) subjects do not have to accomplish simultaneous goals (cognitive and metacognitive task), (2) there is more information generated by collaborative work (broader window into mental activity), and (3) there is no need to rely on successful training of the participants. Goss et al. analyzed data from grammaticality judgments from 52 English-speaking college-level students: 19 students from third semester Spanish, 11 students from seventh semester Spanish, and 18 students (control group) from an introductory linguistics course or a freshman writing seminar. Thirty-seven students performed the test on an individual basis and the rest of the students responded to the test in groups: two dyads from elementary Spanish, one dyad and one triad from advanced Spanish and two dyads from the English courses. The conversational interaction in the joint format groups was recorded and then transcribed. Each group received only one questionnaire to generate discussion about a single appropriate response per group. No time limit was established for the completion of the task. The criterion used by Goss et al. to identify the use of non-genuine linguistic intuition is the identification of

> talk that cites rules, pedagogical or otherwise and accurate or not, the source of which may be an instructor or textbook, or that involves translations into the native language, as indicative of judgments based on something other than real linguistic intuitions (p. 271)

The analysis of the protocols from the students working in groups showed that native speakers assessed the grammaticality of sentences based on "how the sentence sounds upon reading it aloud." In contrast, elementary Spanish students preferred the use of English translation or their metaknowledge about Spanish grammar rules. Advanced learners of Spanish also relied on learned linguistic rules and translation although they also showed signs of relying on feel to a larger extent than elementary students. The major difference between elementary and advanced learners was the higher percentage of accurate responses from the advanced learners. In sum, Goss et al. analyzed three strategies (two which were mentioned by Ellis): feel, memory of learned rules and translation.

Davies and Kaplan (1998) replicated the study of Goss et al. on the use of various strategies by dyads versus individuals. The subjects (37 L1 English speakers enrolled in a fourth semester course of college-level French) had to determine the grammaticality of decontextualized sentences in both their L1 and their L2: 12 sentences in English and 12 sentences in French. 26 subjects were tested in 13 dyads and 11 subjects were tested individually. For the analysis of the strategies used by these students the dyads were tape-recorded and the analysis of the speak-aloud protocols were transcribed. The transcripts were first analyzed to define the types of strategies used by the learners in their judgment of grammaticality. Davies and Kaplan identified seven distinct strategies in the analysis of the L2 data:

1. feel (intuitive response),
2. meaning-based,
3. repair,
4. learned grammar rules,
5. translation,
6. analogy and
7. guess

As pointed out by Davies and Kaplan these strategies match the ones identified by Ellis (1991).[11] More importantly, Davies and Kaplan provided quantitative data about the use of those strategies. Since the analysis of the present study is concerned with the processing of grammatical features of the L2 in a cloze task, and not necessarily the analysis of grammaticality judgments tasks, I will examine only a subset of those strategies: feel, memory of learned rules and translation (e.g., repair and analogy are more relevant for the processing of a grammaticality judgment task). Table 5.7 presents the summary of the above mentioned subset of strategies.

The analysis of the data from Table 5.7 shows a categorical difference in the type of strategies used by L1 English speakers in the processing of their L1 in comparison to the processing of their nonnative language (i.e., French). Similarly, French native speakers, analyzing sentences in French, behave as L1

---

11. Davies and Kaplan make a distinction between translation and meaning-based strategies which I will not consider in the analysis of their data. According to Davies and Kaplan if a translated sentence in English is ungrammatical but students accept it, translation was used as a means to understand meaning. In contrast, when students translate a sentence and determine the grammaticality of the original sentence based on the rendered translation the strategy used was translation. I believe, however, that it may be very difficult to tease apart these two factors when analyzing speak-aloud protocols. In any case, the distinction is irrelevant for the type of task used in this study.

Table 5.7. Distribution of strategies used to judge grammaticality of sentences: n-size refers to number of subjects per group (adapted from Davies & Kaplan, 1998)

	L1 English (n = 133)		L2 French (n = 133)		L1 French (n = 36)	
Feel	115	86.5%	53	39.3%	35	97.2%
Learned	18	9.8%	78	57.8%	5	13.9%
Translation	0	0%	13	9.6%	0	0%
One strategy	89	66.9%	42	31.1%	25	69.4%

English speakers in their analysis of English. Notice that the use of learned rules is highest in the processing of the L2 whereas the use of feel is highest for the processing of the native language. As expected, the use of translation is only apparent in the processing of the L2. As argued by Davies and Kaplan these results are not surprising because their subjects were classroom learners; thus, they were skillful in the application of "rules" in their processing of the grammaticality of L2 decontextualized sentences.

Notwithstanding the claim of Davies and Kaplan, Cowan and Hatasa (1994: 301) argue that the identification of strategies used in the processing of L2 data is to wander "into a dangerous area of subjective judgment." Instead, they encourage researchers to use "objective research techniques that display a high degree of validity and reliability." It may be true that the identification and classification of particular strategies for the processing of nonnative grammars as opposed to native grammars is not as precise as we would like. On the other hand, the specific goal of the studies which attempt to identify processing strategies through various techniques (e.g., Davies & Kaplan 1998; Ellis 1991; Ericsson & Simon 1983; Goss et al. 1994) is precisely the investigation of the potential reliability and validity of widely accepted procedures of data collection, such as grammaticality judgments. For that reason, the analysis of the protocols of the subjects who participated in the longitudinal study will be presented as a means to gain access to the type of on-line processing used during the completion of the cloze test. This analysis is intended to shed some light on the particular constraints that govern the selection of morphological markers of temporality. As such, it presents additional evidence for judging the quantitative data collected from the cross-sectional study. The procedure of data collection used in this study was similar to that of Goss et al., with the exception of the time limits established for the present study. All groups were composed of dyads with the same individuals in Times 1 and 2. The conversational interaction in the joint format groups was recorded and then transcribed. Each group received only one questionnaire to generate discussion about a single appropriate response per group. There were five categories established for the analysis: (1) direct response, (2) rehearsal of response, (3) use of translation, (4) use of learned rules associated with temporality, and (5) use of learned rules associated with areas other than temporality. The categories will be defined more precisely and examples will be shown in the next chapter.

5.3.4 Procedure of data collection

All the data from the main pool of subjects were collected at two different times during the Fall academic semester: mid-September and mid-November. The interval of two months between the two times of data collection was considered to be appropriate to measure the degree of improvement in aspect marking across time within each individual learner.[12] The measurement of language development within specific individuals appears to be more reliable and accurate than the cross-analysis of different levels of experience with different subjects in each level (e.g., Perdue & Klein 1992; Sato 1990; Tarone 1995). Native speakers and near native speakers performed the same tasks in one single session.

The order of the tasks administered in each session was the same for all groups. All participants were interviewed in pairs with other students from their same level. Each session lasted approximately one hour. During the first part of the session the students completed the narration of the selected movie, filled out the academic background questionnaire and completed the individual cloze test (movie Psycho). The tasks were administered in the following order. First, one student (A) watched one of the selected movies alone while the other student (B) completed the academic background questionnaire (approximately 6 minutes). Subsequently, both students and the researcher met and student A narrated the story orally to student B (approximately 6 minutes). Immediately after that, the second student (B) told the story s/he just heard to a third person (a native speaker of Spanish) while the other student (A) completed the individual cloze test (approximately 6 minutes). Subsequently, the students switched tasks and followed the same procedure described above: student B watched the other selected Chaplin movie while student A completed the academic background questionnaire, and so forth. During the second part of the session both students

---

12. The two-month period was the longest period available within one semester of instruction in consideration of the fact that during the first weeks at the beginning and the last weeks at the end of the semester it is not feasible to conduct this type of experiment.

reconvened and they were given the first part of the joint problem-solving task to complete. The participants received a single copy of the fill-in-the-blank version of the joint test and they were asked to work together and agree on a single answer to each item. The participants were asked to discuss the answers in the language in which they felt most comfortable: All participants discussed their answers mostly in English irrespective of level. Each dyad worked in privacy and the session was recorded with the consent of the participants. There was a time limit of 10 minutes to complete the task. All dyads were informed of how much time they had left at five and two minutes before the time limit. At the end of the allotted time the researcher collected the first page and gave them the second part with the editing task. Students were given five minutes to complete the second task. Each dyad received a time warning at two minutes before the end of the time limit.

The participants received specific instructions about the movie narrative task. Based on previous research on the nature of language production evoked in experimental tasks it was important to obtain as spontaneous data as possible (e.g., Tarone 1983, 1988, 1995). For that purpose it was necessary to ascertain that all participants would focus on the communication of the subject matter (i.e., what happened on the street/in the Department store) rather than on correctness of linguistic form (decontextualized language task). The nature of the role-play situation in which this task was embedded makes it a better alternative than simply asking students to narrate what happened in a film.[13] Furthermore, the task put some pressure on the students who narrated the movie first, since they knew that their fellow student would have to rely on their narrative to tell the same story to a third person. To avoid possible extraneous effects created by differences in the order and content of instruction given to each subject the researcher wrote a text which was rehearsed and repeated (not read) almost verbatim to each participant before the task:

> You are going to watch a silent movie of approximately five minutes. I would like to ask you to play the role of the witness who has seen the events that happened yesterday and tell what happened to the detective in charge of the investigation (the other student). Please remember to be as precise as possible because later the detective will have to tell what happened yesterday to the police commissioner.

---

13. I do not claim that the above mentioned task is to be equated to a real event when someone has to give an eyewitness report to the police, but, rather, that it is more likely that the participants will engage in the type of language production that they believe accomplishes that task.

After a student finished watching the movie in private, s/he joined a second student in the adjacent room. The researcher again repeated the instructions to both subjects, but this case in Spanish to make the transition to the narrative task in Spanish easier.

> Tú fuiste testigo (witness) de lo que sucedió ayer en la calle/almacén. Cuéntale (tell) lo que pasó al detective. El detective le debe contar lo que pasó ayer al jefe de policía. Por eso debes ser lo más preciso posible en tu narración.

In the case of the beginning students the instructions were also given in English to ascertain that both students understood the task correctly. In both sets of instructions (English and Spanish) the words yesterday and happened (the latter most salient as a past tense in Spanish: pasó versus pasa) were stressed (under-lined words in text of instructions). Native and near native speakers also received the same set of instructions but only in Spanish, since the language used with them during the interaction (e.g., greetings, small talk) was Spanish.

5.3.5 Classification of verbs: operational tests

For the quantitative analysis of the results of the cloze test the use of Imperfect or Preterite was arbitrarily assigned one of two possible values: 0 for Preterite and 1 for Imperfect (as in the pilot study). This binary system produced a series of proportions of use of Preterite and Imperfect for every item from cloze and editing task. For the quantitative analysis of the movie narrative all verbs were classified according to the actual marking of verbal morphology during the on-line task. Five different categories were considered for this analysis: Preterite, Imperfect, Present, Infinitive and Progressive. The identification of these categories was straightforward. Concomitantly, all verbs were classified accord-ing to their inherent lexical aspectual semantics. This classification was common to both tasks mentioned above. Three categories were considered for this second classificatory system: statives, atelic events, and telic events. Following the rationale presented in Chapter 2 and the analysis of data from Chapter 4, telic events were not classified into punctual and non-punctual events (accomplish-ments and achievements). There are some studies in L1 acquisition which have used a similar three-way classification: Cziko and Koda (1987), Stephany (1981). The classification of each verb in terms of inherent semantic aspect was done by the researcher in accordance with two major criteria: telicity and stativity. Two operational tests were used to distinguish lexical aspectual classes:[14]

The test of stativity distinguished stative versus non-stative verbs: If the verb cannot have a habitual interpretation it is a stative verb.

The test of telicity distinguished telic versus atelic verbs: If you stop in the middle of V-ing have you done the act of V (entailment test)?

These two operational tests are among the most widely used in experimental studies (e.g., Dowty 1979; Hasbún 1995; Shirai 1991) due to their relative robust results compared to similar tests (see Chapter 2). The application of these tests was performed sequentially. That is to say, if a verb is stative, the following test is not relevant. On the other hand, if a verb is non-stative according to the first test, the second test was applied. The application of each test will be shown with the following examples:

(1)   (Ser) horrible su muerte
      Her death (to be) horrible

(2)   Ella (salir) del cuarto
      She (to leave) the room

As shown in the examples above, to ensure impartiality, the classification of verbs was done with the verbs in their infinitive form to avoid the bias of the effect of the specific morphological marker selected by the subject. The preservation of the morphological marker used by the subjects entails circular results. In contrast, the effect of the context of the phrase or sentence in which the verbs were used (both arguments and adjuncts) was considered essential for the adequate classification of verb types. First, we apply the test of stativity: can we use the verb *ser* in a habitual sense in the framework in which it has been embedded? No. Then the verb *ser* is a state verb. The second test becomes irrelevant in this case. The same procedure is applied to the second sentence: can we use the verb *salir* in a habitual sense in the framework in which it has been embedded? Yes. Then it is a non-stative verb. In this case, the second test needs to be applied: if you stop in the middle of leaving the room, have you left the room? (Si paras en el proceso de salir del cuarto, has salido?) No. Then, *salir* is a telic verb.

The reliability of the classification system of lexical aspectual classes was assessed in two different ways: interrater reliability and intrarater reliability

---

14. Robison (1990, 1995) has used three tests per category, but two tests have been used in other studies (e.g., Bergström 1995; Salaberry 1998, 2000).

(I am thankful to Yas Shirai for the suggestion about the use of the intrarater reliability procedure). First, the classification of verbs from the cloze test and a subset of the narratives (four students from four different levels) was compared with the classification made by two other raters on the same subset of verbs. The alternative raters were both native speakers of Spanish. One of the raters had some experience with the classification of lexical aspectual classes in Spanish through previous empirical research of her own. The second alternative rater was a linguistics student who specialized in Spanish syntax and semantics and who was familiar with the classification of lexical aspect. All three raters classified the verbs independently according to the specific operational tests reviewed above. The classification of verbs done by the researcher concurred on 85% of the items classified by each one of the other two raters. The researcher then considered some changes on the application of the operational tests based on the suggestions made by the alternative raters. Subsequently, the classification of all verbs from the narrative was made within a month after the collection of the second set of data (mid-December). Four months after the first overall classification of verbs was finished, a subset of verbs from the narratives (four students from four levels) was classified again by the researcher without access to the previous classification. The comparison of both sets of verb type classification (time 1 and time 2) showed a 96% coefficient of intrarater reliability.

The classification of verbs of the cloze test was fixed; hence, it did not generate any inconsistencies beyond the discrepancies with the other two raters as mentioned above and whose suggestions were used to modify the classification of a small subset of items. On the other hand, the high rate of consistency (intrarater reliability) in the classification of verbs from the free narratives was achieved through the application of a series of established criteria in the scoring procedure of the narrative task. The most important criteria for the assessment of verbs from the narrative task were based on the following five broad categories: (1) aspectual verbs, (2) inception of state versus state, (3) modals and main lexical verbs, (4) verbs following prepositions, and (5) negative clauses.

1. Aspectual verbs constitute an important category because most subjects in the narrative used them fairly frequently. Aspectual verbs may be classified into inchoative verbs (e.g., *empezar*, to start), protractive verbs (e.g., *quedarse*, to remain), cumulative verbs (e.g., *continuar*, to continue) and completive verbs (e.g., *acabar de*, to finish) (see Fleischman 1990: 22; Sebastian & Slobin 1994: 257–8). In all cases the focus of the operational test was the aspectual verb rather than the main lexical verb. The use of inchoative and completive aspectual verbs generated in all cases by definition telic events. The lexical aspectual class

associated with the use of cumulative verbs was indeterminate (high correlation to local context) because verbs such as *continuar* may refer to the actual continuation of an event or to the resumption of the specific activity. For example, *continuar trabajando* (to continue working) may sometimes refer to the beginning of work (after the lunch recess), in which case generates a telic event. Alternatively, *continuar trabajando* may refer to the actual continuation of the activity (atelic) while something else happened (e.g., the visit of the inspector to the production plant while the workers continued their work oblivious to the arrival of the inspector). Unlike inchoative and completive verbs, the determination of the lexical class of cumulative verbs was highly dependent on contextual factors (similar to the dependency of activity verbs). Finally, protractive verbs were usually classified as telic events since they essentially refer to the inception of the protracted state.

2. A major point of discrepancy among previous empirical studies was the status of states versus beginning or end of states (e.g., Bybee 1995; Comrie 1976; Dowty 1986; Guitart 1978; Klein 1994; Smith 1986; Studerus 1989). For example, Hasbún (1995) does not distinguish between inception or end of a state and the state itself, whereas Robison classifies the beginning of a state as a "punctual stative." For this study, the inceptive or completive value of stative verbs was classified as a telic event (beginning or completion of a state). For example item 20 from the cloze test was classified as a telic event and not as a stative verb due to the effect of the adverbial phrase that precedes the verb (inchoative meaning): *después que (saber) la verdad* = after he (find out) the truth.

3. The use of modals, as expected, was extensive. *Poder* (to be able to), *querer* (to desire, to want) and *deber* (to have to, must) were among the most typical modals used by most subjects. Their classification is also controversial. For this study, the operational test of lexical aspectual class was applied to the modal verb and not the main lexical predicate. For instance, to steal (*robar*) is normally classified as a telic event, whereas to be able to steal (*poder robar*) will be classified as a stative verb (most contexts):

(3)   a.   Chaplin (poder) robar
       b.   Chaplin (querer) robar
       c.   Chaplin (deber) robar

If the classification were based on the categorization of the main lexical verb, all the above mentioned examples would have been classified as telic events. However, none of these examples entails the actual realization of the main event, but rather the state conveyed by the modal verb. Similarly, the verb to try (*tratar*) occurs with a main lexical verb. In the latter case, the operational tests determine that, in the majority of cases, *tratar* is an activity verb (event with no inherent end point).

4. The selection of lexical aspectual class was not overridden in cases where there was an incorrect choice of preposition or the absence of the preposition as long as the reference was easily identifiable in the context of the narrative. For instance, in the following sentences the use of the preposition *por* entails that the characters wandered aimlessly around the store (activity verb), whereas the use of the intended preposition *para* (it is clear from the movie clip that the characters were going towards the store) generates a telic event.[15]

(4)   a.   Van por la tienda = (They) wander around the store
       b.   Van para la tienda = (They) go towards the store

Furthermore, certain verbs were not marked for tense or aspectual distinctions because they were embedded in certain matrixes that do not require the marking of the past tense verbal endings. For example, the use of most prepositions generate the use of the infinitive in Spanish irrespective of tense (English requires the use of the gerund):

(5)   después de robar = after stealing

Similarly, some prepositions generated (correctly) the use of the subjunctive (mostly among advanced learners):

(6)   para que viniera = so that (s/he) would come

Verbs preceded by prepositions and correctly marked with either infinitive or subjunctive were not counted for the analysis of the data. However, the majority of verb tokens were marked with past tense verbal morphology.

5. The use of negative expressions was not considered different than affirmative statements for the classification of inherent lexical semantics as a matter of practicality. That is to say, there is a deep epistemological (or otherwise logical) problem created by the assumption of a non-existent situation that would be difficult to classify within the constraints of the present operational tests. On the other hand, if we consider that the constellation of verbal predicate and associated arguments and adjuncts are the major determinants of lexical aspectual classes, we may assume that a negative expression will not necessarily change the lexical semantics of the expression. Furthermore, Klein (1994: 43) argues that

---

15. Incidentally, the classification was not affected by the morphological marker used with the verb; in this case, present tense.

negation functions like a modifying adverb that does not modify the aspectual relation but rather the lexical content of the verb phrase.

5.4   Conclusion

As shown in the previous chapter, there appear to be substantial differences in the research design, data collection and data analysis procedures across studies that investigate the development of verbal morphology among adult L2 learners. The selection of research methodology for the present set of studies was based on the analysis of the results of a pilot study that also provided some preliminary evidence bearing on the claim about the development of past tense verbal morphology. In particular, as shown above, the pilot study provided preliminary evidence that confirms potential discrepancies with the basic claim of the lexical aspect hypothesis insofar the beginning stages of development is concerned. In order to provide a more comprehensive analysis of the theoretical claims of the lexical aspect hypothesis, the research design of the present study incorporates a combination of a cross-sectional and longitudinal study. In addition, the study includes a joint-problem solving task in order to investigate the potential effect of consciously learned rules in the selection of past tense verbal morphology in a written task.

Chapter 6

Analysis of data sets

In this chapter I present the analysis of the three sets of data (i.e., movie narrative, cloze and editing task, and speak-aloud protocols) that will be used as empirical evidence to substantiate the claim to be advanced in Chapter 7 (already previewed in the analysis of data from the pilot study discussed in the preceding chapter). The analysis of the protocols of the movie narratives is based on the analysis of both cross-sectional (four levels of experience with L2 Spanish) and longitudinal data (collected from the same speakers at the beginning and end of a two-month interval). The analysis of the written tasks (cloze and editing tests) is based on a cross-sectional analysis (two levels of experience with the L2 and a control group of monolingual native speakers). Finally, the analysis of the speak-aloud protocols of 20 nonnative speakers and four native speakers provides information about the processing of the material presented in the written tasks mentioned above. The discussion of the findings of all studies will be presented in the following chapter.

6.1   Results from movie narrative task

Tables 6.1 through 6.4 display a summary of the results from the analysis of the protocols from the movie narratives. Sample narratives from four levels of academic instruction (beginners to advanced) are presented in Appendix H. A total of 2,054 verb tokens were analyzed in the data from all four groups of students. Table 6.1 displays the raw counts of verb tokens across lexical aspectual classes by level.

The results from both native and near native speakers are absent from the analysis because both groups of subjects narrated the movies using present instead of past tense. In addition, the data from one subject from the advanced group of students (subject 311.3) were also eliminated from the summary of results because she also narrated the movies using only present tense. As

Table 6.1. Raw counts of morphological marking by lexical class for Times 1 and 2 (movie retelling)

	Time 1				Time 2			
	Telic	Activ.	State	ALL	Telic	Activ.	States	ALL
Beginner (*n* = 4)								
Preterite	28	12	7	47	61	5	9	75
Imperfect	0	0	1	1	2	0	2	4
Present	55	9	27	91	41	9	20	70
Infinitive	10	1	0	11	10	7	0	17
Total	93	22	35	150	114	21	31	166
Interm-low (*n* = 4)								
Preterite	150	24	29	203	124	13	12	149
Imperfect	14	8	20	42	10	0	19	29
Present	23	5	40	68	33	1	34	68
Infinitive	2	1	0	3	4	0	0	4
Progressive	1	13	2	16	6	5	0	11
Total	190	51	91	332	177	19	65	261
Interm-high (*n* = 4)								
Preterite	87	7	8	102	94	6	5	105
Imperfect	4	5	38	47	2	3	25	30
Present	9	2	26	37	12	11	21	44
Infinitive	1	1	0	2	1	0	0	1
Progressive	0	5	1	6	1	2	1	4
Total	101	20	73	194	110	22	52	184
Advanced (*n* = 3)								
Preterite	164	8	3	175	148	14	10	172
Imperfect	6	6	73	85	12	4	76	92
Present	59	14	39	112	42	7	27	76
Infinitive	0	0	0	0	0	0	0	0
Progressive	7	13	0	20	10	25	0	35
Total	236	41	115	392	212	50	113	375

mentioned in the previous chapter, Spanish present tense does not show any overt morphological marking of aspectual contrasts (present tense is inherently Imperfective). Hence, the use of present instead of past tense renders the data uninformative. It is important to point out, however, that all subjects received the same type of instructions (see previous chapter) irrespective of level or native language. Therefore, differences in the use of present versus past tense should not be attributed to methodological deficiencies, but rather, to normal tendencies found in narrative tasks. The above-mentioned findings are, in fact, relevant for the general assessment of the data and will be discussed in the following chapter. For the analysis of the data from the non-native speakers a Chi-square test of independence between lexical aspect and morphological marking was selected as the appropriate statistical procedure to test the null hypotheses (following the rationale of previous studies such as Hasbún 1995). The analysis of the data, however, revealed that the use of the Chi-square procedure of statistical analysis is not valid because two of the five general assumptions of the Chi-square test were not met: (1) there is no independence of data within each cell, and (2) a high percentage of expected cell frequencies falls below five (Hatch & Lazaraton 1991: 406–410; Minium & Clarke 1982: 381–382). The first assumption was not met because some students contributed more data to some cells than other students. That is to say, the combined data are not reflective of the data from any individual subject. This is not an unexpected outcome in consideration of the fact that (1) the subjects were not constrained in the use of types of verbs in their narratives, and (2) the films were narrated online under obvious time constraints, which made more prominent individual differences. The second assumption was not met because some students did not use all morphological markers to the same extent. This was particularly clear in some cases were students narrated the story using exclusively Preterite to the detriment of Imperfect (i.e., beginners, Time 1).[1] Analysis of the descriptive data without the test of statistical significance is the only appropriate procedure in this case (Hatch & Lazaraton 1991: 409–410; R. Schwagger, personal communication, March 27, 1997). It is important to point out that the previous outcome of this study is the result of a more ecologically valid procedure of data collection. Furthermore, the quantitative data from the cloze test and editing task to be presented in the following section provide the type of cross-reference data with associated measurements of statistical significance, which complement the type of descriptive analysis from the oral narratives.

The analysis of Table 6.1 reveals the following: (1) the number of verb tokens increases with the level of experience of the students, (2) the number of verb tokens per level remains almost unchanged from Time 1 to Time 2, (3) the number of verb tokens is unequally distributed across lexical aspectual classes

---

1. In some studies (e.g., Hasbún 1995; Robison 1995) the Chi-Square statistical procedure was applied to the summation of data from all subjects as could have been done in the present case with the data shown in Table 1 as well. However, that procedure has no statistical validity.

irrespective of level, and (4) the beginners group is the only one which does not show a contrast of past tense morphological marking by means of the use of both Preterite and Imperfect (with the exception of three tokens with Imperfective morphology out of a total of 316 tokens for both times). First, the number of verb tokens is correlated to the length of the narrative produced by each student, whereas the length of the narratives increases with the level of experience with the language. In general, the number of verb tokens increases steadily from lowest (beginners) to highest level (advanced) with the exception of the intermediate level whose production at both Times 1 and 2 is higher than the intermediate-high (but lower than advanced). Second, the number of verb tokens remains stable across time except for intermediate whose production decreases by approximately 25% from Time 1 to Time 2 (from 332 tokens to 261 tokens). Third, the number of verb tokens is unequally distributed across lexical aspectual classes across all levels. Table 6.2 presents these differences in terms of percentages of the total number of verb tokens within each level for stative verbs and telic events.

Table 6.2. Percentage of stative and telic verbs out of total number of verb of tokens per level

	Percentage of stative verbs		Percentage of telic verbs	
	Time 1	Time 2	Time 1	Time 2
Beginners	23%	19%	62%	69%
Interm.	27%	25%	57%	68%
Interm-high	38%	28%	52%	60%
Advanced	29%	30%	60%	57%

Table 6.2 shows that the most stable distribution of verb tokens according to lexical aspectual classes across time corresponds to advanced students. The production of these subjects remains almost unchanged from Time 1 to Time 2: roughly 30% of all verbs are stative verbs and approximately 60% are telic verbs. The remaining 10% of verbs used by advanced students are verbs classified as atelic events (activity). The data from the other groups reflect a similar distribution — although less stable — within ten percentage points of difference with the data from advanced. In other words, the use of telic verbs far surpasses the use of stative verbs irrespective of experience with the target language. Incidentally, the high degree of stability of the selection of verb types

across time of the advanced students is correlated to the stability of other indicators of language use in the movie narratives of this group as will be shown next.

Finally, the analysis of Table 6.1 shows that at Time 1 the use of the Imperfect is nonexistent among beginner students and that they do not produce any significant amount of Imperfective marking of past tense verbs in their oral narratives at Time 2 (three tokens out of a total of 316 tokens). The absence of the Imperfect verbal ending in this group is particularly important at Time 2 because the Imperfect had been introduced as a formal grammatical topic — and had been practiced — during the two weeks prior to the collection of the movie narratives at Time 2. In contrast, the data from the other three groups of learners reveals that the Imperfect was used across all lexical aspectual classes. However, the distribution was not equally balanced for all groups. The comparison of total number of verb tokens with past tense morphology shows that for the intermediate group the use of Imperfect corresponds to 17% (42 out of 245 tokens) and 16% (29 out of 178 tokens) of all verbs used in past tense at Times 1 and 2 respectively. For the intermediate-high group the use of Imperfect corresponds to 32% and 22% of all verbs marked with past tense morphology at Times 1 and 2 respectively. The use of the Imperfect among advanced students corresponds to 37% and 35% at Times 1 and 2 respectively. In sum, the use of the Imperfect increases according to level of experience with the L2 from non-use of the Imperfect (beginners) to employing the Imperfect with roughly 35% of all verbs marked with past tense morphology (advanced).

For the analysis of the results of the narrative data across levels and across time the raw counts of verb tokens from Table 1 were converted into percentages in Tables 6.3 and 6.4. Table 6.3 presents the percentage of use of verbal morphology within each lexical aspectual class of verb (e.g., all verbal endings used with telic verbs only). The analysis of Table 6.3 shows that the beginning and intermediate-low groups show distinct signs of change across time. The data from the beginners group show the following changes from Time 1 to Time 2: (1) the use of Preterite increases for both stative (from 20% to 29%) and telic verbs (from 30% to 59%), (2) the use of Imperfect remains largely unchanged with both stative (increase from 3% to 6%) and telic verbs (increase from 0% to 2%), and (3) the use of Preterite decreases significantly for atelic verbs (from 55% to 24%). In essence, the first signs of change in the morphological marking of verbs is not necessarily associated with lexical aspectual classes: the relative increase in use of both markers of past tense (i.e., Preterite and Imperfect) at Time 2 is accounted for in both the stative and telic events categories. The results from the group intermediate-low show the following changes from Time 1 to Time 2: (1) for stative verbs a decrease in the use of Preterite (from 32% to

Table 6.3. Distribution of morphological marking within lexical aspectual class (movie task)[a]

	Time 1			Time 2		
	Telic	Activ.	States	Telic	Activ.	States
Beginners (n = 4)						
Preterite	30%	55%	20%	54%	24%	29%
Imperfect	0%	0%	3%	2%	0%	6%
Present	59%	41%	77%	36%	43%	65%
Infinitive	11%	5%	0%	9%	33%	0%
Progressive	0%	0%	0%	0%	0%	0%
Tokens	93	22	35	114	21	31
Interm. (n = 4)						
Preterite	79%	47%	32%	70%	68%	18%
Imperfect	7%	16%	22%	6%	0%	29%
Present	12%	10%	44%	19%	5%	52%
Infinitive	1%	2%	0%	2%	0%	0%
Progressive	1%	25%	2%	3%	26%	0%
Tokens	190	51	91	177	19	65
Interm-high (n = 4)						
Preterite	86%	35%	11%	85%	27%	10%
Imperfect	4%	25%	52%	2%	14%	48%
Present	9%	10%	36%	11%	50%	40%
Infinitive	1%	5%	0%	1%	0%	0%
Progressive	0%	25%	1%	1%	9%	2%
Tokens	101	20	73	110	22	52
Advanced (n = 3)						
Preterite	69%	20%	3%	70%	28%	9%
Imperfect	3%	15%	63%	6%	8%	67%
Present	25%	34%	34%	20%	14%	24%
Infinitive	0%	0%	0%	0%	0%	0%
Progressive	3%	32%	0%	5%	50%	0%
Tokens	236	41	115	212	50	113

[a] Percentages add up to 100% by columns.

18%) is associated with an increase in the use of Imperfect (from 22% to 29%), (2) for atelic verbs an increase in the use of Preterite (from 47% to 68%) is associated with a decrease in the use of Imperfect (from 16% to 0%), and (3) for telic verbs a slight decrease with the use of Preterite (from 79% to 70%) is associated with no change in the use of Imperfect (from 7% to 6%). The data from this group appear to show the first signs of the effect of inherent lexical aspectual meaning in the use of past tense verbal morphology: the Preterite becomes associated with the non-stative category and the Imperfect is restricted primarily to the stative category.

In contrast, the results from the other two, more advanced, groups of learners (intermediate-high and advanced) show remarkably similar distributions of morphological marking across lexical aspectual classes from Time 1 to Time 2. For the intermediate-high group the use of Preterite (86%), Imperfect (4%) and present (9%) with *telic verbs* at Time 1 remains almost unchanged at Time 2: Preterite (85%), Imperfect (2%) and present (11%). Likewise, the use of Preterite (11%), Imperfect (52%) and present (36%) with *stative verbs* at Time 1 also remains unchanged at Time 2: Preterite (10%), Imperfect (48%) and present (40%). Similarly, for the advanced group the use of Preterite (69%), Imperfect (3%) and present (25%) with *telic verbs* at Time 1 remains almost unchanged at Time 2: Preterite (70%), Imperfect (6%) and present (20%). On the other hand, the use of Preterite (3%) and present (34%) with *stative verbs* at Time 1 reflects some change at Time 2: Preterite (9%) and present (24%), whereas the use of Imperfect remains largely unchanged from Time 1 to Time 2: 63% to 67%. In sum, both advanced groups show a relatively high degree of stability in the production of morphological markers of temporality across lexical aspectual classes in the oral narratives across time (two-month period).

The above-mentioned preliminary analysis may be corroborated by means of an alternative analysis of the data based on the distribution of lexical aspectual classes which is associated with each morphological marker. This alternative analysis is a better indicator of potential changes in the development of verbal morphology because it uses, as a point of departure, the verbal endings used by the subjects (e.g., Preterite and Imperfect), instead of the classification of lexical aspectual classes (e.g., telic event, atelic event). The latter classification is, as I have shown in Chapters 2 and 4, highly debatable (e.g., Hasbún 1995: 186). Hence, Table 6.4 presents the percentages of distribution of morphological markers across levels and across time (e.g., all verbs marked with Preterite across all lexical aspectual classes). Table 6.4 shows that the effect of lexical aspectual categories is associated with level of experience in the L2 up to the point where the consequences of such an effect start to diminish (concurrent examination of both longitudinal and cross level analyses).

The increase in the use of the Preterite with telic verbs is consistent and gradual both across time within each group and across levels. Hence, if we

Table 6.4. Distribution of lexical aspectual class within morphological marking

	Time 1				Time 2			
	Telic	Activ.	State	Token	Telic	Activ.	State	Token
Beginners (n = 4)								
Preterite	60%	26%	15%	47	81%	7%	12%	75
Imperfect	0%	0%	100%	1	50%	0%	50%	4
Present	60%	10%	30%	91	59%	13%	29%	70
Infinitive	91%	9%	0%	11	59%	41%	0%	17
Progressive	0	0	0	0	0	0	0	0
Intermediate (n = 4)								
Preterite	74%	12%	14%	203	83%	9%	8%	149
Imperfect	33%	19%	48%	42	34%	0%	66%	29
Present	34%	7%	59%	68	49%	1%	50%	68
Infinitive	67%	33%	0%	3	100%	0%	0%	4
Progressive	6%	81%	13%	16	55%	45%	0%	11
Interm-high (n = 4)								
Preterite	85%	7%	8%	102	90%	6%	5%	105
Imperfect	9%	11%	81%	47	7%	10%	83%	30
Present	24%	5%	70%	37	27%	25%	48%	44
Infinitive	50%	50%	0%	2	100%	0%	0%	1
Progressive	0%	83%	17%	6	25%	50%	25%	4
Advanced (n = 3)								
Preterite	94%	5%	2%	175	86%	8%	6%	172
Imperfect	7%	7%	86%	85	13%	4%	83%	92
Present	53%	13%	35%	112	55%	9%	36%	76
Infinitive	0%	0%	0%	0	0%	0%	0%	0
Progressive	35%	65%	0%	20	29%	71%	0%	35

follow the change in the percentage of the use of Preterite with telic events we identify a change from 74% (intermediate, Time 1) to 83% (intermediate, Time 2) to 85% (intermediate-high, Time 1) to 90% (intermediate-high, Time 2), and finally to 94% (advanced, Time 1). However, in the movement from Time 1 to Time 2 within the advanced group the direction of change has been reversed: 86% of verbs marked with the Preterite are telic events. This slight change may plausibly signal a tenuous attempt at marking point-of-view aspect (non-proto-typical marking of lexical aspectual classes). In fact, this reversal in the constant increase towards complete marking of verbal morphology according to lexical aspect was shown in previous studies on academic learning of L2 Spanish as well (e.g., Hasbún 1995; Ramsay 1990). A similar trend is evident in the use of the Imperfect: a consistent and gradual increase both across time and across levels towards complete correspondence of Imperfect morphology with lexical aspect. In this case we identify a change of 48% (intermediate, Time 1) to 66% (intermediate, Time 2) to 81% (intermediate-high, Time 1) to 83% (intermediate-high, Time 2), and finally to 86% (advanced, Time 1). Once again, we notice that in the movement from Time 1 to Time 2 within the advanced group the direction of change is reversed with the percentage moving slightly back to the mark of 83%. In sum, the above mentioned argument about the association of the effect of lexical aspectual class with level of experience in the target language is substantiated with the analysis of both morphological markers of past tense in parallel (concurrent effects).

6.2   Results from cloze and editing task

The analysis of longitudinal oral data presented in the previous section was correlated to data collected among an extended group of subjects from two of the academic levels represented in the analysis of the oral movie narratives: intermediate-low and advanced (along with a control group of native speakers). In fact, the participants who narrated the movies were fellow classmates of the subjects whose data will be analyzed in this section.[2] The data from the cloze and editing tasks to be described shortly were collected in between Time 1 and Time 2 (i.e., mid-October) of the data collection procedure from the movie narrative. The cross-sectional quantitative data are important because, unlike the less controlled task presented in the previous section, it may be examined through statistical tests of significance. Importantly, the reliability of the written tests was fairly high as measured on the cloze test: Cronbach's alpha of 0.93. Table 6.5 shows the average scores per verb type in both cloze and editing tests for the three groups of subjects. The number of items representative of each lexical aspectual category is included in the Table as the N-size for each category. As mentioned in the previous chapter the results are displayed in percentages of use of Imperfect of total use of past tense across lexical aspectual class (i.e., the

---

2. The main pool of 16 volunteers was excused from the completion of the in-class written tasks since they had completed the above mentioned tests during the out-of-class sessions.

difference between 100% and the percentage for Imperfect corresponds to the use of Preterite). For instance, advanced students marked 63% of all stative verbs in the cloze test with the Imperfect (the remaining 37% corresponds to states marked with the Preterite). We must bear in mind that these are aggregate data: The average percentages associated with each lexical aspectual class reflect the overall tendency of all subjects to mark the number of items that were classified within each lexical aspectual category. The analysis of the data will be presented in the following order: cloze test only, editing task only and differential scores between cloze test and editing task.

Table 6.5. Use of imperfect as percentage of total use of past tense

Verb Type (n)	Cloze test			Editing task		
	123	311	Natives	123	311	Natives
Stative (10)	27%	63%	25%	44%	59%	42%
Activity (14)	15%	40%	30%	49%	62%	64%
Telic (17)	8%	18%	18%	38%	39%	53%

Note: 123 refers to the intermediate course and 311 refers to advanced course

6.2.1 *Cloze test*

The data from the cloze task are presented in graphical format in Figure 6.1. This graphical depiction of the data show that the association of morphological marking and lexical aspect is apparent in both groups of L2 Spanish learners. The magnitude of that association, however, is more noticeable in the data from the advanced group. In contrast, the distribution of scores of native speakers is not strongly determined by lexical aspectual class. In order to answer the two main research questions, the raw scores of the dependent variable in the cloze test (selection of Imperfect or Preterite) were submitted to an Analysis of Variance (ANOVA). The experiment was based on a 3×3 factorial design (three levels of aspectual class × three levels of experience with Spanish). The results of the ANOVA procedure are presented in Table 6.6. The results of the factorial ANOVA revealed significant main differences for lexical aspect ($F(2,21.236) = 0.001$), Spanish level ($F(2,22.207) = 0.001$), and also interaction effects between lexical aspect and L2 knowledge ($F(4,4.779) = 0.001$). Most important, the squared multiple R associated with the data is 0.465. In other words, the effect of the factors selected for the analysis (i.e., lexical aspectual classes and level of

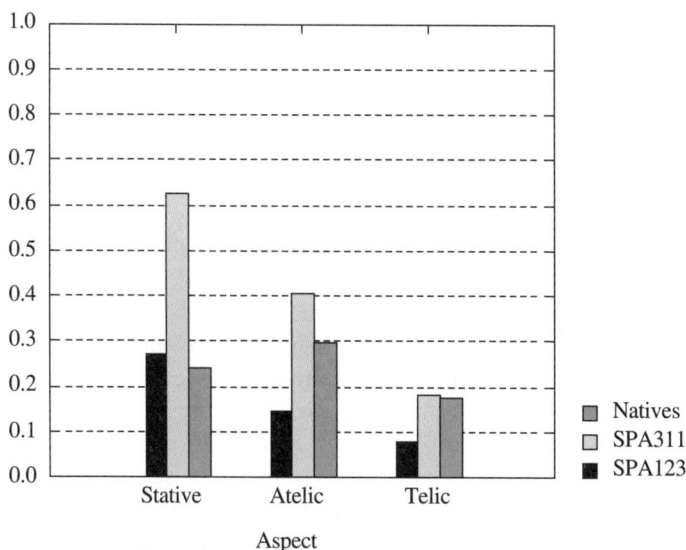

Figure 6.1. Distribution of scores for all items by lexical aspectual class in cloze test (score of 0 represents preterite and score of 1 represents imperfect)

Table 6.6. Results of ANOVA test of statistical significance (cloze test)

Source	Sum squares	DF	Mean squares	F-ratio	p-value
lexical aspect	1.106	2	0.553	21.236	0.001*
L2 experience	1.157	2	0.578	22.207	0.001*
interaction	0.498	4	0.125	4.779	0.001*
error	2.970	114	0.026		

experience with the L2) on the scores of the cloze test account for approximately 50% of all the variation present in these data. A post hoc analysis (Tukey) showed that the differences in scores were statistically significant for comparison between all lexical aspectual classes: stative versus atelic events ($p = 0.035$), stative versus telic events ($p = 0.001$), and atelic events versus telic events ($p = 0.001$). Similarly, a post hoc analysis (Tukey) applied to levels of experience showed that the differences in scores were statistically significant for the comparison across all levels except for the contrast between native speakers and intermediate ($p = 0.109$). The other two contrasts were statistically significant: intermediate and advanced ($p = 0.001$), and advanced and natives ($p = 0.001$). In sum, the morphological marking of verbs is associated with the lexical aspectual class of the verb for the advanced group only. A preliminary conclusion from the analysis of these data indicates that the use of verbal endings among intermediate learners is associated with the discrimination of tense, rather than lexical aspectual classes.

The analysis of the average scores from all items combined within each lexical aspectual class can be analyzed in finer detail if we classify the scores from each item separately and range them into groups of scores according to the strength of response associated with each item. Table 6.7 presents the summary of items in terms of three ranges of percentages of use of Imperfect by level (i.e., the higher the percentage, the more use of the Imperfect). The low range scores are the ones below the 40% marker, mid-range scores cover the middle band between 40% and 60%, and the upper-band is represented by scores above the 60% marker. Extreme scores (upper and lower bands) reflect a clear stand taken by the speaker about the possible morphological marker associated with each specific item: high preference for either Preterite (below 40%) or the Imperfect (above 60%). Mid-range scores reflect a degree of uncertainty about the specific morphological marker of particular items. In sum, scores below 40% reflect a distinct selection of Preterite, scores above 60% reflect the distinct selection of Imperfect, and scores between 40% and 60% reflect a wide range of responses among individuals within the group (ambiguity of the item or uncertainty about the selection of verbal morphology).

Table 6.7. Distribution of ranges of scores per item across levels

	Intermediate			Advanced			Natives		
	Sta.	Act.	Tel.	Sta.	Act.	Tel.	Sta.	Act.	Tel.
< 40%	10	14	17	0	6	16	6	9	16
40–60%	0	0	0	6	3	0	4	5	1
> 60%	0	0	0	4	5	1	0	0	0

Table 6.7 shows that the average scores for all items from the intermediate Spanish group fall below the 40% division irrespective of lexical aspectual class. In other words, the data from intermediate learners show a categorical marking of Preterite irrespective of lexical aspectual classes. In contrast, the average

scores from the advanced learners shift progressively according to lexical aspectual class: Imperfect marking (above 60%) is mostly restricted to stative and activity verbs, whereas Preterite (below 40%) is restricted to nonstative verbs. The data from the advanced students show an outlier: item 36 represents the only telic verb marked with a score higher than 60% (non-prototypical marking of telic verbs). Notice, however, that item 36 corresponds to the verb *saber* (to know), a typical stative verb which was classified as a telic event according to the operational tests of lexical aspectual classes. It is plausible that the advanced students were particularly sensitive to the distributional bias associated with this particular verb, and that they selected the verbal ending most commonly associated with that verb (irrespective of the outcome of the operational test).

Finally, it is important to notice that the apparent similarities across groups in the number of items under the telic events category marked with the Preterite (i.e., scores below 40%) are not accidental. Across all groups the default marker of past tense morphology seems to be the Preterite. In this respect, notice that the Imperfect is not used as a default among the advanced students (nor the native speakers for that matter): stative verbs are not categorically marked with high percentages (i.e., above 60%). In sum, the data from the written task used in this study reveal that the aspectual distinctions represented in the form of lexical aspectual classes may be relevant for the use of inflectional morphology in the advanced stages of tutored L2 development.

6.2.2 *Editing task*

As mentioned above, all subjects completed the editing task after they finished the cloze test. The data from the editing task are presented in graphical format in Figure 6.2. The raw scores of the dependent variable (selection of Imperfect or Preterite) in the editing task were analyzed with an ANOVA. The analysis was based on a 3×3 factorial design (three levels of aspectual class × three levels of experience with Spanish). The results of the ANOVA procedure are presented in Table 6.8. The results of the factorial ANOVA did not reveal any significant differences for lexical aspect ($F(2,2.284) = 0.107$), L2 experience ($F(2,1.087 = 0.341$), or interaction between lexical aspect and L2 experience ($F(4,0.759) = 0.554$). In fact, the value for the squared multiple R obtained from this analysis was 0.081. Concomitantly, the analysis of the graphical information from Figure 6.2 shows a "flat contour" of the data from all levels and across lexical aspectual classes. In sum, the selected factors (aspectual class and level of experience) provide hardly any explanatory value of the present results.

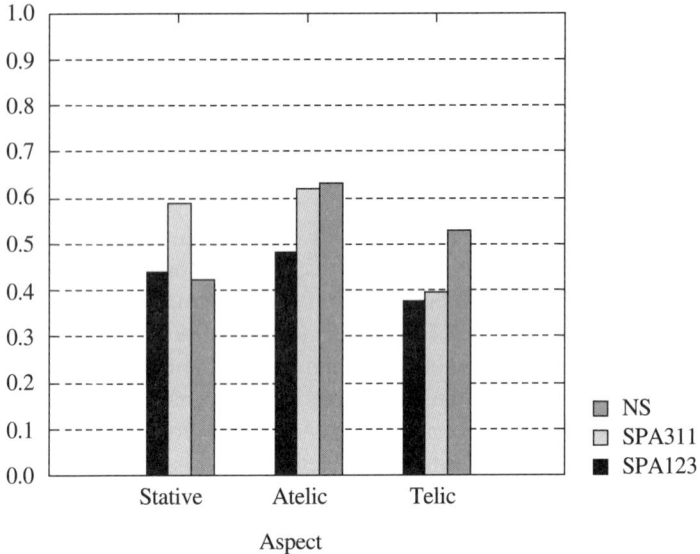

Figure 6.2. Distribution of scores for all items by lexical aspectual class (editing task)

Table 6.8. Results of ANOVA test of statistical significance (editing task)

Source	Sum squares	DF	Mean squares	F-ratio	p-value
lexical aspect	0.503	2	0.251	2.284	0.107
L2 experience	0.239	2	0.120	1.087	0.341
interaction	0.334	4	0.084	0.759	0.554
error	12.551	114	0.110		

6.2.3 *Differential scores*

An alternative analysis of the results from the editing task is based on the examination of the change in the selection of verbal morphology from cloze to editing task within each individual and for each item. The advantages of this analysis is predicated on the fact that it measures the subjects' performance on the same items; thereby, showing the relative degree of stability of the previous selection of verbal endings. For that purpose all scores from the cloze task were subtracted from the scores obtained in the editing test. The differential scores are presented in graphical format in Figure 6.3. The results of a 3 × 3 factorial design ANOVA (three levels of aspectual class × three levels of experience with

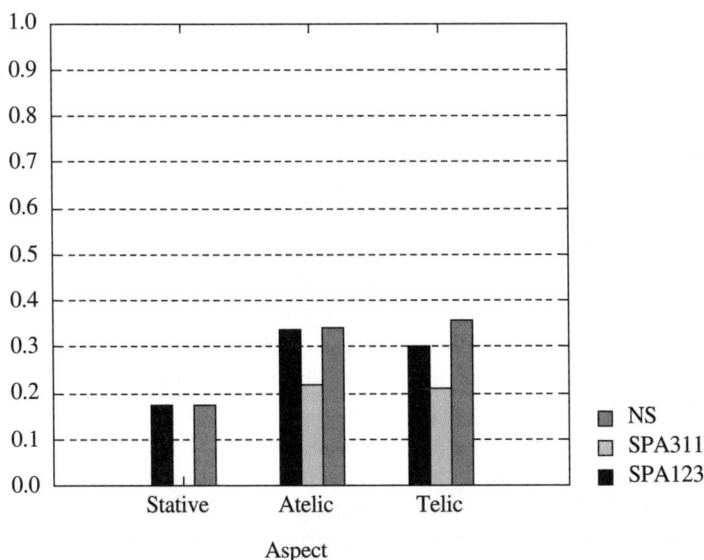

Aspect
Figure 6.3. Distribution of differential scores for all items by lexical aspect

Spanish) in the selection of Imperfect or Preterite between cloze and editing task are presented in Table 6.9.

Table 6.9. Results of ANOVA test of statistical significance (differential scores)

Source	Sum squares	DF	Mean squares	F-ratio	p-value
lexical aspect	0.814	2	0.407	5.304	0.006*
L2 experience	0.585	2	0.292	3.809	0.025*
interaction	0.054	4	0.014	0.177	0.950
error	8.752	114	0.077		

The results of the factorial ANOVA revealed significant differences for the main factors: lexical aspect ($F(2, 5.304 = 0.006)$, and L2 experience ($F(2, 3.809 = 0.025)$. There were no interaction effects between lexical aspect and L2 experience ($F(4, 0.177 = 0.950)$. Indeed, Figure 6.3 shows that the pattern of change in the selection of verbal morphology across lexical class is almost the same (i.e., no interaction between level of experience and aspectual class). A post hoc analysis (Tukey) showed that the contrasts in differential scores were statistically significant for the comparison between stative versus atelic events ($p = 0.011$), and stative versus telic events ($p = 0.013$). However, the contrast between atelic events and telic events was not significant ($p = 0.984$). A second post hoc analysis (Tukey) on level of experience with the L2 showed that the comparison between native speakers and advanced students ($p = 0.035$) was statistically significant. However, the other two contrasts: native speakers and intermediate ($p = 0.955$) and intermediate and advanced ($p = 0.070$) were not significant. The statistical analysis of the average change of selection of Preterite or Imperfect from cloze to editing task (for all items within each aspectual class) masks the fact that those averages do not represent similar profiles of change for all items. That is to say, the data from native speakers show a wide range of differential scores above and below the average degree of change for each individual item, whereas the data from nonnative speakers show a minimum range of variation from the average. The range of differences will be subdivided into three sub-groups to investigate the categorical or non-categorical nature of the subjects' decision with respect to the marked options of aspectual values. Table 6.10 shows the distribution of differential scores in terms of three percentages which cover minimum (0%) to maximum change (69%) reported in these data.

Table 6.10. Differences in selection of verbal morphology across cloze and editing task by level

	intermediate		advanced		Natives	
0%–19%	14/41	34%	12/41	29%	14/41	34%
20%–39%	13/41	32%	17/41	42%	0/41	0%
40%–up	14/41	34%	12/41	29%	27/41	66%

The low range spans changes from 0% to 19%, the middle range from 20% to 39% and the high range from 40% to 69%. The direction of the change (i.e., from Preterite to Imperfect or from Imperfect to Preterite) is not computed since what is important for this analysis is the decision of the subjects to change a previously selected option irrespective of morphological marking. The analysis of Table 6.10 shows that changes of morphological markers of temporality (from cloze task to editing task) were categorical for native speakers only (i.e., highest or lowest ranges only). On the other hand, nonnative speakers seem to be less categorical about their decisions. The data presented in Table 6.10 do not include the effect of lexical aspectual class within each level of experience with the target language. That is to say, they show the changes of selection in all lexical aspectual classes combined. However, the distinction across lexical classes is

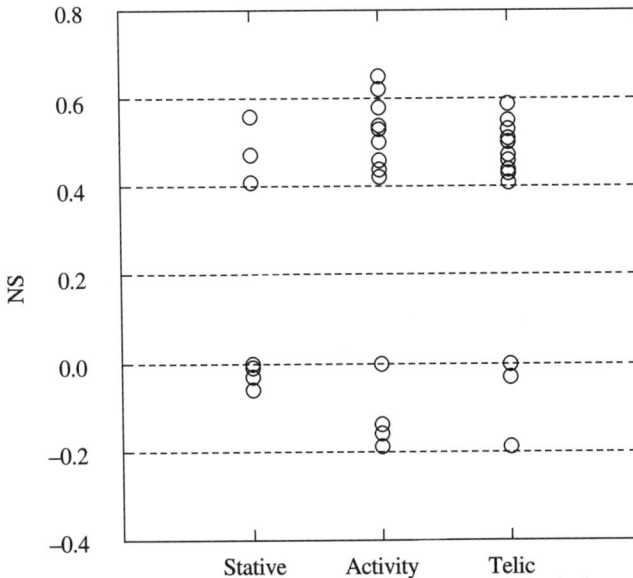

Figure 6.4. Distribution of differential scores for all items by lexical aspectual class: Native speakers

crucial to determine the validity of the claim of the lexical aspect hypothesis. To discriminate the effect of both lexical aspect and level of experience it is useful to plot the data from all 123 observations (differential scores of averages of 41 items × 3 levels of experience) in graphical format.

Figures 6.4 through 6.6 show the distribution of the observations by lexical aspectual class and level of experience with the target language. All Figures include the information about the magnitude of the change (as in Table 6.10), but also the direction of the change. Positive values indicate a change towards Imperfect (i.e., selection of Preterite in cloze test shifts to Imperfect in editing task). Negative values indicate a change from Imperfect to Preterite. The data from native speakers show (1) clustering of all items within two narrow bands of 20 percentage points each, (2) categorical change towards Imperfect, and (3) tenuous change towards Preterite. In sum, the distribution of the differential among native speakers is not directly affected by the inherent lexical semantics of the verbal predicate. On the other hand, there is a tendency towards a categorical change in verbal morphology from Preterite to Imperfect (across lexical class) reflected in the differential scores ranging from 40% to approximately 65%. The change towards Preterite is also similar across lexical classes,

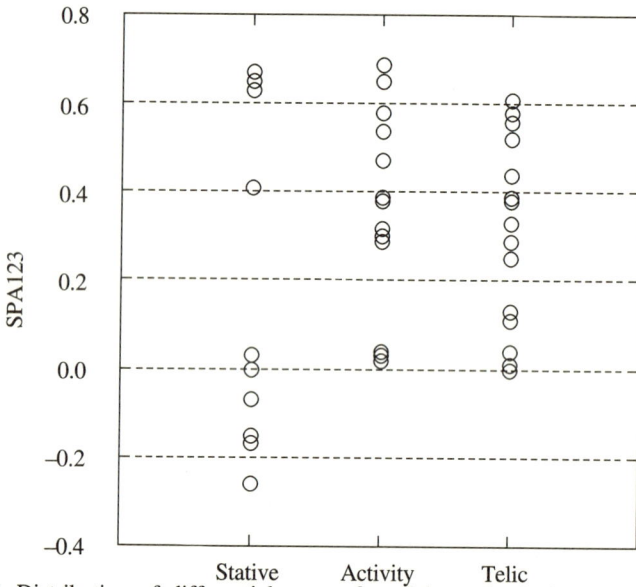

Figure 6.5. Distribution of differential scores for all items by lexical aspectual class: SPA123

but less dramatic: from no change to approximately 20%. Similarly, the results from both nonnative speakers' groups do not show any effect for lexical aspectual classes: changes in verbal morphological marking occur across all classes. However, there is a tendency among intermediate students to change only in the direction of the Imperfective marking for atelic and telic events. In contrast, the changes among the advanced students cover a wide range of magnitudes across lexical classes as shown before in Table 6.10.

6.3   Results from joint writing task

6.3.1 *Individual task*

During the first session (Time 1) the main group of subjects who completed the movie narrative was requested to complete a cloze task accompanied by a series of pictures describing some events from the Hitchcock movie Psycho. Each picture matched one particular group of sentences describing each scene (Appendix B). The results of the cloze test are summarized in Tables 6.11 to 6.13. The results

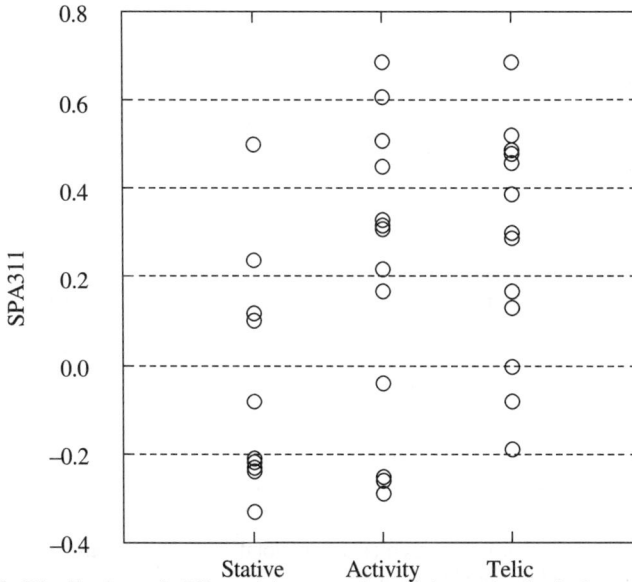

Figure 6.6. Distribution of differential scores for all items by lexical aspectual class: SPA311

are displayed in percentages of use of Imperfect of total use of past tense across lexical aspectual class (i.e., the difference between 100% and the percentage for Imperfect corresponds to the use of Preterite). The data from the four volunteers from the lowest level (beginners) is not presented because two participants conjugated all the verbs in present tense, and the other two used only Preterite (no morphological contrast of aspect). Most subjects performed similarly within their own groups. In particular, the comparison between subjects 1 and 2 and separately subjects 3 and 4 within each group is important because those subjects were later paired up for the completion of the joint problem solving task. All of those pairs performed similarly. Only one notable discrepancy in the selection of morphological marking is evident in the comparison of the individual and group results of the dyad composed by 311.3 and 311.4. This discrepancy will be important for the analysis of the interaction of this dyad during the joint problem-solving task.

6.3.2 *Joint task*

The quantitative data from the protocols of the students working in pairs will be

Table 6.11. Use of imperfect as percentage of total use of past tense for level 311 by individual (test based on movie Psycho plot)

Verb type	311.1	311.2	311.3	311.4	Average
Stative (8)	100%	88%	13%	88%	72%
Activity (7)	57%	43%	0%	57%	39%
Telic (12)	0%	0%	0%	0%	0%

Table 6.12. Use of imperfect as percentage of total use of past tense for level 203 by individual (test based on movie Psycho plot)

Verb type	203.1	203.2	203.3	203.4	Average
Stative (8)	88%	100%	88%	100%	94%
Activity (7)	71%	86%	71%	71%	75%
Telic (12)	8%	25%	0%	0%	8%

Table 6.13. Use of imperfect as percentage of total use of past tense for level 123 by individual (test based on movie Psycho plot)

Verb type	123.1	123.2	123.3	123.4	Average
Stative (8)	63%	88%	25%	38%	53%
Activity (7)	86%	86%	14%	43%	57%
Telic (12)	17%	8%	0%	8%	8%

presented to assess possible changes in the use of strategies. The validity of the assessment of the change in students' responses from time 1 to time 2 is predicated on the assumption that the participants did not remember their response from the first test in order to select a response in the second test. As mentioned in the previous chapter, the internal validity of the procedure (i.e., potential pretest effects on posttest results) was established by way of two different constraints of the data collection methodology: (1) there was a delay of two months between test 1 and test 2, and (2) the order of presentation of the passages in the cloze test was randomized. For the second test the original order of presentation of the passages (1, 2, 3 and 4) was presented in the following alternative order: 4, 3, 1, and 2. Even though it is difficult to categorically assess the success of these procedures, the reaction of the students during the completion of the second test (explicit comments of several dyads) revealed that the effect of time and randomization of passages prevented learners from using memorized routines employed in the first test. For example, in the following excerpt the dyad composed by participants 123.3 and 123.4 recognized the identity of the passages only by the time they were finishing the processing of their second passage:

123.3: Vivía su vida
123.4: Isn't this the same one? vivía su vida dedicada a los pobres,
123.3: a los pobres, ayudaba, yeah
123.4: Remember? .. she died .. the people she helped her life (laugh)
123.3: Yeah, I think so

In fact, one of the groups of advanced students did not realize that the texts were the same until they got to work on the third passage. Notice also that student 311.3 was not completely sure about the exact identity of the two tests:

311.3: Vivía (unison). It sure sounds familiar
311.4: Sure, it's the same one (laugh)
311.3: But I don't remember this part at all, do you?
311.4: Yeah
311.3: Ok (laugh)
311.4: Yes
311.3: I remember the part with Susan was boring

In sum, it is apparent that the participants of this study did not rely on their memory of the responses provided for specific items of the first test to decide their choices in the second test. The fact that many students changed their responses to the same items from time 1 to time 2 may be considered additional support for the lack of memorization of previous responses even though it would be difficult to discriminate the effect of learning during the previous two months (change of selection) and the effect of memorization of previous responses.

To facilitate comparison of both sets of data (i.e., individual and joint tests) a summary of the results from the joint problem-solving task is presented in Tables 6.14 to 6.17.[3] The comparison of these two sets of data reveal that (1) the selection of morphological marking of verbs is similar whether students work individually or in pairs (joint problem solving task) and (2) the trend associated with lexical aspectual class seems to be strong across all levels — with the

---

3. It is not likely that we would obtain similar averages because (1) the number of subjects is small, and (2) the number of items in the first test (movie Psycho) is low (26) compared to the second test (41).

Table 6.14. Use of imperfect as percentage of total use of past tense for all items within each lexical aspectual class per dyad (advanced)

Verb type	Time 1		Time 2	
	311.1/311.2	311.3/311.4	311.1/311.2	311.3/311.4
Stative (10)	80%	70%	80%	60%
Activ. (14)	50%	43%	78%	50%
Telic (17)	12%	0%	35%	18%

Table 6.15. Use of imperfect as percentage of total use of past tense for all items within each lexical aspectual class per dyad (interm-high)

Verb type	Time 1		Time 2	
	203.1/203.2	203.3/203.4	203.1/203.2	203.3/203.4
Stative (10)	80%	70%	90%	50%
Activ. (14)	50%	36%	71%	50%
Telic (17)	24%	0%	29%	17%

Table 6.16. Use of imperfect as percentage of total use of past tense for all items within each lexical aspectual class per dyad (intermediate)

Verb type	Time 1		Time 2	
	123.1/123.2	123.3/123.4	123.1/123.2	123.3/123.4
Stative (10)	60%	50%	70%	90%
Activ. (14)	50%	50%	50%	57%
Telic (17)	18%	18%	23%	29%

exception of the beginners students who marked all verbs with Preterite. These results corroborate previous findings about the performance of students working in dyads or individually (e.g., Davies & Kaplan 1998; Goss et al. 1994).

6.3.3 Processing of joint problem solving task

To perform a quantitative analysis of the preferred strategies used by the participants in the processing of the cloze task the data from all protocols were classified into five categories: (1) direct response, (2) rehearsal of response, (3)

Table 6.17. Use of imperfect as percentage of total use of past tense for all items within each lexical aspectual class per dyad beginners)

Verb type	Time 1		Time 2	
	112.1/112.2	112.3/112.4	112.1/112.2	112.3/112.4
Stative (10)	0%	0%	40%	0%
Activ. (14)	0%	0%	50%	0%
Telic (17)	0%	0%	23%	0%

use of translation, (4) use of learned rules associated with temporality, and (5) use of learned rules associated with areas other than temporality. A direct response was defined as the provision of a response without any explicit comments about the reasons that guided that decision. Rehearsal was characterized by the use of a minimum of three repetitions of the specific word under analysis (or variations of the verb conjugation patterns). The use of translations was assessed on the translation of either the target verbal predicate or the associated context surrounding the predicate. Finally, the classification of learned rules was based on the identification of explicit statements about grammatical rules. The following transcriptions from various protocols provide examples of each one of the above mentioned strategies:

Direct response (no discussion of reasons for the selection):

    203.2: Pensaba?

    203.1: Yeah

Rehearsal (at least three repetitions of the verb or its associated variants):

    112.2: the wind until de romperse until de .. rom- pó rompar maybe

    112.1: Rompieron?

    112.2: Rompieron (scribbling)

Translation (predicate or associated arguments):

    123.2: Loma . the hill

    123.1: Uhm .. then

    123.2: We went/

    123.1: We went\ (inaudible).. fui?

    123.2: Fuimos

Use of learned rule about temporality (the notion of ongoing action is a pedagogical rule for use of Imperfect):[4]

123.4: Qué es papalote though? Cuando volar is to fly right? So if you're flying then .. it was something that was ongoing .. cuando volaba/

123.3: Sure, OK

Use of learned rules other than temporality (a grammatical notion not related to temporality — number — is what determines the selection):[5]

112.3: Hacer

112.4: Haceron?

112.3: Haceron, yeah\ No nos hacimos nos es we so

112.4: No, it's el air so it's haci- hació

112.3: El nos?

112.4: Yeah, right\ but the subject is el air, aire I think it's like the air helped us laugh or something like that.

112.3: Oh, OK

For the quantitative analysis the use of a direct response, by definition, was considered to be exclusionary of the use of any one of the other categories. In contrast, the use of the other strategies was considered to be non-exclusionary of the use of other procedures. In fact, when faced with difficult items it was common for all subjects to use several strategies concurrently (e.g., translation in conjunction with learned rule about temporality). One of the problems raised by the use of multiple strategies is to determine which particular strategy determined the final selection of the subject. It is difficult to reach a categorical decision on this issue because the nature of the data collection procedure entailed that subjects were not requested to specifically say or not say anything in particular. On the other hand, this is one of the advantages of the joint problem solving methodology over the traditional single subject think-aloud procedure. In think-aloud tests subjects are given precise instructions on what they should do to accomplish the task (e.g., Ericsson & Simon 1983).[6]

---

4. In this case translation is used concurrently.

5. In this case translation is used concurrently.

6. Liskin-Gasparro (1997) implemented a data collection procedure which may provide information about the strategies which trigger the students' decisions. Liskin-Gasparro interviewed L1 English speakers in L2 Spanish (intermediate and advanced speakers) and later showed them a video tape of their interview. The researcher explicitly asked the students to comment on the decision to use specific morphological markers of temporality at some points during their interview. This type of post-hoc analysis of subjects' introspection may be instrumental in determining which type of strategy

The summary of the quantitative analysis of the strategies used by all participants is presented in Table 6.18. The data from near native and native speakers are presented separately in Table 6.19. The analysis of the use of strategies in the joint task reveal the following: (1) only inexperienced learners (beginners) show extended use of rehearsal and translation strategies, (2) in contrast, near native and native speakers rarely use rehearsal or translation strategies, (3) the use of translation increases significantly from time 1 to time 2 for beginners (a similar increase occurs in only one of the more advanced students' dyads: 203.1), (4) the use of the rehearsal strategy is similar across the more experienced learners (intermediate to advanced), (5) the use of rehearsal strategies does not change from time 1 to time 2 (across all groups of learners), (6) the consistent use of strategies across time is evident only among advanced students, (7) the use of learned grammar rules is similar across all groups, and (8) the use of learned grammar rules about non-temporal phenomena is highest among the native speakers' group.

The types of learned rules of temporality mentioned by the students are similar across levels. However, the level of sophistication of the explanations increases according to experience with the language (see above). Almost all of the learned rules are almost verbatim transcriptions from the students' protocols. The explicit rules mentioned by the students in association with the use of *Preterite* in all protocols are: (1) definite action (specific action) in the past, (2) once, one instance, a certain instance, it happened one time, (3) (a series of) actions, (4) succession of movements, (5) an instant thing, (6) a specific or special time, (7) a dialogue, and (8) special lexical translations (e.g., I found out for *supe*). In contrast, the explicit rules mentioned by the students in association with the use of *Imperfect* in all protocols are: (1) ongoing action, (2) translation of *used to*, (3) description, (4) every other time, from time to time, (5) all night, during her life, etc., (6) background, (7) habitual, frequentative, (8) paraphrases of "*it was happening*," "*while something else was happening*," and (9) a state verb (mentioned only once by dyad 203.3 and 203.4 with item #19). The latter was the only instance in which students explicitly referred to the particular lexical semantics of the verb. In most cases, those rules reflect the type of metalinguistic talk characteristic of classroom instruction. Notice also that, in general, such rules refer to notions associated with the narrative-based foreground-background contrast (i.e., description, sequence of actions, habitual, while, etc.), or the use of approximate translations to the L1 (i.e., *used to, found out*)

(among many) triggered the specific response of the subject.

Table 6.18. Summary of overt strategies used by student dyads

	Time 1							
	112.1	112.2	123.1	123.2	203.1	203.2	311.1	311.2
Direct	20	14	12	22	24	17	22	22
Rehearsal	16	24	6	6	3	3	5	8
Translat.	7	2	21	13	4	11	7	4
Tempor.	0	0	5	13	9	10	15	4
Other	1	11	4	1	1	3	2	2
	Time 2							
	112.1	112.2	123.1	123.2	203.1	203.2	311.1	311.2
Direct	3	6	16	27	17	18	22	27
Rehearsal	20	19	6	7	9	7	8	4
Translat.	30	25	18	9	17	13	4	8
Tempor.	5	15	6	6	14	9	11	7
Other	4	2	2	3	3	2	2	0

Table 6.19. Summary of overt strategies: natives and near-natives

	Nearnatives		Natives	
Direct	33	31	28	35
Rehearsal	1	0	1	0
Translation	1	4	0	0
Temporality	9	8	6	5
Other	0	1	7	2

The use of particular sets of strategies may be compared with the actual selection of past tense marking by each dyad (Tables 6.14 to 6.17). As shown in the previous section the majority of students shifted slightly towards the use of the Imperfect during the second session. This was an expected outcome especially among the lower level students. However, one of the remarkable features of these data is that one of the dyads from the lower level 112 never used the Imperfect. In fact, the analysis of the protocols from both times of data collection reveals that these students did not even consider the use of the Imperfect except for one isolated circumstance:

Dyad 112.3 and 112.4 (time 2, item 21):

112.3: Ok, my aunt María uhm .. it was horrible, .. her death was horrible her death was horrible/ yeah, .. su su muerte, so her death, so it would be, what's ser in past tense? (laugh, unison) I can't remember these things

112.4: It's like estaba, it's like tuve or tener, it's like ..

112.3: Uhm, wait, I forgot, no me acuerdo uhm at least we got the verb in the past tense .. e- era/

112.4: Era/

112.3: Fuera/ (laugh, unison)

In the end this dyad chose the Preterite form even though the recorded conversation leads one to believe that they settled for the subjunctive.[7] In sum, there was only one instance in which these two students considered the use of the Imperfect, even though that consideration was eventually rejected. Remarkably none of the items from both tests from these subjects was marked with the Imperfect even though the beginners sections had received explicit focused grammatical instruction on the Imperfect during the two weeks prior to the second session.[8] In contrast, the dyad composed by students 112.1 and 112.2 preferred to use the Imperfect with a large number of items in the second test (all items in the first test were marked with the Preterite). In most cases the choice of the Imperfect was based on the explicit formulation of a learned rule:

Dyad 112.1 and 112.2 (time 2, item 22):

112.2: So she lived, right? so how do you say? vi- vivió?

112.1: It's probably, she .. it's not, it's not vivir, vivía? vivía?

112.2: Oh yeah she used to live, true

112.1: Vi- vía, right (murmur) .. ayu-

In some cases, the increased amount of experience with the target language does not necessarily make the task easier for the students. For example, the dyad composed by 203.3 and 203.4 was quick to determine that *volver* (item 31) was to be marked with the Preterite at time 1. Two months later, the decision becomes more complicated because the students considered the option of using the conditional instead of simply Preterite or Imperfect:

Dyad 203.3 and 203.4 (time 1, item 31):

Tía María .. volvió (unison)

wait .. returned from the death .. volvió

---

7. The analysis of the rest of the protocol does not reveal that the students ever returned to this item to correct it.

8. Subject 112.4 dropped the course halfway between the two sessions. However, there is no evidence in the protocols that 112.3 ever engaged in a discussion on the possible use of the Imperfect, nor that subject 112.4 dominated the discussion; thereby, biasing the results.

Dyad 203.3 and 203.4 (time 2, item 31):

203.3: .. my aunt, right? my aunt María/ would return .. vol- vuera
203.4: Volvió\
203.3: .. volvió?
203.4: ... uh uh
203.3: Oh! it's conditional!
203.4: pero .. fue .. it's supposed to be in past tense .. pero fue
203.3: Ok
203.4: Tía María está .. o .. es past tense .. estuvo/ ..
203.3: Estuvo muerta
203.4: Ok

Later in the session these students revised their response to this item. Their concern about the possible use of the conditional is again triggered by the obvious effect of the translation to English (*would* is normally equated with the conditional pattern of conjugation in Spanish, but also with Imperfect):

203.4: I think it should be Imperfect, like I was thinking that my aunt was .. like returning from the dead
203.3: Aha .. I think it's volvía
203.4: Aha
203.3: Do you think it could be p- uh conditional
203.4: No
203.3: I was thinking that she would return .. that she would come, she would ..
203.4: Let's just put that

It is obvious that these students were more sophisticated in their discussions at time 2 since they were able to consider a wider range of options about the morphological marking of verbs. But, as mentioned above, the wide range of options considered by these subjects does not necessarily mean that the task became easier. If anything, the task becomes more difficult when the number of options has expanded. Additional evidence is provided by the data from the advanced speakers

Dyad 311.1 and 311.2 (time 1, item 5):

311.1: It's gotta be Preterite because there seems to be an action occurring when the wind... ..
311.2: Ok, Yeah ... (murmur) is that dragged by the wind (murmur) That's a definite action, OK?
311.1: But it could be a continuing, uh like a description of a continuous

action while it was happening, like a description of a continuous action while it was happening

Dyad 311.1 and 311.2 (time 2, item 5):

311.2: ... entonces se nos .. íbamos/ ... no!, se nos uh iba iba that's like leaving us, yeah/ like the string of the kite
311.1: Uhm, ye::ah
311.2: What do you think?
311.1: Yeah, I guess,
311.2: Iba
311.1: Iba

Another feature of the processing of data revealed in the analysis of the joint task was that in the second session some students engaged in an extended discussion of the morphological endings associated with certain items without necessarily changing the selection made the first time. In the following case it is remarkable how the discussion from the first time is reproduced almost exactly (same comments made by same subjects during the first three turns) in the second instance. However, the discussion turns out to be longer and more sophisticated the second time without any change in the outcome.

Dyad 311.3 and 311.4 (time 1, item 19):

311.4: Estaba/
311.3: Estaba despierto toda la noche, Estuvo! ... toda la noche, estuvo?
311.4: The whole night .. he was awake (laugh) (Whispering: I don't know)
311.3: Estuvo despierto toda la noche después que ...

Dyad 311.3 and 311.4 (time 2, item 19):

311.4: Estaba/
311.3: Estuve or estaba/
311.4: I think it's for the whole night, .. like a long thing
311.3: Aha, but it is a
311.4: It is a definite amount of time
311.3: Por la noche
311.4: Ok, maybe it's estuve
311.3: Estuvo/
311.4: Estuvo, yeah
311.3: Estuve/
311.4: Wait ...
311.3: Estuve/ .. estuve despierto toda la noche después
311.4: Yeah

Among native speakers discussions were less centered on the analysis of grammatical rules but rather on the overall meaning of the passages. In fact, it is apparent that the native speakers do not even have the type of metalanguage that nonnative speakers possess to talk about the grammatical distinction between Preterite and Imperfect. For example, in one of the few instances when NS1 and NS2 discussed the above mentioned distinction they switched to English to describe the contrast.

> NS1: pero yo lo pondría para ponerlo como como en más pasado todo en pasado pasado .. yo pensé .. en ti Susana cuando volamos ..
> NS2: Pero está está en pasado ... está más continuo
> NS1: Sí.
> NS2: I was doing en vez de I did. Es eso.
> NS1: Sí, bueno pe- pero I was doing no es past tense .. es past es past continuous tense .. tiene otro nombre
>
> NS1: But I would put it to put it like like more in past all in past past .. I thought (PRE) .. in you Susana when we flew (PRE)
> NS2: But it is it is in past ... it is more continuous
> NS1: Yes
> NS2: I was doing instead of I did. That's it
> NS1: Yes, well, bu- but I was doing is not past tense .. it is past it is past continuous .. it has another name
> (phrases originally in English are underlined)

These native speakers seem to be unable to use the metalanguage to explain grammar rules in their native language. The switch to English appears to be related to the fact that both NS1 and NS2 learned explicit rules of grammar in their nonnative language (i.e., English). This is not an uncommon phenomenon in the literature. For example, in the discussion of their data, Davies and Kaplan (1998) speculate that their L2 French subjects may have had "more explicit French grammar rules (correctly or incorrectly formulated) at their disposal than they have explicit English grammar rules." From the type of judgments offered by all native speakers who acted as controls in this study it is clear that their explicit metaknowledge of Spanish grammar rules is limited.

Finally, the analysis of the proportion of use of learned rules associated with temporality vis-à-vis the use of learned rules associated with other grammatical phenomena provides another perspective on the analysis of the data. Table 6.20 presents the distribution of use of learned rules across all groups of subjects and the percentage of use of other than temporal rules.

Table 6.20. Distribution of explicit mention of grammar rules across groups

	112	123	203	311	NNS	NS
Temporality	16	12	23	18	17	11
Other	6	5	5	2	1	9
Percentage Temp.	73%	71%	82%	90%	94%	55%

Table 6.20 shows that the more advanced the learners, the more attention they pay to temporal instead of non-temporal features of verbal morphology. The proportional mention of explicit temporal rules (in contrast with non-temporal rules) increases from approximately 70% for the less experienced learners to roughly 80% for the intermediate learners, to approximately 90% for the advanced learners and finally peaks at 94% among near native speakers. The continuum is broken in the transition to the native speakers' data whose use of temporality rules is 55% of the total number of explicit rules mentioned during the cloze task. In essence, the native speakers do not seem to be overly concerned about grammar rules based on temporality phenomena as opposed to other grammatical phenomena. This finding confirms the claim made by Coppieters (1987) with reference to the distinctive nature of different grammar rules.

CHAPTER 7

Developmental stages in the acquisition of Spanish past tense morphology

In this chapter I present an extended analysis of the development of tense and aspect morphology among L2 adult learners by addressing three major questions: (1) what is the developmental pattern of acquisition of past tense verbal morphology among tutored (academic) learners? (2) what are the factors which may account for the particular distribution of morphological endings at any given stage?, and (3) how does instruction affect the movement from one stage to the next? The present chapter will address the previous questions through an analysis of the findings of the studies presented in the previous chapter and a reassessment of findings from other empirical studies already described in Chapter 4. In the first section I discuss the results of the longitudinal and cross-sectional studies presented in Chapter 6. The analysis provides a reassessment of the general claim of the lexical aspect hypothesis and proposes some minor changes (affecting mostly principle 1, as described in Shirai & Kurono 1998) that may render the hypothesis more appropriate for, especially, L2 clasroom learning. In the second section, I compare those findings with previous empirical data from both classroom and naturalistic studies. The comparison will be useful to reach a more comprehensive picture of the phenomenon of grammatical marking of temporality in adult L2 acquisition and to identify the factors that may have an effect on the particular stages of tense and aspect development as proposed in the previous section.

7.1 Summary of findings

With regards to the two sets of null and alternative hypotheses (see Chapter 5) we can conclude the following. First, the statistical significance of the findings from the written task and the supporting evidence from the oral data (as well as data from the pilot study) do not lead to the rejection of the first null hypothesis.

That is, the early appearance of past tense morphological marking (both Preterite and Imperfect) in L2 Spanish of adult tutored learners is independent of the effect of inherent lexical aspectual value of verbal predicates. Second, the statistical significance of the findings from the written task and the supporting evidence from the oral data lead to the rejection of the second null hypothesis. In other words, the selection of Spanish past tense morphological marking among advanced tutored learners is not independent of the effect of inherent lexical aspectual value of verbal predicates. In essence, the previously mentioned findings can be summarized in the following way: The data from the movie narratives from students from the beginning and intermediate-low levels (beginning of language development) show that the use of past tense does not appear to be guided by aspectual, but rather by tense constraints. In contrast, the data from the oral narratives of the students from intermediate-low through advanced levels reveal that the effect of lexical aspect becomes stronger in direct correlation with level of experience in the target language. Similarly, the data from the written tasks show that the selection of past tense verb endings among intermediate learners was largely independent of lexical aspect, but, that among students in the advanced sections, it was closely associated with lexical aspectual classes (prototypical marking). In sum, both sets of data (movie narratives and written task) show that the effect of tense is stronger than lexical aspect during the early stages of acquisition of L2 Spanish among English-speaking adult classroom learners. In the following sections I will address the theoretical significance of the previous summary of findings for each set of data.

7.1.1 Oral movie narratives

7.1.1.1 A default marker of past tense
One of the most important findings of the analysis of the data from the oral narratives is the fact that the lowest level learners appear to be using a single marker of past tense across lexical aspectual classes: a default past tense marker. However, the results were not categorical because along with the Preterite, Present tense forms were also used. Hence, it is important to consider two potential criticisms as to the value of the proposal of a default marker of past tense. First, it is possible, as Shirai (1997) claims, that the use of past tense morphology among beginning students did not reflect *knowledge* of such morphological marker: "[students were] trying their best to produce not-yet-acquired Preterite forms using conscious effort." Shirai adduces that this is the likely outcome of the demands of the task in terms of memory and communicative demands. In fact, the increased communicative demands of the task constituted

an explicit feature of the research methodology design of the study. Even though Shirai's assumption about the underlying nature of the cognitive process that led students to use past tense marking with some verbs, may be valid, it may not necessarily be the appropriate way to analyze these data.[1] I will elaborate on an alternative interpretation of these data along the lines of the potential existence of a default marker of past tense.

As Shirai argues, the use of past tense in the narratives of the less proficient subjects signals that temporal relations are an important concept to mark in the use of the target language (whether learners are successful in marking them or not). And, as shown in the previous section, the data revealed that the beginning students were not capable of marking past tense on all verb phrases. However, it is not the extent to which these learners failed to mark past tense verbal morphology that matters, but the extent to which they succeeded. In other words, these students did mark past tense with some verb phrases, *and in so doing they relied on one single marker of past (Preterite).* Notice also that this happened despite the fact that instruction on the use of the alternative morphological marker of past (Imperfect) was introduced (and practiced) during the two weeks prior to the second time of data collection. In sum, the requirements of the task (triggered by the conditions established by the data elicitation procedure) did not allow the beginning students to successfully use past marking with all verbs. And when they did use past marking, it was in the form of a single past form (Preterite). The latter is in accordance with the claim that these students used a default marker of past tense. In passing, notice that it is possible to speculate that instruction has a delayed effect on learning. In that case, instruction on the use of the Imperfect would not be reflected in the learners' production of the target grammatical item until sometime later than two weeks. However, current theoretical and empirical research on cognitive processes of language acquisition (e.g., Leeman, Arteagoitia, Fridman, & Doughty 1995; Harley 1989; Schmidt 1990, 1995; Schmidt & Frota 1986) may also lead us to speculate the opposite: that the explicit focus on a particular grammatical item will increase its production immediately following instruction. Further research including the analysis of delay effects for periods longer than two weeks would be necessary to empirically address this issue. Alternatively, one could also claim that there is task variation and that the Imperfect may first surface in relatively planned tasks rather than spontaneous production (e.g., written versus oral tasks). However, this

---

1. In fact, Shirai's interpretation could also be unwarranted depending on the operationalization of the concept of "knowledge" of morphological markers (e.g., is such operationalization based on a competence-performance distinction?).

is not the case as the findings from the written task reviewed above provide evidence against such assumption.

A second potential counterclaim to the proposed existence of a default marker of past tense refers to the theoretical nature of such construct. For instance, the notion of Preterite as a default marker of past tense could be indistinguishable from Andersen and Shirai's (1994, 1996) notion of an overlap of the prototypes of perfective and past. Notice, however, that a default marker of past tense (i.e., Preterite for Spanish) does not discriminate aspectual contrasts (it only marks tense contrasts). Hence, such a default marker of past tense will be used with verb phrases of all lexical aspectual classes (from telic events to statives) when the learner wants to make reference to past time events. This is in fact verified in the analysis of the data from the beginning students (for similar analysis of L2 Italian see Wiberg 1996, for L2 Spanish data see Hasbún 1995, and for L2 English data see Salaberry 2000). In contrast, the overlap of the prototypes of perfective and past — as proposed in Andersen and Shirai (1994, 1996) — does not predict the use of Preterite with verbs that, according to the Congruence Principle, should be associated with the Imperfect (typically stative verbs). This is the crucial factor that discriminates the claims made by either hypothesis and makes them empirically verifiable. Accordingly, it can be argued that the data from the present study showed preliminary support for the proposal that at the beginning stages learners use a default marker of past tense to mark verbal endings conveying past time reference.

7.1.1.2 *Developmental patterns: Underapplication, overgeneralization and regression*

The analysis of the longitudinal data of the oral protocols from the movie narratives is informative about the first signs of a stage of development not directly addressed by the research hypotheses. That is, the association between atelic verbs with Imperfect and telic verbs with Preterite in the use of past tense verbal morphology, among advanced students at Time 1, reaches a degree of association higher than normally found among native speakers. The degree of prototypical association of past tense inflectional morphology and lexical aspectual classes, however, begins to subside after two months (Time 2, advanced students). In other words, after the ceiling of prototypical marking of verbal morphology has been reached (data from written task and oral narrative from Time 1), advanced learners become less dependent on lexical aspectual values and begin to mark some verbs according to viewpoint aspect (non-prototypical) (oral narrative, Time 2). Even though the data on this proposed reversal effect is not particularly strong, it is important to point out that they corroborate the results from previous studies which included L2 Spanish students with more experience in the target language (e.g., Hasbún 1995; Ramsay 1990). Furthermore, the statistical significance of the quantitative analysis of the data from the written cloze tests from the larger group of subjects (intermediate and advanced groups) confirms that the degree of association between lexical aspectual classes and inflectional morphology increases with time to the point that it overgeneralizes to a level that surpasses the distributional bias represented among native speakers in the control group.

This phenomenon of overgeneralization is not new in studies of language development, both among first and second language learners (e.g., McLaughlin 1990 and Skehan 1998 for a general review). In this particular case, the route followed by these students is the following: underapplication, overgeneralization, and regression. During the the first stage learners rely on a single marker of past tense verbal morphology (i.e., Preterite), which, arguably, depicts tense distinctions. That is, there is an underapplication of the rule for past tense formation in Spanish because the use of both Preterite and Imperfect is necessary to mark past tense in Spanish verbal morphology. Eventually, students pick up on the necessity of using two different markers of past tense, and in conformity with the tenets of the lexical aspect hypothesis, they use them according to specific constraints related to the inherent lexical semantics associated with verb types (i.e., lexical aspect). As shown in the analysis of data from the previous chapter, students eventually overgeneralize the use of past tense markers associated with specific lexical aspectual classes (prototypical) to the point that their distribution surpasses what one may find in the data from native speakers. Finally, with more experience and practice with the target language, students are able to focus on language-specific discursive-pragmatic factors that provide them with information about when to go against the use of prototypical marking of verbal morphology.

There are cogent reasons why classroom students would follow the above-mentioned sequence. First, a contrastive analysis of Spanish and English reveals that for L1 English speakers tense distinctions are more transparent than aspectual ones. For instance, Giorgi and Pianesi (1997) claim that dynamic verbs in English are marked with the aspectual feature [+perfective]. That entails that the feature [−perfective] is not relevant, or, alternatively, that English lacks the functional category AspP. In either case, it follows that simple past tense morphology in English only marks tense distinctions (see Slabakova & Montrul, forthcoming for extended analysis). Furthermore, the need to mark tense through morphological means naturally follows the knowledge that English speakers already have from their L1 (i.e., the bound morpheme -ed signals past tense). To this we could add that classroom instruction, by its very nature, focuses students

Table 7.1 Sequential development of past tense morphology in Spanish among classroom learners

Stages	Description
Stage 0	No past tense marking
Stage 1	Past tense is marked with Preterite only
Stage 2	Imperfect is used with stative verbs (limited set)
Stage 3	Imperfect extended to atelic and telic events
Stage 4	All verbs may be marked with Imperfect or Preterite

on the use of morphosyntactic means to convey notions of temporality in the L2. Second, the notion of prototypes, as cogently argued for in Andersen and Shirai (1994, 1996), provides a useful theoretical framework to understand why, during a subsequent stage of development, learners would rely so heavily on the association of specific markers of past tense (e.g., Preterite and Imperfect) with specific lexical aspectual classes (e.g., telic events and statives). Finally, the complexity of discourse-pragmatic factors that underlie the native-like use of past tense markers in Spanish may account for the late incorporation of this type of information to the process learners follow to select verbal endings in past tense.

The previous analysis of the data shows a sequence of developmental stages different from the one proposed by Andersen (1986), the latter based on data from two adolescent learners in the natural environment. Table 7.1 presents a possible alternative sequence of development of past tense verbal morphology for academic learners of Spanish. The length of time that learners spend at Stage 0 may be relatively short, since English-speaking adults are particularly encouraged to mark the present-past tense distinction in the L2 — a distinction overtly represented in the L1 as well. In fact, several studies of classroom learning have shown rapid progress towards some type of past tense marking by the end of the second semester of academic instruction (e.g., Bergström 1995; Hasbún, Salaberry 1998). Stage 1 (tense distinctions) may represent a relatively more extended period of time for some learners because it reconciles the student's need to mark tense distinctions with the extended use of the most prominent marker of past tense in a narrative: Preterite. At this stage foreground-background distinctions may be marked by means of a contrast between the Preterite and the present tense. At the end of stage 1 target-like aspectual marking is gradually incorporated into the nonnative system by means of a few lexically-determined decisions: imperfective is associated with stative verbs only. The late appearance of the Imperfect in association with a constrained number of verbal predicates has been shown in empirical studies of L1 acquisition (e.g., Bloom, Lifter & Hafitz 1980), tutored L2 acquisition (e.g., Bardovi-Harlig & Bergström 1996; Schmidt & Frota 1986; Wiberg 1996), and untutored L2 acquisition (e.g., Andersen 1986, 1991). In essence, the transition from stage 1 to stage 2 does not represent a sharp developmental change except for the fact that the learner uses Imperfect with the verbs which are most commonly marked as such in the input available to them (e.g., Bardovi-Harlig & Bergström 1996; Hasbún 1995; Kaplan 1987). Stage 3, in contrast, represents a qualitatively distinct stage in the developmental sequence because learners start to rely on grammar rules instead of lexically-based decisions to determine the appropriate verb endings. During this stage learners start to develop a more stable system which allows them to use either Imperfect or Preterite with the same verbs in a more consistent and principled way (Ramsay 1990). To reach the final stage of the proposed developmental sequence, L2 learners must be able to mark aspectual distinctions irrespective of the inherent lexical semantics of the predicate, according to point of view (e.g., Binnick 1991; Ramsay 1990; Smith 1991). Non-prototypical aspect marking (point-of-view aspect) was not apparent in the data from the selected academic learners, except for some tenuous indications in the reversal of the trend among the most advanced group of speakers (oral data from movie narratives). The above-mentioned sequence of developmental stages for academic learners differs from the sequences previously proposed to account for the natural acquisition of nonnative languages (e.g., Andersen 1986, 1991), or natural tutored learners (e.g., Bardovi-Harlig 1992, 1995a). It is more likely to be followed by classroom learners for two obvious reasons: (1) the heavy emphasis on the use of inflectional morphology in academic settings, and (2) lack of access to consistent contacts with the use of the L2 in a natural environment of communication.

7.1.1.3 *Present versus past tense marking*
The analysis of the data from the oral movie narratives also revealed some interesting findings not directly specified by the formal hypotheses, but which bear directly on the focus of inquiry of this study. In particular, the use of almost exclusive present tense by both native and near-native speakers of Spanish in their oral narratives of the movies was almost exceptionless. On the other hand, beginning to advanced students narrated the movies using past tense marking (i.e., Preterite or Imperfect or both). As mentioned in the previous chapter, one of the students from the advanced group was not included in the analysis of the movie narratives because she also exclusively used present instead of past tense marking. Interestingly, another student (311.2) from the same group used present

tense during the first narrative but switched to past tense when he had to retell the plot of the movie as narrated by another student in past tense. It appears that this student was influenced by the selection of past instead of present tense by the other student. That is, the choice of tense of student 311.2 was unstable compared with the selection made by native speakers (see comment on selection of tense by NS2 below). This outcome is even more significant if we consider the fact that in the case of one native speaker the researcher probed the strength of the reliance on the use of present tense by making explicit requests to the subject to use past tense. The researcher stopped the native speaker twice to remind him of the instructions. The first time the reminder was subtle, but the second time, the speaker was specifically requested to narrate the story in the past tense (morphological marking) and not the present tense. In spite of the number and explicitness of the requests the native speaker remained impervious to the researcher's prodding: the first time NS1 did not realize that the researcher was asking him to use past tense, and, the second time NS1 used past tense for a number of instances, but immediately fell back on the use of present tense. As a further note, it should be pointed out that the native speaker who was present during this first exchange narrated her movie afterwards and did so exclusively in present tense.

As a consequence of the above-mentioned contrast, the data from the oral movie narratives of the native and near-native speakers did not provide information about the effect of lexical aspectual classes on aspectual marking. In effect, Spanish present tense is inherently imperfective; hence, it does not show any aspectual contrast in verbal morphology as is the case in Spanish past tense marking with the distinction of Preterite versus Imperfect (Bybee 1995; Bybee & Dahl 1989; Giorgi & Pianesi 1997). The corollary of such outcome was that the effect of lexical aspectual classes on the marking of past tense verbal morphology among classroom learners could not be compared with the effect of lexical aspect in the data from native and near-native speakers. However, what at first blush appeared to be a setback and a loss of data, constituted in fact a significant finding with (potential) important consequences for the research design of subsequent studies. The significance of the above mentioned outcome is predicated on the fact that all subjects (learners, native and near-native speakers) recounted the movies under the same experimental conditions. Most important, they all received the same set of instructions irrespective of course level or native language. The important question to ask is: why would L2 Spanish students not recount the movie in present tense as native and near-native speakers did? Or, alternatively, why would native and near-native speakers not recount the movie using past tense instead of present tense?

As a first approximation we may assume — justifiably so — that the native and near-native speakers provide the norm. In other words, the movie should have indeed been recounted in present and not past tense. In effect, the use of what has been called the "historical present" in the narratives of native speakers seems to be the norm rather than the exception (e.g., Chafé 1980; Fleischman 1990; Silva-Corvalán 1983; Wiberg 1996). For instance, Fleischman (1990: 285) makes a distinction between historical present and narrative present. The latter constitutes spontaneous use of the present tense (with time reference in the past) that "occurs consistently in alternation with tenses of the past and is linked to a performative mode of oral story telling." In contrast, the historical present is a "stylistic feature of narrative writing" (compare with Klein's classification of narrative present and epic Preterite below). Similarly, Klein (1994: 133–40) classifies the use of the present instead of past tense into: (1) narrative present (based on personal narratives, mostly oral), (2) time travel (not related to vividness as in personal narratives), (3) fact listing (series of historical facts), (4) epic Preterite (especially literary texts), (5) retelling (movies), and (6) pictured past (series of pictures).[2] I believe that the strongest discrimination between types of texts which use present tense marking (in a context of past time reference) may be the distinction among pictured past, narrative present (possibly including time travel and epic Preterite as well) and retelling of movies (perhaps including fact listing). This is because the differences among these categories are predicated on their distinct sources of information: picture, personal stories, and plots. In fact, Frawley and Lantolf (1984) and Sebastian and Slobin (1994) comment on the use of the pictured past as being different from personal or movie narratives (although the authors reach different conclusions in their analysis). Furthermore, the data from the pilot study presented in Chapter 5 showed that personal and movie narratives generated distinct responses insofar as the choice of verb types and morphological marking was concerned (see also analysis of data from Robison 1995 in Chapter 4). Most important, however, the data from the main study, provided empirical evidence that substantiated the claim that movie narratives are recounted in present and not past tense. These distinctions should be considered for the implementation of experimental tasks as they may affect the results of the empirical study. Due to the fact that this study did not attempt to analyze the contrast between personal and movie narratives it

---

2. This classification, however, is open to debate. For example, the distinction between (1) and (2), and even (4) may not be so clear since vividness need not be restricted to personal narration, and written literary texts need not differ substantially from spoken everyday language (as far as use of present tense is concerned).

is difficult to make strong generalizations (but see Salaberry 1999). For the sake of the present analysis, however, we may rely on such information to make sense of what native speakers did vis-à-vis non-native speakers.

Indeed, the previous argument provides a valid foundation for the analysis of potential reasons that account for the — categorically — distinct response of native speakers vis-à-vis the reaction of classroom learners to the procedure of data elicitation. One potential answer may be based on the distinct perception of these two populations about the genre of the narrative. In fact, it is likely that classroom learners assessed this (laboratory) task as they normally assess any other classroom task: a language practice activity implemented as a role-play. As such, it was not difficult for students to realize — despite the attempt to make it as real-life as possible — that the task required the narration of events that happened in past time; thereby, requiring past tense marking. In contrast, it is likely that the distinct behavior of the native speakers (as well as near-native speakers) corresponds to a different assessment of the task: the retelling of a movie plot. And, as previous research has shown movie plots are not narrated in past tense, but in present tense (e.g., Chafé 1980; Fleischman 1989, 1990; Silva-Corvalán 1983; Wiberg 1996). However, for that argument to hold, one must also account for the fact that the exclusive use of present tense among the control group of native speakers (and the near-native groups as well) in the present study was not reported in previous ones. A detailed reanalysis of the data from previous studies, however, reveals discrepancies that cast doubts on the purported exclusive use of past tense among native speakers (e.g., Hasbún 1995; Ramsay 1990). In fact, at a minimum, previous data show a stronger tendency among native speaker control groups in previous analyses (compared to classroom learners) to use present instead of past tense (see reviews of studies presented in Chapter 4). The categorical nature of the use of historical present among native and near-native speakers in the present study, compared to the less categorical results from previous ones, may plausibly be attributed to differences in data collection procedure and other methodological constraints. For instance, it is likely that the distinct behavior of native speakers and students in the present study represents an indirect consequence of the effect of test modality (oral versus written data) and the functional requirements of the task (communicative relevance). In effect, the data collection procedure of the oral narrative task explicitly accounted for the operationalization of the concepts of communicative demands (Tarone 1983, 1985) and monitoring of form (Ellis 1989). Such constraints appear to be especially relevant in two ways. First, they highlight particular functional constraints of the intended task as normally carried out in normal social activities (i.e., role-play adds more veracity to the task). Second, the cognitive demands of the task (e.g., oral narratives allow for less monitoring of form) were more likely to prevent L2 learners rather than native speakers from appropriately assessing the functional requirements of the task. In contrast, previous studies (e.g., Hasbún 1995; Ramsay 1990) have not explicitly controlled for the above-mentioned factors.

7.1.2 Cloze and editing written tasks: confirmatory data

As mentioned above, the data from the cross-sectional written task confirmed the findings obtained in the longitudinal analysis of oral movie narratives. First, the results from the cloze test revealed that the range of scores across lexical aspectual classes was markedly different for the advanced Spanish learners (24 students) compared to the intermediate students (23 students). As was the case in the longitudinal study, the average marking of verbal endings among advanced students reflects a clear relationship between lexical aspectual classes and past tense verbal endings: the use of Imperfect was associated with stative verbs (63%) and the use of Preterite was associated with telic events (82%). In contrast, the morphological marking of verbs among the intermediate students was not necessarily correlated with lexical aspectual types: the use of Imperfect was not associated with stative verbs (27%). On the other hand, the use of Preterite was strongly associated with telic events (92%), but, also with stative verbs (73%). The use of the Imperfect — instead of the Preterite — would be expected with statives if the lexical aspectual class of the verbs indeed had an effect on the selection of verbal endings (cf. tenet 1 of the lexical aspect hypothesis). In essence, among intermediate students the use of the Preterite was extended to all lexical aspectual categories (i.e., the Preterite acts as a default marker of past tense). Interestingly, native speakers (32 speakers) seemed to pair up with less experienced speakers (intermediate) in their selection of morphological marking: 82% of telic events were marked with Preterite and 75% of stative were also marked with Preterite. This outcome appears to reinforce even more the above-mentioned claim about the process of overgeneralization adduced to underlie the performance of the more advanced group of students.

Another important measurement in the analysis of the cross-sectional data is the range of use of morphological markers across lexical aspectual categories. For instance, if we consider the use of the Imperfect, we can see that the overall range of scores across lexical aspectual classes varies across levels. For the advanced students the range of scores for the Imperfect spans an overall scope of 45 percentage points: from 18% of use with telic verbs to 63% of use with statives. Furthermore, the differential scores for the use of Imperfect between each two lexical aspectual classes for the advanced students is proportional: 22 percentage points of a difference between telic and atelic events, and 23 percentage points between atelic events and statives. In contrast, the overall range of scores of use of Imperfect for the other two groups is much more restricted: 12 percentage points for native speakers (from 18% for telic events to 30% for atelic events) and 19 percentage points for intermediate students (from 8% for telic events to 27% for statives). In sum, the data from the cloze task may be considered representative of a particular sequence of development in which aspectual distinctions are relevant for morphological marking in the advanced stages rather than in beginning stages of academic learning. In contrast, the results from the editing task show that the association of morphological marking and lexical aspect is apparent in both groups of L2 Spanish learners. The magnitude of that association, however, is substantial for the advanced group of students only. On the other hand, the distribution of scores of native speakers is not strongly determined by lexical aspectual class (i.e., limited sequential distribution of inflectional markers according to lexical aspectual classes).

Finally, the comparison of data from the cloze and editing tasks revealed substantial differences in the use of past tense markers among native speakers and students. Native speakers showed a tendency to accept the new option (non-prototypical) as a valid alternative. Conversely, both groups of nonnative speakers were less certain about the grammaticality of the new options (non-prototypical) offered by the editing task. The differential scores between cloze and editing task of the less experienced group of learners were evenly divided across range differentials, whereas the ones from more experienced learners showed even more uncertainty. Notice that the less categorical decision of nonnative speakers in García and vanPutte's (1988) data mirrors the results obtained from the analysis of the differential scores between cloze and editing task in this study. In essence, advanced students were not approximating the profile of native speakers. If anything, advanced students were more uncertain about previously made selections of morphological marking (see also analysis of oral data in previous section). This does not necessarily mean that advanced nonnative speakers were not able to make a valid selection of verbal morphology in past tense contexts, but rather that they were — most likely — aware of the complexities of aspectual marking in past tense Spanish. These results correlate with previous findings about near native speakers' perception of their control of discursive-semantic phenomena in the target language (e.g., Birdsong 1992; Coppieters 1987; García & vanPutte 1988; Paradis 1994; Schmidt 1995).

7.1.3 *Speak-aloud task: metalinguistic rules*

The data from the speak-aloud task were important to gain access to the on-line decision-making process followed by the participants while doing the fill-in-the-blanks cloze test. The analysis of the speak aloud protocols (joint problem solving task) revealed that the judgments of the classroom students were preceded by extended metalinguistic talk. Such outcome stands in contrast with the data from native and near-native speakers who rarely used such metalinguistic talk. It was further concluded that the students' metalinguistic talk was heavily influenced by the type of pedagogical rules normally available in classroom instruction. Few of those rules, however, were associated with specific comments about the lexical semantics of verb classes. Most of the students' comments were associated with notions of narrative grounding restricted to the local sentence level (or the level of a few related sentences at most). In contrast, native speakers rarely engaged in a metalinguistic analysis of the selections of verbal morphology; instead, they relied on direct responses (implicit judgments) associated with the global analysis of the texts (cf., García & vanPutte 1988). Furthermore, native speakers made few references to markers of temporality.

As mentioned above, students were prone to rely on the use of metalinguistic rules to determine the selection of verbal morphological markers denoting temporality (e.g., Preterite and Imperfect) more regularly than other linguistic categories (e.g., person and number). Moreover, the types of learned rules of temporality mentioned by the students were similar across levels. The level of sophistication of the explanations, however, increased according to experience with the language. This continuum of use of explicit rules associated with temporality among L2 learners is what we would expect according to previous analyses of the acquisition of Romance languages among L1 English speakers (e.g., Paradis 1994; Schmidt 1995). That is, as learners become more experienced with the L2 they are able to handle certain features of the target language better than others. Logically, learners will be more concerned about the most difficult features of the target language; therefore, they will be more likely to rely on metalinguistic judgments if they are not entirely sure about their intuitions. It appears that learners pay more attention to the more demanding feature of tense-aspectual distinctions rather than non-temporal phenomena in the marking of Spanish verbal morphology (see Chapter 1). In contrast, native speakers are not overly concerned with the explicit formulation of grammar rules based on temporality: native speakers pay as much attention to temporal as well as non-temporal phenomena in their explicit formulation of grammar rules. Finally, in spite of the fact that the data from near native speakers reveal potential ultimate attainment in the use of Spanish tense-aspect morphology, the cognitive process-ing that underlies such performance need not necessarily coincide with the processing that underlies the native speakers' performance (cf. Birdsong 1992; Coppieters 1987). This proposal, however, must remain speculative at this stage due to the limited amount of data bearing on this issue (there were also some differences between dyads within each level).

7.2   Significance of the present findings in the context of previous studies

It is important to point out that previous theoretical interpretations of L2 acquisition data have pointed in the direction of the conclusions reached by the present study (e.g., Bardovi-Harlig 1992; Buczowska & Weist 1991; Meisel 1987; Robison 1990; Wiberg 1996). For example, in an analysis of tutored learners, Bardovi-Harlig (1992: 274) concluded that the learners of her study "also marked tense fairly consistently across aspectual classes." Meisel (1987: 220) makes a similar claim regarding natural learners: "... learners do not systematically use an aspectual system. It may well be that this is a very marginal phenomenon, occurring only occasionally ..."Additionally, as men-tioned in previous chapters, some researchers have explicitly claimed that tense contrasts will be instantiated in verbal morphology before lexical aspectual information from verbal predicates (e.g., Buczowska & Weist 1991; Wiberg 1996). Most important, it should be pointed out that the original proposal on the relevance of the lexical aspect hypothesis (Andersen 1991) or the primacy of aspect hypothesis (Robison 1990) for the overt marking of verbal morphology has been modified. Such modifications have been necessary to account for contradictory findings revealed by empirical data, or, alternatively, to develop a comprehensive theoretical appraisal of the development of verbal morphology. For example, Robison changed his original standpoint on the effect of the primacy of lexical aspect during the beginning stages of acquisition, and adopted the more conservative position that such effect will happen during "some stage of development" (Robison 1990: 330). The analysis of the data reported in the previous chapter confirms Robison's prediction. On the other hand, with reference to the development of theoretical frameworks, Andersen and Shirai (1994) considered the role of discourse-based phenomena (the effect of ground-ing) and the distributional bias of verbal morphology among native speakers (input bias) as two alternative forces which have an impact on the development of past tense verbal morphology among nonnative speakers. Furthermore, Shirai and Andersen (1995) acknowledge that it is difficult to argue that aspect develops before tense in cases like Spanish where the markers of both tense and aspect are both fused into a single morphological ending

Another way to address potential contradictions between empirical data and the basic prediction of the lexical aspect hypothesis is to reassess the validity of each one of the tenets that comprise this hypothesis (see Chapter 4, Section 4.2.1). That is, it is possible that some of its basic principles will remain valid, whereas others will be contradicted by the analysis of recent empirical data. In that case, we may preserve the basic claim of the lexical aspect hypothesis by way of modifying at least one of the three tenets that are relevant to the analysis of L2 development (principle 4 is only applicable to L1 acquisition: see Shirai & Kurono 1998). In effect, it may be the case that, for classroom learners of L2 Spanish, perfective past marking (i.e., Preterite) is used across all lexical aspectual classes during the beginning stages of acquisition. Principles 2 and 3 could be maintained as they refer to the appearance and use of imperfective marking (i.e., Imperfect) or the periphrastic Progressive.

Finally, it is important to point out that contrasts in methodology and data collection procedures may account for potential differences across studies. For that purpose, the following specific features of the procedure of data collection from the present study should be taken into account: (1) all learners of Spanish were native speakers of a single language (i.e., English), (2) all subjects were young adults (college-level students), (3) exposure to the target language was mainly through academic instruction at the college level, (4) the films used for the narrative task were shown only once (less planning), (5) the film narratives were delivered in oral instead of writing format (less time for monitoring form), (6) the data on movie narratives were collected at two different times to obtain longitudinal as well as cross sectional data, (7) the written task contained an analysis of acceptance or rejection of non-prototypical markings of aspect, and (8) the native speakers who acted as control group for the extended analysis of the cloze test and editing task were monolinguals instead of bilinguals (tested in home country). Despite the above mentioned methodological differences in the data collection procedure, it is remarkable that some general constraints of the development of tense aspectual systems are similar across studies as shown in the data from Bergström, Hasbún and Leeman et al.

The findings from the present study highlight the level of complexity in the analysis of the development of verbal morphology in a second language. Thus, it appears that the tenets of the lexical aspect hypothesis need to be further assessed against the background of the contradictory empirical data reviewed in Chapter 4 as well as the data from the present study. Such analysis points in the direction of several areas of research that need to be pursued further in order to obtain a better understanding of the development of tense and aspect in L2 acquisition. Therefore, it is important to identify crucial features in the research design across two important dimensions: (a) learning environments and (b) data collection/data analysis procedures. In terms of learning environment, it is important to account for the potential confounding effects of the following factors:

1. setting effects (e.g., natural versus academic environments),
2. instruction effects (instructed versus non-instructed learners),
3. age effects (e.g., adults, children and adolescents), and
4. language typology effects (e.g., all subjects share the same L1).

In terms of data collection and analysis the consideration and control of the following factors is essential for the appropriate design of future research studies:

1. grouping factors (i.e., levels of L2 proficiency of selected subjects),
2. selection of longitudinal versus cross-sectional analysis,
3. classification of verbal predicates (i.e., operational tests),
4. data elicitation procedures (e.g., role play setting),
5. use of oral versus written data,
6. selection of discrete item grammar tests versus narrative tasks,
7. use of personal versus movie narratives,
8. use of sentence level versus discourse level grammar tests,
9. use of introspective studies, and
10. type of data analysis (e.g., analysis within or across lexical classes)

On the other hand, it is important to point out several limitations in the research design of the present study that limit the generalization of findings. First, the results from a limited longitudinal study with only two anchor points should be validated with longer longitudinal experiments to verify the proposed sequence based on data from the present study. Second, the analysis based on the protocols from the joint problem solving task may be cross-validated with similar types of analyses (e.g., Liskin-Gasparro 1997). Third, the cross-linguistic investigation of two languages functioning as both source and target language (two-way analysis) should provide an even stronger base for the investigation of language specific effects. Fourth, the review of the literature on the use of present instead of past tense revealed that not all narrative plots are marked with present tense. Fleischman (1990: 105) claims that the retelling of narrative plots from novels and films are normally recounted in the present tense, but plots of television serials tend to be recounted in the past tense in response to a question similarly posed in the past tense. This particular constraint could also be investigated by means of experimental conditions in future studies. Fifth, the analysis of the development of past tense marking in a target language whose aspectual system is similar to the source language may provide another type of evidence for the investigation of the cognitive processing of inflectional morphology among academic learners. For instance, the development of L2 Spanish past tense morphosyntax among French native speakers may provide another source of evidence as is already the case in studies of natural learners (cf., Trévise 1987). Finally, it is important to mention that the methodology of this study did not include any comprehensive measurement of motivation beyond some general exploratory questions about perceived usefulness of the target language in the future, reasons for taking an academic course in Spanish, etc. (see background questionnaires, Appendix D). It is possible, however, that communication requirements are not necessarily conducive to development of verbal morphology as shown by data from studies that track the development of verbal morphology among natural learners (e.g., Perdue & Klein 1992; Klein et al. 1995). Pienemann, Johnston and Meisel (1993: 498) state that "for every study that finds a positive relationship between one external factor and SLA one can find another study to show the contrary." Furthermore, motivation constitutes such a complex factor in the acquisition of language that it is too ambitious to try to offer a detailed analysis of such explanatory phenomenon in language acquisition within the scope of the discussion of findings presented in the previous chapter (see Crookes & Schmidt 1989; Skehan 1989; inter alia).

7.3   Conclusion

The development of tense-aspect inflectional morphology among second language learners represents an area of studies that is gaining rapid popularity for both theoretical and practical reasons. In this study, (1) I described the concept of tense-aspect in general and how it is represented in verbal morphology in Spanish and English, (2) I reviewed previous empirical studies on the acquisition of inflectional morphology in both L1 and L2 acquisition and potential theoretical accounts of how the process occurs (especially the lexical aspect hypothesis which has been used as the foundation for a large number of studies), and (3) I analyzed original data from classroom learners that bear on the development of L2 Spanish past tense marking (Preterite–Imperfect). The results of the analysis of the data — although far from conclusive — reveal that the strong version of the lexical aspect hypothesis (especially the Relevance Principle and the Congruence Principle) may represent an incomplete explanation of the development of L2 Spanish among L1 English speakers in an instructed setting — at least for the beginning stages. The present study appears to reveal more clearly a preliminary stage in the development of past tense verbal morphology in L2 Spanish that may not be accounted for in the framework provided by the lexical aspect hypothesis. It appears likely that modifications to the lexical aspect hypothesis — along the lines of the proposed default marker of past tense — would represent a viable way to develop a more comprehensive theoretical explanation of the processes behind the selection of past tense verbal morphology among L2 classroom learners.

Appendices

Appendix A
Transcription Conventions

Terminal pitch direction
Fall \
Rise /

Pause
Long ...
Medium ..
Short .

Vowel elongation
: colon following vowel indicates elongated vowel sound
:: extra colon indicates longer elongation

Additional symbols
(?) inaudible or unintelligible utterance

Appendix B
Psycho script

Please, conjugate the verbs in parentheses in the past tense:

1. El jefe _____**(1)**_____ (darle) dinero a la empleada para depositar en el banco.
    _____**(2)**_____ (Trabajar) para la compañía, pero no _____**(3)**_____ (estar)
    contenta y _____**(4)**_____ (querer) otro trabajo.

2. La mujer _____**(5)**_____ (hacer) las maletas y _____**(6)**_____ (poner) el dinero
    en la bolsa.

3. _____**(7)**_____ (Salir) de la ciudad en coche pero _____**(8)**_____ (tener) miedo
    de la policía. Por eso _____**(9)**_____ (buscar) un hotel.

4.   _____(10)_____ (Llegar) al Hotel Bates. _____(11)_____ (Pensar) que _____(12)_____ (ser) un lugar seguro. _____(13)_____ (Haber) una casa grande cerca. _____(14)_____ (Llover) mucho.

5.   _____(15)_____ (Conocer) a Norman. _____(16)_____ (Hablar) unos minutos, _____(17)_____ (escribir) su nombre y _____(18)_____ (tomar) la llave de su habitación.

6.   _____(19)_____ (Subir) a su habitación. _____(20)_____ (Tener) hambre, y _____(21)_____ (pensar) salir a cenar más tarde, pero _____(22)_____ (decidir) ducharse primero.

7.   Norman _____(23)_____ (estar) un poco loco porque su madre _____(24)_____ (estar) muerta. Entonces, Norman _____(25)_____ (disfrazarse) de su madre, y _____(26)_____ (entrar) a la habitación de la mujer.

8.   Mientras ella _____(27)_____ (ducharse) Norman _____(28)_____ (matarla).

Appendix C
Cloze (and editing) test

Please, conjugate verbs in parentheses in PAST TENSE. Words in italics have been translated.

Text 1: Yo _____(1)_____ (pensar) en ti Susana. Cuando _____(2)_____ (volar) *papalotes.* _____(3)_____ (oir) allá abajo el rumor del pueblo mientras _____(4)_____ (estar) encima de él, arriba de la *loma,* en tanto se nos _____(5)_____ (ir) el hilo del papalote *arrastrado* por el *viento.* 'Ayúdame, Susana.' Y unas manos suaves _____(6)_____ (apretarse) a mis manos. El aire nos _____(7)_____ (hacer) reír; _____(8)_____ (juntar) la mirada de nuestros ojos, mientras el *hilo* _____(9)_____ (correr) entre los dedos del viento, hasta que _____(10)_____ (romperse) con un "crack". Y allá arriba, el pájaro de papel _____(11)_____ (caer) arrastrando su *cola,* perdiéndose en el verde de la loma.

arrastrado = dragged   *cola = tail*   *dedos = fingers*
hilo = thread   *loma = hill*   *papalote = kite viento = wind*

Text 2: En su inseguro *sueño,* la imaginación le _____(12)_____ (reproducir) todo lo que había hecho aquella noche, desfigurándolo sin alterarlo en su esencia. _____(13)_____ (oir) el reloj de la catedral; _____(14)_____ (ver) con alegría a la *criada,* durmiendo en su cama. _____(15)_____ (salir) del cuarto muy despacio para no hacer ruido; _____(16)_____ (bajar) la escalera tan suavemente que no _____(17)_____ (mover) un pie hasta no estar segura de poder evitar el más imperceptible ruido. _____(18)_____ (salir) a la *huerta,* deteniéndose un momento para mirar al cielo.

criada = maid   *huerta = vegetable garden*
sueño = dream

Text 3: _____(19)_____ (Estar) despierto toda la noche después que _____(20)_____ (saber) la verdad sobre mi tía María. _____(21)_____ (Ser) horrible su muerte. _____(22)_____ (Vivir) su vida dedicada a los pobres y los _____(23)_____ (ayudar) desinteresadamente. ¡Qué irónico! _____(24)_____ (Ser) uno de ellos — a quienes tanto _____(25)_____ (ayudar) — quien la _____(26)_____ (matar). _____(27)_____ (Tener) sueños horribles toda la noche. Aunque _____(28)_____ (tomar) muchas píldoras no _____(29)_____ (poder) dormir. _____(30)_____ (Pensar) que tía María _____(31)_____ (volver) de la muerte, ... pero _____(32)_____ (ser) un sueño.Tia María _____(33)_____ (estar) muerta definitivamente.

Text 4: _____(34)_____ (oir) de vez en cuando el sonido de las palabras, y _____(35)_____ (notar) la diferencia. Porque las palabras que había oido — entonces lo _____(36)_____ (saber) — no _____(37)_____ (tener) ningún sonido, no _____(38)_____ (sonar); _____(39)_____ (sentirse); pero sin sonido, como las que se oyen durante los sueños. — ¿Quién será? — _____(40)_____ (preguntar) la mujer. — Quién sabe — _____(41)_____ (contestar) el hombre.

Appendix D
Academic background questionnaire (students)

(1) Academic experience with Spanish (_please, count present semester as 1_).
High School (in years): 1   2   3   4   5
College (in semesters): 1   2   3   4   5

(2) Have you ever traveled in a Spanish-speaking country?
Countries:
Length of time:
Use of Spanish (hours/day):
0   1–2   3–5   6 or more

(3) Did you have regular contact with Spanish while you were growing up?
(a) all the time   (b) at home   (c) at school   (d) never

(4) How many hours (**average per week**) do you devote to studying Spanish? Please, circle one:
0–2   3–5   6–8   9 or more

(5) On a scale from 1 to 5 (lowest to highest), how do you rate your proficiency in Spanish?
(Low) 1   2   3   4   5   (High)

(6) Do you use Spanish outside of class? Please specify (e.g. friends, family, associations, etc.)

Appendix E
Post-test questionnaire (volunteers)

(1) Which is your native language?

(2) What other languages do you speak fluently?

(3) What other languages have you studied?

(4) Why are you studying Spanish? Please, circle one:
     (a) requirement   (b) personal interest (c) both

(5) Are you planning to use your knowledge of Spanish in the future?
     (a) very much so (b) once in a while   (c) not likely   (d) never

(6) How do you think your knowledge of Spanish will be useful? (may circle more than one)
     (a) business purposes (b) family/friends (c)job placement/improvement

(7) Has classroom training in Spanish been useful (have you learned Spanish)?

(8) Do you think you can communicate (e.g. negotiate prices, order a meal, etc.) using only Spanish with ...
     –   your teacher
     –   a classmate
     –   a native speaker of Spanish on the street

(9) Can you guess what specific structures of Spanish grammar the researcher is studying?

(10) Were the tasks difficult? Please explain.
     –   Movie narrative:
     –   Retell of the students' narrative:
     –   Joint problem solving task:
     –   Interview

(11) Were the tasks interesting or enjoyable?

(12) Did you learn anything from your participation in this study?

(13) Would you like to get further information about the study?

Appendix F
Academic Background Questionnaire (natives)

(1) ¿Cuál es tu lengua materna (lengua que aprendiste hasta los 5/6 años de edad)? (Puedes marcar más de una si eres bilingüe desde la infancia))

(2) ¿Cuántas lenguas hablas aparte de español? Por favor, marca tu conocimiento en cada una usando una escala de 1 (muy poco) a 5 (excelente dominio)

(3) Si sabes inglés, ¿cómo lo aprendiste? (puedes marcar más de una opción)
(a) escuela o liceo (b) instituto de lenguas (c) viajes al extranjero (d) autodidacta (e) familia o amigos

(4) En una escala de 1 (muy poco) a 5 (excelente) califica tu conocimiento de idioma español:
1   2   3   4   5

(5) En una escala de 1 (casi nunca) a 5 (casi siempre) determina la frecuencia con la cual escribes en español:
1   2   3   4   5

(6) En una escala de 1 (casi nunca) a 5 (casi siempre) determina la frecuencia con la cual lees libros en español:
1   2   3   4   5

Appendix G
Movie plots

Alone and hungry

A young woman in ragged clothes walks by a bakery at the same time that a bakery worker is unloading bread from a truck. The young woman steals a loaf of bread and flees the scene. The employee pursues the lady until they bump into Charlie Chaplin. Chaplin says he was the thief and he is arrested by the police. Subsequently a lady who saw the events tells the police that the lady was the thief and not Chaplin. The lady is taken by the police and Charlie is set free. Charlie goes to a cafeteria and eats two trays of food without paying. The police arrests him and he is taken by the police car. A few minutes later the police car stops to pick up the young lady Charlie had tried to save before. After Charlie and the young lady exchange smiles the police car has an accident and everyone is on the street. Charlie and the young lady escape while the policeman is unconscious on the floor.

At the department store

Charlie Chaplin is hired as a night guardian at a department store. At night she brings a woman whom he has befriended in the previous film clip. They visit various sections of the store, they eat cake, and they smoke cigars. After a while the woman goes to sleep and Chaplin goes to check the store is closed. In the meantime some thiefs break into the store. They see Chaplin and they fire their guns. The shots hit a big barrel of rum above Chaplin. Charlie Chaplin ends up getting drunk because he drinks most of the liquid coming out of the barrel. The next morning Chaplin's friend wakes up and realizing how late it was flees the scene. In the meantime a customer in search for a piece of fabric discovers Charlie with a hangover under a huge piece of fabric. The police comes in and arrests Charlie.

Appendix H
Sample narratives: Alone and Hungry (time 1)

SPA112 student

NNS: Ayer uh uh en el medio de la día un mujer necesita uhm <u>necesita</u> … uhm un comida .. uhm así tom- uhm así <u>tomá</u> un uh how do you say bread?
R: pan
NNS: toma un pan de una …
R: camión? truck?
NNS: de un camión que fue uh uh que <u>fue está dando</u> .. pan a la tienda uhm uhm .. un otro mujer uhm uhm <u>míro</u> uhm uhm la mujer y uhm uhm <u>apeló</u> a un policía yeah un policía uhm la la mujer uhm co- <u>corré</u> y uhm …
R: eh tropezar es el verbo tropezar
NNS: y tropezar <u>tropezá</u> en en un .. hombre uhm ellos … (gesture)
R: caer?
NNS: ellos caer <u>caé</u> uh y uhm la policía uh uh uhm la policía uh .. (inaudible) la policía (inaudible) la policía le no la los <u>busquéa</u> uhm el hombre el hombre <u>dice</u> a la policía que uhm uhm él uh to- <u>tomá</u> el pan uhm uhm después el otro mujer uhm <u>dice</u> la policía no la mujer <u>toma</u> el pan uhm uhm la policía uhm to- tomá la tomá la <u>tomá</u> y después la .. el hombre uh va a un <u>va</u> a un restaurante y .. y comé <u>comó</u> un una muy grande comida y uh uhm no <u>pagó</u> Así un policía tomá el no <u>tomá</u> en el
R: camión
NNS: camión de la policía la mujer y el y el hombre uhm uhm … y el hombre ni el de y el hombre se le cada otro cada otro uh fall out
R: caerse es el verbo
NNS: caer uhm .. ellos caén ellos <u>caén</u> el vehículo y cuan la policía (laugh) .. la policía <u>son</u> inconsciente por un poco tiempo y el hombre y uh la mujer <u>corren</u>.

NOTE: NNS: Nonnative speaker
               R: Researcher

SPA123 Student

NNS: <u>Fue</u> una muchacha .. <u>robió</u> un autobus de pan. La dueño del autobús de pan .. <u>es</u> muy furioso y uhm la muchacha uhm <u>corrieron</u> a la calle uhm y la dueño co- <u>corrió</u> después de ella y uhm el Chaplin oh! cuando el dueño encuen- encuentre <u>encontró</u> la muchacha uhm Chaplin <u>dije</u> que él uhm .. uhm <u>dije</u> que él robió el autobús de pan y él él <u>dije</u> la muchacha no <u>robió</u> el pan y uhm .. then la policía <u>venía</u> y uhm … aaaah <u>tenía</u> y … ahm lle- lle- I'm trying to ?? the past tense <u>llevaba</u> Chaplin a la carcel para <u>creía</u> que Chaplin <u>robió</u> el pan. Uhm, la muchacha uhm <u>caminaba</u> por la calle en el otro direcc- de la policía y … uhm .. an- después de una muchacha otro de la muchacha de <u>robió</u> el pan <u>veí</u> uhm .. la muchacha <u>veí</u> la policía <u>tomaba</u> Chaplin a la carcel y <u>dije</u> que no <u>es</u> Chaplin <u>es</u> la muchacha si? uhm uhm sí pues la policía <u>corrieron</u> a la muchacha por la calle y .. I can't remember what hapenned (Hx) y oh but pero no: uhm no no to- <u>tomaba</u> a la carcel la muchacha y Chaplin uhm cuando: uhm cuando él con la policía <u>robió</u> la tienda/ otra/ y: <u>tomaba</u> uhm how do you say cigarettes?

R: Cigarros

NNS: Cigarros y uhm .. y después what's (???) again?

R: Eh almacén

NNS: y postales y so y <u>robió</u> la tienda otro y la policía uhm <u>tiene</u> uhm … uhm <u>tiene</u> tomar a la carcel pero … uhm (laugh) .. porque Chaplin quiero <u>querío</u> ir a la carcel para uhm ver la muchacha y uhm … so then/ en el automo- autobús que: <u>ir</u> a la carcel con los criminales en el autobús y uhm Chaplin <u>veía</u> la muchacha y la muchacha <u>se encanta</u> con Chaplin porque uhm él <u>dije</u> que ella no <u>es</u> la criminal uhm después lo dos los dos uhm .. <u>corrieran</u> a la autobús de criminales y uhm cae caien fall <u>caien</u> en la calle y de-<u>decidieron</u> uhm correran uhm de la policía.

SPA203 student

NNS: Ayer uhm <u>había</u> una mujer pobre que <u>quería</u> el pan y ella <u>robó</u> el pan de una un una camión en la calle y una otra mujer uh la la <u>vió</u> y ella le <u>dijo</u> a la policia Ch. la <u>vió</u> también y Ch. dijo le dijo le <u>dijo</u> al a la policía que uhm .. él <u>robó</u>/ el pan pero la mujer le <u>dijo</u> al policia que <u>fue</u> la mujer y entonces la policía <u>tomó</u> la la mujer en uh .. su .. coche para ir a la estación y .. entonces fui <u>fue</u> a un restaurante y <u>comió</u> mucho pero no <u>pagó</u> la cuenta y <u>dijo</u> le <u>dijo</u> a un policía que no <u>podía</u> pagar la cuenta y la policía uhm .. lo <u>tomó</u> uh y .. Ch. uhm <u>entró</u> al coche también y entonces Ch. y la mujer <u>se</u> <u>encontraron</u> y .. uh … <u>estaban</u> contentos <u>había</u> un una confrontación entre las personas en el coche y Ch. y la policía y la mujer <u>se cayeron</u>/ y .. no .. en la calle y uh la policía no .. la policeia <u>se sentía</u> mal no .. estaba <u>estaba</u> durmiendo y Ch. y la mujer <u>se fueron</u> y .. uh es todo.

SPA311 student

NNS: El cuento <u>empezó</u> en una panadería y <u>vino</u> un camión que con un hombre que <u>traía</u> la el pan para la panadería. Mientras él <u>estaba</u> por la tienda una mujer <u>vino</u> que y ella <u>tenía</u> mucha hambre y ella <u>decidió</u> robar uh un pedazo de pan del camión, entonces después de robar un pedazo de pan ella se <u>marchó</u> pero <u>había</u> una testiga uh y ella y ella <u>dijo</u> al hombre que que la mujer ro- <u>robó</u> un pedazo de pan de de su camión entonces el hombre uh <u>corrió</u> uh para para buscar la mujer que <u>robó</u> el el pan. mientras la mujer estaba corriendo ella se encontró con Ch.Ch. y él estaba caminando uh en la otra dirección y los dos <u>se chocaron</u> y y Ch. Ch. <u>tomó</u> el pedazo de pan de la mujer entonces mientras mientras las dos los dos <u>estaban</u> allí <u>vinieron</u> el hombre con uh con la policía y y … qué más? ah! el hombre <u>acusó</u> a uno de uno de los dos de robar un pedazo de pan. Entonces Ch. Ch. <u>dijo</u> a la policía que que que yo ten- uh yo <u>tuvo</u> la culpa, yo <u>robó</u> el pedazo de pan entonces uh uh la policía uh … uh se <u>se detuvo</u> a a Ch. Ch. y uh puso se puso <u>lo puso</u> en el camión de la policía. pero después <u>vino</u> la mujer que uh uh la testiga que <u>vió</u> todo y ella <u>dijo</u> al hombre que <u>era</u> la mujer que <u>robó</u> el pedazo de pan. Entonces, el hombre uh el chofer del camión <u>corrió</u> para encontrar la policía y él <u>explicó</u> a la policía que no <u>era</u> Ch. Ch. pero <u>era</u> la mujer, entonces la policía uhm <u>regresaron</u> para uh para detener a la la mujer uh … let's see mientras tanto Ch. Ch. <u>se fue</u> y uh <u>fue</u> a una cafetería y él <u>estaba</u> ahí comiendo todo lo que lo que <u>quería</u> uhm .. pero después de comer descubrió que que no tenía mucha din- que no tenía ninguna dinero ningún dinero uh y entonces él llamó, él gritó uh para que viniera la policía y la policía vino y Ch. Ch. dijo al al empleado de la de la cafetería que la policía iba a pagar su su cuenta. Ah, entonces la policía uh estaba muy enfadado y uh .. dijo que que sí pagaba la cuenta pero tenía que detenerse a Ch. Ch. Ah .. entonces uh se detuvo a Ch. Ch. y uh uh lo puso en en el camión de la policía y .. qué pasó? Oh! no no no uh .. la policía y Ch. Ch. salió uh .. salió de la tien- de la cafetería y y lapolicía fue a buscar un teléfono para llamar al camión de policía para que viniera a recoger recoger Ch.Ch., entonces mientras la policía estaba en el teléfono Ch. Ch. descubrió una tienda pequeña que tenían revistas y cigarros y él decidí comprar una revista y unos cigarros y decidió comprar un cigarro para un un niño que vió ahí uh uh y después cuando la policía terminó con su conversación en el en el teléfono descubrió que Ch. Ch. uh uh había comprado las cosas que uhm .. que él no podía pagar porque (laugh) Ch. Ch. no podía pagar la cuenta de nuevo entonces la policía tenía que pa- pagar por todas las cosas que Ch. Ch, compró. Ah por fin, vinio el camión de policía y uh .. uh lo lo puso a Ch. Ch. en el camión y había otros criminales ahí, uh un borracho y un viejo y unos ladrones y entonces se fueron de ahí y y procedieron a otra esquina donde recogió la mujer que originalmente robó el pedazo de pan del camión uhm .. uhm entonces cuando la mujer entró en el camión los dos empezaron a discutir como podrian escapar y Ch. Ch, .. le sugirió que había una manera en que podrían escapar y .. uh .. no sé exactamente pero el, .. ah sí los dos uhm uh se se pusieron a a un lado de del camión entonces éste causó el camión a su lado en la calle uhm ... y el el chofer del camión de policía se se se puso inconsciente/

R: Sí, perder la consciencia

NNS: Entonces uhm uh los dos tenían la oportunidad de escapar y y la mujer uh Ch. Ch. dijo a la mujer que que si tú puedes escapar vayate entonces la mujer corrió a la esquina pero ella paró y gritó a Ch. Ch. que tú puedes escapar conmigo entonces Ch. Ch, uh se escapó con ella y eso eso termina sí.

References

Andersen, R. 1986. El desarrollo de la morfología verbal en el español como segundo idioma. In *Adquisición del Lenguaje — Acquisição da Linguagem*, edited by J. Meisel. Frankfurt: Klaus-Dieter Vervuert Verlag.

Andersen, R. 1989. The theoretical status of variation in interlanguage development. In *Variation in Second Language Acquisition Volume II: Psycholinguistic Issues*, edited by S. Gass, C. Madden, D. Preston and L. Selinker. Clevedon, Avon: Multilingual Matters.

Andersen, R. 1990. Models, processes, principles and strategies: second language acquisition inside and outside the classroom. In *Second Language Acquisition-Foreign Language Learning*, edited by B. VanPatten and J. Lee. Bristol: Multilingual Matters Ltd.

Andersen, R. 1991. Developmental sequences: the emergence of aspect marking in second language acquisition. In *Crosscurrents in Second Language Acquisition and Linguistic Theories*, edited by T. Huebner and C. A. Ferguson. Amsterdam: John Benjamins.

Andersen, R. 1994. The insider's advantage. In *Italiano lingua seconda/lingua straniera*, edited by A. Giacalone-Ramat and M. Vedovelli. Rome: Bulzoni.

Andersen, R., and Y. Shirai. 1996. The primacy of aspect in first and second language acquisition: the pidgin-creole connection. In *Handbook of Second Language Acquisition*, edited by B. Laufer and W. Ritchie: Academic Press.

Andersen, R, and Y. Shirai. 1994. Discourse motivations for some cognitive acquisition principles. *Studies in Second Language Acquisition* 16: 133–156.

Antinucci, F., and R. Miller. 1976. How children talk about what happened. *Journal of Child Language* 3: 169–189.

Bardovi-Harlig, K. 1992. The relationship of form and meaning: a cross sectional study of tense and aspect in the interlanguage of learners of English as a second language. *Applied Psycholinguistics* 13: 253–278.

Bardovi-Harlig, K. 1994. Anecdote or evidence? Evaluating support for hypotheses concerning the development of tense and aspect. In *Research Methodology in Second-Language Acquisition*, edited by E. Tarone, S. Gass and A. Cohen. Hillsdale, NJ: Lawrence Erlbaum.

Bardovi-Harlig, K. 1995a. A narrative perspective on the development of the tense/aspect system in second language acquisition. *Studies in Second Language Acquisition* 17: 263–289.

Bardovi-Harlig, K. 1995b. The interaction of pedagogy and natural sequences in the acquisition of tense and aspect. In *Second language acquisition theory and pedagogy*, edited by F. Eckman, D. Highland, P. Lee, J. Mileham and R. Rutkowski. Mahwah, NJ: Laurence Erlbaum.

Bardovi-Harlig, K. 1997. Narrative structure and lexical aspect: competing or conspiring factors in the second language acquisition of tense/aspect morphology? Paper read at Cornell University, at Ithaca, NY.

Bardovi-Harlig, K., and A. Bergström. 1996. Acquisition of tense and aspect in second language and foreign language learning: learner narratives in ESL and FFL. *Canadian Modern Language Review* 52: 308–330.

Bardovi-Harlig, K, and D. Reynolds. 1995. The role of lexical aspect in the acquisition of tense and aspect. *TESOL Quarterly* 29: 107–131.

Bayley, R. 1994. Interlanguage variation and the quantitaive paradigm: past tense marking in Chinese-English. In *Research Methodology in Second-Language Acquisition*, edited by E. Tarone, S. Gass and A. Cohen. Hillsdale, NJ: Lawrence Erlbaum.

Bergström, A. 1995. The expression of past temporal reference by English-speaking learners of French. Unpublished Ph.D. dissertation, The Pennsylvania State University.

Bialystok, E. 1988. Psycholinguistic dimensions of second language proficiency. In *Grammar and Second Language Teaching*, edited by W. Rutherford and W. Sharwood-Smith. Rowley, MA: Newbury House.

Bickerton, D. 1981. *Roots of Language*. Ann Arbor, MI: Karoma Publishers.

Binnick, R. J. 1991. *Time and the Verb*. Oxford: Blackwell.

Birdsong, D. 1989. *Metalinguistic Performance and Interlinguistic Competence*. Berlin: Springer-Verlag.

Birdsong, D. 1992. Ultimate attainment in second language acquisition. *Language* 68: 706–755.

Bley-Vroman, R. 1989. The logical problem of second language learning. In *Linguistic Perspectives on Second Language Learning*, edited by S. Gass and J. Schachter. Cambridge: Cambridge University Press.

Bley-Vroman, R. 1991. Processing constraints on acquisition and the parsing of ungrammatical sentences. In *Point Counterpoint: Universal Grammar in the Second Language*, edited by L. Eubank. Amsterdam: John Benjamins.

Bloom, L., Lifter, K., and J. Hafitz. 1980. Semantics of verbs and the development of verb inflection in child language. *Language* 56: 386–412.

Bloom, L., and L. Harner. 1989. On the developmental contour of child language: A reply to Smith & Weist. *Journal of Child Language* 16: 207–216.

Blyth, C. 1997. A constructivist approach to grammar: teaching teachers to teach aspect. *Modern Language Journal* 81 (i): 50–66.

Bolinger, D. 1963. Reference and inference: inceptiveness in the Spanish preterite. *Hispania* 46: 128–135.

Bronckart, J. P., and H. Sinclair. 1973. Time, tense, and aspect. *Cognition* 2: 107–130.

Brown, R. 1973. *A First Language: The Early Stages*. Cambridge, MA: Harvard University Press.

Buczowska, E., and R. Weist. 1991. The effects of formal instruction on the second language acquisition of temporal location. *Language Learning* 41: 535–554.

Bull, W. 1960. *Time, Tense and the Verb*. Berkeley: University of California Press.

Bull, W. 1965. *Spanish for Teachers: Applied Linguistics*. New York: The Royal Press Company.

Bybee, J. 1985. *Morphology: a Study of the Relation between Meaning and Form*. Philadelphia: John Benjamins.

Bybee, J. 1995. Spanish tense and aspect from a typological perspective. In *Studies in Language Learning and Spanish Linguistics*, edited by P. Hashemipour, R. Maldonado and M. van Naerssen. New York: McGraw Hill.

Bybee, J., and O. Dahl. 1989. The creation of tense and aspect systems in the languages of the world. *Studies in Language* 13: 51–103.

Carter, R., and M. McCarthy. 1995. Grammar and the spoken language. *Applied Linguistics* 16: 141–157.

Chafe, W., ed. 1980. *The Pear Stories: Cognitive, Cultural, and Linguistic Aspects of Narrative Production*. Norwood, NJ: Ablex.

Chomsky, N. 1959. A review of B. F. Skinner's Verbal Behavior. *Language* 35: 26–58.

Christie, K., and J. Lantolf. 1992. The ontological status of learner grammaticality judgments in UG approaches to L2 acquisition. *Rassegna Italiana de Linguistica Applicata* 24 (3): 31–52.

Chung, S., and A. Timberlake. 1985. Tense, aspect, and mood. In *Language Typology and Syntactic Description III: Grammatical Categories and the Lexicon*, edited by T. Shopen. Cambridge: Cambridge University Press.

Clark, E. 1985. The acquisition of Romance, with special reference to French. In *The Crosslinguistic Study of Language Acquisition, Vol. 1*, edited by D. Slobin. Hillsdale, NJ: Lawrence Erlbaum.

Clark, E. 1987. The principle of contrast: a contrast on language acquisition. In *Mechanisms of Language Acquisition*, edited by B. MacWhinney. Hillsdale, NJ: Laurence Erlbaum.

Clements, J. 1985. Verb classification and verb class change in Spanish. Unpublished Ph.D. dissertation, University of Washington, Seattle, WA.

Comrie, B. 1976. *Aspect*. Cambridge: Cambridge University Press.

Coppieters, R. 1987. Competence differences between native and near-native speakers. *Language* 63: 544–573.

Cowan, R., and Y. Hatasa. 1994. Investigating the validity and reliability of native speaker and second-language learner judgments about sentences. In *Research Methodology in Second-Language Acquisition*, edited by E. Tarone, S. Gass and A. Cohen. Hillsdale, NJ: Lawrence Erlbaum.

Crookes, G., and R. Schmidt. 1989. Motivation: reopening the research agenda. *University of Hawai'i Working Papers in English as a Second Language* 8: 217–256.

Cziko, G. A., and K. Koda. 1987. A Japanese child's use of stative and punctual verbs. *Journal of Child Language* 14: 99–111.

Dahl, O. 1985. *Tense and aspect systems.* Oxford: Basil Blackwell.

Davies, W., and T. Kaplan. 1998. Native speaker vs. L2 learner grammaticality judgments. *Applied Linguistics* 19: 183–203.

de Lemos, C. 1981. Interactional processes in the child's construction of language. In *The child's construction of language,* edited by W. Deutsch. London: Academic Press.

de Miguel, E. 1992. *El Aspecto en la Sintaxis del Español: Perfectividad e Imperfectividad.* Madrid: Ediciones de la Universidad Autónoma de Madrid.

DeKeyser, R. 1994. Learning second language grammar rules: an experiment with a miniature linguistic system. *Studies in Second Language Acquisition* 17: 379–410.

DeKeyser, R. 1996. Critical period phenomena as a function of verbal aptitude. Paper read at SLRF 1996, at University of Arizona, Tucson, AZ.

DeKeyser, R. 1998. Beyond focus on form: cognitive perspectives on learning and practicing second language grammar. In *Focus on Form in Classroom Second Language Acquisition,* edited by C. Doughty and J. Williams. New York: Cambridge University Press.

Delgado-Jenkins, H. 1990. Imperfect vs. preterit: a new approach. *Hispania* 73: 1145–1146.

Depraetre, I. 1995. On the necessity of distinguishing between (un)boundedness and (a)telicity. *Linguistics and Philosophy* 18: 1–19.

Desclés, Jean-P. 1989. State, event, process, and typology. *General Linguistics* 29 (3):159–200.

Dietrich, R., W. Klein, and C. Noyau. 1995. *The Acquisition of Temporality in a Second Language.* Philadelphia, PA: John Benjamins.

Dowty, D. 1972. *Studies in the Logic of Verb Aspect and Time Reference in English.* Austin: University of Texas.

Dowty, D. 1979. *Word Meaning and Montague Grammar.* Dordrecht: D. Reidel.

Dowty, D. 1986. The effects of aspectual class on the temporal structure of discourse: semantics or pragmatics? *Linguistics and Philosophy* 9: 37–61.

Dry, H. 1983. The movement of narrative time. *Journal of Literary Semantics* 12: 19–53.

Ellis, N. 1996. Sequencing in SLA: phonological memory, chunking and points of order. *Studies in Second Language Acquisition* 18: 91–126.

Ellis, R. 1987. Interlanguage variability in narrative discourse: style shifting in the use of the past tense. *Studies in Second Language Acquisition* 9: 1–20.

Ellis, R. 1991. Grammaticality judgments and second language acquisition. *Studies in Second Language Acquisition* 13: 161–186.

Ellis, R. 1997. Item versus system learning: explaining free variation. Paper read at Annual Meeting of AAAL 1997, at Orlando, FL.

Ericsson, K., and H. Simon. 1984. *Protocol Analysis: Verbal Reports as Data.* Cambridge, MA: MIT Press.

Faerch, C., and G. Kasper, eds. 1987. *Introspection in Second Language Research.* Clevedon: Multilingual Matters.

Fantuzzi, C. 1996. The acquisition of tense and temporal reference. Paper read at Twentieth Boston University Conference on Language Development, at Boston, MA.

Fleischman, S. 1989. Temporal distance: a basic linguistic metaphor. *Studies in Language* 13: 1–50.

Fleischman, S. 1990. *Tense and Narrativity.* London: Routledge.

Flynn, S., and S. Manuel. 1991. Age-dependent effects in language acquisition: an evaluation of 'critical period' hypotheses. In *Point Counterpoint: UG in the Second Language*, edited by L. Eubank. Philadelphia, PA: John Benjamins.

Frantzen, D. 1995. Preterite/Imperfect half-truths: problems with Spanish textbook rules for usage. *Hispania* 78: 145–158.

Frawley, W. 1992. *Linguistic Semantics.* Hillsdale, NJ: Lawrence Erlbaum.

Frawley, W., and J. Lantolf. 1984. Speaking and self-order: a critique of orthodox L2 research. *Studies in Second Language Acquisition* 6: 143–159.

Frawley, W, and J. Lantolf. 1985. Second language discourse: a Vygotskyan perspective. *Applied Linguistics* 6: 19–44.

García, E., and F. vanPutte. 1988. The value of contrast: contrasting the value of strategies. *IRAL* 26: 263–281.

Garey, H. 1957. Verbal aspect in French. *Language* 33: 91–110.

Gass, S. 1994. The reliability of second-language grammaticality judgments. In *Research Methodology in Second-Language Acquisition*, edited by E. Tarone, S. Gass and A. Cohen. Hillsdale, NJ: Lawrence Erlbaum.

Gass, S., and J. Ard. 1984. Second language acquisition and the ontology of language universals. In *Language Universals and Second Language Acquisition*, edited by W. Rutherford. Amsterdam: John Benjamins.

Giacalone-Ramat, A. 1992. Grammaticalization processes in the area of temporal and modal relations. *Studies in Second Language Acquisition* 14: 297–322.

Giorgi, A., and F. Pianesi. 1997. *Tense and Aspect: From semantics to morphosyntax.* Oxford: Oxford University Press.

Givón, T. 1982. Tense-aspect-modality: The Creole prototype and beyond. In *Tense-Aspect: Between Semantics and Pragmatics*, edited by P. J. Hopper. Amsterdam: John Benjamins.

Goldowsky, B., and E. Newport. 1992. Modelling the effects of processing limitations on the acquisition of morphology: the less is more hypothesis. In *The Proceedings of the 24th Annual Child Language Research Forum*, edited by E. Clark. Stanford, CA: Center for the Study of Language and Information.

Gonzalez, P. 1995. Progressive and nonprogressive imperfects in Spanish discourse. *Hispanic Linguistics* 7: 61–92.

Goss, N, Z. Ying-Hua, and J. Lantolf. 1994. Two heads may be better than one: mental activity in second-language grammaticality judgments. In *Research Methodology in Second-Language Acquisition*, edited by E. Tarone, S. Gass and A. Cohen. Hillsdale, NJ: Lawrence Erlbaum.

Guitart, J. 1978. Aspects of Spanish aspect: a new look at the preterit/imperfect distinction. In *Contemporary Studies in Romance Linguistics*, edited by M. Suñer. Washington, DC: Georgetown University Press.

Guitart, J. 1995. Preterit and imperfect in a nutshell. Unpublished Manuscript, SUNY Buffalo.

Harley, B. 1989. Functional grammar in French immersion: a classroom experiment. *Applied Linguistics* 10: 331–359.

Hasbún, L. 1995. The role of lexical aspect in the acquisition of the tense/aspect system in L2 Spanish. Unpublished Ph.D. dissertation, Indiana University, Bloomington.

Hatch, E., and A. Lazaraton. 1991. *The Research Manual: Design and Statistics for Applied Linguistics*. New York: Newbury House.

Hernán, L. 1994. VIPI, Visualización del pretérito y del imperfecto. *Hispania* 77–2: 280–286.

Hernandez Pina, F. 1984. *Teorías Psicolingüísticas y su Aplicación a la Adquisición del Español como Lengua Materna*. Madrid: Siglo XXI.

Hernanz, M. 1991. Spanish absolute constructions and aspect. *Catalan Working Papers in Linguistics* 4: 45–92.

Hopper, P. 1979. Aspect and foregrounding in discourse. In *Syntax and Semantics. Vol. 12*, edited by T. Givón. New York: Academic Press.

Hopper, P. 1982. *Tense-Aspect: Between Syntax and Pragmatics*. Philadelphia: John Benjamins.

Housen, A. 1994. Tense and aspect in second language learning: the Dutch interlanguage of a native speaker of English. In *Tense and Aspect in Discourse*, edited by C. Vet and C. Vetters. Berlin: Mouton de Gruyter.

Huebner, T. 1995. The effect of overseas language programs: report on a case study of an intensive Japanese course. In *Second Language Acquisition in a Study Abroad Context*, edited by B. Freed. Amsterdam/Philadelphia: John Benjamins.

Hulstijn, J., and W. Hulstijn. 1984. Grammatical errors as a function of processing constraints and explicit knowledge. *Language Learning* 34: 23–43.

Jacobsen, T. 1986. ¿Aspecto antes que tiempo? Una mirada a la adquisición temprana del español. In *Adquisición de lenguaje. Aquisição da linguagem*, edited by J. M. Meisel. Frankfurt: Vervuert.

Jakobson, R. 1957. Shifters, verbal categories, and the Russian verb. In *Selected Writings, Volume 2: Word and Language*, edited by R. Jakobson. The Hague: Mouton.

Johnson, K. 1996. *Language Teaching and Skill Learning*. Oxford: Blackwell.

Jourdenais, R. 1996. The limitations of think-alouds. Paper read at Annual Meeting of AAAL 1996, at Chicago, IL.

Jourdenais, R, M. Ota, S. Stauffer, B. Boyson, and C. Doughty. 1995. Does textual enhancement promote noticing? a think aloud protocol analysis. In *Attention and Awareness in Foreign Language Learning*, edited by R. Schmidt. Honolulu, HI: University of Hawai'i.

Kachru, Y. 1995. Cultural meaning and rhetorical styles: toward a framework for contrastive rhetoric. In *Principle and Practice in Applied Linguistics. Studies in*

Honor of H. G. Widdowson, edited by G. Cook and B. Seidlhofer. Oxford: Oxford University Press.

Kamp, H., and C. Rohrer. 1983. Tense in texts. In *Meaning, Use and Interpretation of Language*, edited by R. Bäuerle, C. Schwarze and A. von Steechow. Berlin: Walter de Gruyter.

Kaplan, M. 1987. Developmental patterns of past tense acquisition among foreign language learners of French. In *Foreign Language Learning: A Research Perspective*, edited by B. VanPatten. Rowley, MA: Newbury House.

Karmiloff-Smith, A. 1986. From metaprocesses to conscious access: evidence from children's metalinguistic and repair data. *Cognition* 23: 95–147.

Kellerman, E. 1979. Transfer and non-transfer: where are we now? *Studies in Second Language Acquisition* 2: 37–57.

Kenny, A. 1963. *Action, Emotion and Will*. New York: Springer.

Klein, E. 1995. Evidence for a 'wild' L2 grammar: when PPs rear their empty heads. *Applied Linguistics* 16 (1): 87–117.

Klein, W. 1986. *Second Language Acquisition*. Cambridge: Cambridge University Press.

Klein, W. 1990. A theory of language acquisition is not so easy. *Studies in Second Language Acquisition* 12: 219–231.

Klein, W. 1994. *Time in Language*. London: Routledge.

Klein, W. 1995. A time-relational analysis of Russian aspect. *Language* 71: 669–695.

Klein, W., R. Dietrich, and C. Noyau. 1995. Conclusions. In *The Acquisition of Temporality in a Second Language*, edited by R. Dietrich, W. Klein and C. Noyau. Philadelphia, PA: John Benjamins.

Klein, W., and C. Perdue, eds. 1992. *Utterance structure: Developing Grammars Again*. Amsterdam: John Benjamins.

Kramsch, C. 1986. From language proficiency to interactional competence. *Modern Language Journal* 70: 366–372.

Krashen, S. 1982. *Principles and Practice in Second Language Acquisition*. New York: Pergamon Press.

Krashen, S., and T. Terrell. 1983. *The Natural Approach: Language Acquisition in the Classroom*. Oxford: Pergamon.

Krasinski, E. 1995. The development of past marking in a bilingual child and the punctual-nonpunctual distinction. *First Language* 15: 239–276.

Kuczaj, S. 1989. On the search for universals of language acquisition: a commentary on Cziko. *First Language* 9: 39–44.

Kumpf, L. 1984. Temporal systems and universality in interlanguage: A case study. In *Universals of Second Language Acquisition*, edited by F. R. Eckman, L. H. Bell and D. Nelson. Rowley, MA: Newbury House.

Labov, W. 1972. *Sociolinguistic Patterns*. Philadelphia: University of Pennsylvania Press.

Lafford, B. 1996. The development of tense/aspect relations in L2 Spanish narratives: evidence to test competing theories. Paper read at SLRF 96, at Tucson, AZ.

Langacker, R. 1982. Remarks on English aspect. In *Tense-Aspect: Between Syntax and Pragmatics*, edited by P. Hopper. Philadelphia: John Benjamins.

Lantolf, P., and G. Appel. 1994. Theoretical framework: an introduction to Vygotskian perspectives on second language research. In *Vygotskian Approaches to Second Language Research*, edited by P. Lantolf and G. Appel. Norwood, NJ: Ablex.

Leeman, J., I. Arteagoitia, B. Fridman, and C. Doughty. 1995. Integrating attention to form with meaning: Focus on form in content-based Spanish instruction. In *Attention and Awareness in Foreign Language Learning*, edited by R. Schmidt. Honolulu, HI: University of Hawai'i.

Levy, E., and K. Nelson. 1994. Words in discourse: a dialectical approach to the acquisition of meaning and use. *Journal of Child Language* 21: 367–389.

Lightbown, P. 1987. Classroom language as input to second language acquisition. In *First and Second Language Acquisition Processes*, edited by C. W. Pfaff. Cambridge, MA: Newbury House.

Liskin-Gasparro, J. 1996. Narrative strategies: a case study of developing storytelling skills by a learner of Spanish. *Modern Language Journal* 80: 271–286.

Liskin-Gasparro, J. 1997. The acquisition of temporality in Spanish oral narratives: exploring learners' perceptions. Paper read at Annual Meeting of AAAL 97, at Orlando, FL.

Long, M., and P. Robinson. 1998. Focus on form: theory, research, and practice. In *Focus on Form in Classroom Second Language Acquisition*, edited by C. Doughty and J. Williams. New York: Cambridge University Press.

Loschky, L., and R. Bley-Vroman. 1993. Grammar and task-based methodology. In *Tasks and Language Learning: Integrating Theory and Practice*, edited by G. Crookes and S. Gass. Clevedon, GB: Multilingual Matters Ltd.

Lunn, P. 1985. The aspectual lens. *Hispanic Linguistics* 2: 49–61.

Lyons, J. 1968. *Introduction to Theoretical Linguistics*. Cambridge: Cambridge University Press.

Maingueneau, D. 1994. *L'Enonciation en Linguistique Française*. Paris: Hachette.

Mapstone, E., and P. Harris. 1985. Is the English progressive unique? *Journal of Child Language* 12: 431–441.

McCarthy, M. 1991. *Discourse Analysis for Language Teachers*. New York: Cambridge University Press.

McLaughlin, B. 1990. Restructuring. *Applied Linguistics* 11: 113–128.

Meisel, J. 1987. Reference to past events and actions in the development of natural second language acquisition. In *First and Second Language Acquisition*, edited by C. Pfaff. New York: Newbury House.

Minium, E., and R. Clarke. 1982. *Elements of Statistical Reasoning*. New York, NY: Wiley and Sons.

Montrul, S., and R. Salaberry. forthcoming. The development of Spanish past tense morphology: Developing a research agenda. In *Studies in Spanish Second Language Acquisition: State of the Science*, edited by B. Lafford and R. Salaberry. Washington, DC: Georgetown University Press.

Morales, A. 1989. Manifestaciones de pasado en niños puertorriqueños de 2–6 años. *Revista de Lingüística Teórica y Aplicada* 27: 115–131.

Mourelatos, A. 1981. Events, processes, and states. In *Syntax and Semantics, vol. 14: Tense and Aspect*, edited by P. Tedeschi and A. Zaenen. New York: Academic Press.

Musatti, T., and M. Orsolini. 1993. Uses of past forms in the social pretend play of Italian children. *Journal of Child Language* 20: 619–639.

Nagata, H. 1987. The relativity of linguistic intuition: the effect of repetition on grammaticality judgments. *Journal of Psycholinguistics research* 17: 1–17.

Newport, E. 1990. Maturational Constraints on Language Learning. *Cognitive Science* 14: 11–28.

Newport, E., Gleitman, H., and L. Gleitman. 1977. Mother, I'd rather do it myself: Some effects and non-effects of maternal speech style. In *Talking to Children: Language Input and Acquisition*, edited by C. Snow and C. A. Ferguson. Cambridge: Cambridge University Press.

Nishida, C. 1994. The Spanish reflexive clitic se as an aspectual class marker. *Linguistics* 32: 425–458.

Ocampo, F. 1990. El subjuntivo en tres generaciones de hablantes bilingües. In *Spanish in the United States: Sociolinguistic Issues*, edited by J. Bergen. Washington, DC: Georgetown University Press.

Ochs, E. 1979. Planned and unplanned discourse. In *Syntax and Semantics, Vol 12: Discourse and Semantics*, edited by T. Givón. New York: Academic Press.

Olsen, M. 1997. *A Semantic and Pragmatic Model of Lexical and Grammatical Aspect*. New York: Garland Publishing.

Ozete, O. 1988. Focusing on the preterit and imperfect. *Hispania* 71: 687–691.

Paradis, M. 1994. Neurolinguistic aspects of implicit and explicit memory: implications for bilingualism and SLA. In *Implicit and Explicit Learning of Languages*, edited by N. Ellis. London: Academic Press.

Patkowski, M. 1990. Age and accent in a second language: a reply to James Emil Flege. *Applied Linguistics* 11: 73–89.

Perdue, C., and W. Klein. 1992. Why does the production of some learners not grammaticalize? *Studies in Second Language Acquisition* 14: 259–272.

Pienemann, M. 1985. Learnability and syllabus construction. In *Modelling and Assessing Second Language Acquisition*, edited by K. Hyltenstam and M. Pienemann. Clevedon, England: College Hill Press.

Pienemann, M. 1986. Psychological constraints on the teachability of languages. In *First and Second Language Acquisition Processes*, edited by C. W. Pfaff. Rowley, MA: Newbury House.

Pienemann, M. 1988. Constructing an acquisition-based procedure for second language assessment. *Studies in Second Language Acquisition* 10: 217–243.

Pienemann, M. 1989. Is language teachable? psycholinguistic experiments and hypotheses. *Applied Linguistics* 10: 52–79.

Pienemann, M, M. Johnston, and J. Meisel. 1993. The Multidimensional Model, linguistic profiling, and related issues. *Studies in Second Language Acquisition* 15: 495–503.

Pinker, S. 1991. Rules of Language. *Science* 253: 530–535.

Ramsay, V. 1989. On the debate over the acquisition of aspect before tense: setting the record straight. Paper read at Annual Conference of the AAAL 1989, at Washington, DC.

Ramsay, V. 1990. Developmental stages in the acquisition of the perfective and the imperfective aspects by classroom L2 learners of Spanish. Unpublished PhD dissertation, University of Oregon.

Reichenbach, H. 1947. *Elements of Symbolic Logic.* New York: The MacMillan Company.

Reid, W. 1980. Meaning and narrative structure. *Columbia University Working Papers in Linguistics* 5: 12–20.

Reinhart, T. 1984. Principles of Gestalt perception in the temporal organization of narrative texts. *Linguistics* 22: 779–809.

Rispoli, M. 1990. Lexical assignability and perspective switch: the acquisition of verb subcategorization for aspectual inflections. *Journal of Child Language* 17: 375–392.

Rispoli, M., and L. Bloom. 1985. Incomplete and continuing: theoretical issues in the acquisition of tense and aspect. *Journal of Child Language* 12: 471–474.

Robison, R. 1990. The primacy of aspect: aspectual marking in English interlanguage. *Studies in Second Language Acquisition* 12:315–330.

Robison, R. 1995. The aspect hypothesis revisited: a cross sectional study of tense and aspect marking in interlanguage. *Applied Linguistics* 16:344–371.

Rohde, A. 1996. The aspect hypothesis and the emergence of tense distinctions in naturalistic L2 acquisition. *Linguistics* 34:1115–1137.

Rutherford, W. 1987. *Second Language Grammar: Learning and Teaching.* London: Longman.

Salaberry, R. 1998. The development of aspectual distinctions in classroom L2 French. *Canadian Modern Language Review* 54 (4):504–542.

Salaberry, R. 1999. The use of Spanish past tense morphology in narratives based on fictional and personal stories. Paper read at 19th meeting of SLRF, at Minneapolis, MN.

Salaberry, R. 2000. The acquisition of English Past tense in an instructional setting: irregular and frequent morphology. *System* 28:1–18.

Salaberry, R., and N. López-Ortega. 1998. Accurate L2 production across language tasks: focus on form, focus on meaning and communicative control. *Modern Language Journal* 82:114–157.

Salaberry, R., and Y. Shirai. forthcoming. *Tense-aspect Morphology in L2 acquisition.* Amsterdam: John Benjamins.

Sankoff, G. 1990. The grammaticalization of tense and aspect in Tok Pisin and Sranan. *Language Variation and Change* 2:295–312.

Sato, C. 1988. Origins of complex syntax in interlanguage development. *Studies in Second Language Acquisition* 10:371–395.

Sato, C. 1990. *The syntax of Conversation in Interlanguage Development.* Tübingen: Gunter Narr Verlag.

Schmidt, R. 1990. The role of consciousness in Second Language Learning. *Applied Linguistics* 11 (2):129–158.

Schmidt, R. 1995. Consciousness and foreign language learning: a tutorial on the role of attention and awareness in learning. In *Attention and Awareness in Foreign Language Learning*, edited by R. Schmidt. Manoa, HI: University of Hawai'i.

Schmidt, R., and S. Frota. 1986. Developing basic conversational ability in a second language: a case study of an adult learner of Portuguese. In *Talking to Learn: conversation in Second Language Acquisition*, edited by R. Day. Rowley, MA: Newbury House.

Schumann, J. 1987. The expression of temporality in basilang speech. *Studies in Second Language Acquisition* 9:21–41.

Schwartz, B. 1986. The epistemological status of second language acquisition. *Second Language Research* 2:120–159.

Schwartz, B. 1993. On explicit and negative data effecting and affecting competence and linguistic behavior. *Studies in Second Language Acquisition* 15:147–163.

Sebastian, E., and D. Slobin. 1994. Development of linguisitc forms: Spanish. In *Relating Events in Narrative*, edited by R. Berman and D. Slobin. Hillsdale, NJ: Laurence Erlbaum.

Sharwood-Smith, M. 1993. Input enhancement in instructed SLA: Theoretical bases. *Studies in Second Language Acquisition* 15:165–179.

Shirai, Y. 1991. Primacy of aspect in language acquisition: Simplified input and prototype. Unpublished PhD Dissertation, UCLA, Los Angeles.

Shirai, Y. 1994. On the overgeneralization of progressive marking on stative verbs: bioprogram or input? *First Language* 14:67–82.

Shirai, Y. 1995. Tense-aspect marking by L2 learners of Japanese. Unpublished Manuscript, Daito Bunka University.

Shirai, Y., and R. Andersen. 1995. The acquisition of tense-aspect morphology: a prototype account. *Language* 71 (4):743–762.

Shirai, Y., and A. Kurono. 1998. The acquisition of tense-aspect marking in Japanese as a second language. *Language Learning* 48 (2):245–279.

Silva-Corvalán, C. 1983. Tense and aspect in oral Spanish narrative: context and meaning. *Language* 59:760–80.

Silva-Corvalán, C. 1986. A speech event analysis of tense and aspect in Spanish. In papers from the XII LSRL, edited by P. Baldi. Amsterdam: John Benjamins.

Simões, M., and C. Stoel-Gammon. 1979. The acquisition of inflections in Portuguese: a study of the development of person markers on verbs. *Journal of Child Language* 6:53–67.

Sinclair, A., R. Jarvella, and W. Levelt. 1978. *The Child's Conception of Language*. Berlin: Springer-Verlag.

Skehan, P. 1989. *Individual Differences in Second-Language Learning*. London: Edward Arnold.

Skehan, P. 1998. *A Cognitive Approach to Language Learning*. Oxford: Oxford University Press.

Slabakova, R. 1997. The L2 acquisition of telicity in English: a parametric approach. Paper read at SLRF 97, at Michigan State University, East Lansing, MI.

Slabakova, R. 1999. The parameter of aspect in second language acquisition. *Second Language Research* 3:283–317.

Slabakova, R., and S. Montrul. forthcoming. Aspectual tenses in Spanish L2 acquisition: A UG perspective. In *Tense-Aspect Morphology in L2 acquisition*, edited by R. Salaberry and Y. Shirai. Philadelphia: John Benjamins.

Smith, C. 1983. A theory of aspectual choice. *Language* 59:479–501.

Smith, C. 1991. *The Parameter of Aspect*. Dordrecht: Kluwer Academic Press.

Smith, C., and R. Weist. 1987. On the temporal contour of child language: A reply to Rispoli & Bloom. *Journal of Child Language* 14:387–392.

Stephany, U. 1981. Verbal grammar in modern Greek early child language. In *Child Language: an International Perspective*, edited by P. Dale and D. Ingram. Baltimore: University Park Press.

Stokes, J. 1985. Effect of student monitoring of verb inflection in Spanish. *Modern Language Journal* 69:377–384.

Studerus, L. 1989. On the role of Spanish meaning changing preterites. *Hispanic Linguisitcs* 3:131–145.

Stutterheim, C. von, and W. Klein. 1987. A concept-oriented approach to second language studies. In *First and Second Language Acquisition Processes*, edited by C. Pfaff. Cambridge, MA: Newbury House.

Suñer, M. 1990. Impersonal se passives and the licensing of empty categories. *Probus* 2:209–233.

Swain, M. 1985. Communicative Competence: some roles of comprehensible input and comprehensible output in its development. In *Input in Second Language Acquisition*, edited by S. Gass and C. Madden. Rowley, Mass.: Newbury House.

Swain, M. 1992. Manipulating and complementing content teaching to maximize learning. In *Foreign/Second Language Pedagogy Research*, edited by E. Kellerman, R. Phillipson, L. Selinker and M. Sharwood-Smith. Clevedon: Multilingual Press.

Swain, M., and S. Lapkin. 1995. Problems in output and the cognitive processes they generate: a step towards second language learning. *Applied Linguistics* 16 (3):371–391.

Tarone, E. 1983. On the variability of interlanguage systems. *Applied Linguistics* 4:142–163.

Tarone, E. 1988. *Variation in Interlanguage*. London: Edward Arnold.

Tarone, E. 1995. A variationist framework for SLA research: examples and pedagogical insights. In *Second language acquisition theory and pedagogy*, edited by F. Eckman, D. Highland, P. Lee, J. Mileham and R. Rutkowski. Mahwah, NJ: Laurence Erlbaum.

Taylor, R. 1989. *Linguistic Categorization: Prototypes in Linguistic Theory*. Oxford: Oxford University Press.

Tenny, C. 1994. *Aspectual Roles and the Syntax-Semantics Interface*. Dordrecht: Kluwer Academic Press.

ter Meulen, A. 1995. *Representing Time in Natural Language: the Dynamic Interpretation of Tense and Aspect*. Cambridge, MA: MIT Press.

Terrell, T., M. Rogers, B. Barnes, and M. Wolff-Hessini. 1993. *Deux Mondes, Second Edition.* New York: McGraw Hill.

Teutsch-Dwyer, M., and A. Fathman. 1997. Temporal reference in tutored and untutored learner varieties. Paper read at Annual Meeting of AAAL 97, at Orlando, FL.

Towell, Richard, and Roger Hawkins. 1994. *Approaches to Second Language Acquisition.* Clevedon: Multilingual Press.

Trévise, A. 1987. Toward an analysis of the (inter)language activity of referring to time in narratives. In *First and Second Language Acquisition Processes*, edited by C. Pfaff. Cambridge, MA: Newbury House.

van Lier, L. 1996. *Interaction in the Language Curriculum: Awareness, Autonomy and Authenticity.* New York: Longman.

Vendler, Z. 1967. *Linguistics in Philosophy.* Ithaca, NY: Cornell University Press.

Verkuyl, H. 1993. *A Theory of Aspectuality: the Interaction between Temporal and Atemporal Structure.* Cambridge: Cambridge University Press.

Véronique, D. 1987. Reference to past events and actions in narratives in L2: insights from North African workers' French. In *First and Second Language Acquisition Processes*, edited by C. Pfaff. Cambridge, MA: Newbury House.

Vet, C., and C. Vetters. 1994. *Tense and Aspect in Discourse.* Berlin: Mouton de Gruyter.

Villamil, B. 1985. Desarrollo de las categorías tempo-aspectuales en niños puertorriqueños entre las edades de 1,0 a 3,2 años. Unpublished Master's Thesis, Universidad de Puerto Rico.

Wallace, S. 1982. Figure and ground: the interrelationships of linguistic categories. In *Tense-Aspect: Between Syntax and Pragmatics*, edited by P. Hopper. Philadelphia: John Benjamins.

Weist, R. 1989. Time concepts in language and thought: filling the Piagetian void from two to five years. In *Time and Human Cognition: a Life Span Perspective*, edited by I. Levin and D. Zakay. Amsterdam: Elsevier.

Weist, R., H. Wysocka, and P. Lyytinen. 1991. A cross-linguistic perspective on the development of temporal systems. *Journal of Child Language* 18:67–92.

Weist, R., H. Wysocka, K. Witkowska-Stadnik, E. Buczowska, and E. Konieczna. 1984. The defective tense hypothesis: On the emergence of tense and aspect in child Polish. *Journal of Child Language* 11:347–374.

Weist, R. 1983. Prefix versus suffix information processing in the comprehension of tense and aspect. *Journal of Child Language* 10:85–96.

Westfall, R., and S. Foerster. 1996. Beyond aspect: new strategies for teaching the preterite and the imperfect. *Hispania* 79:550–560.

White, Lydia. 1989. *Universal Grammar and Second Language Acquisition.* Philadelphia: John Benjamins.

Wiberg, E. 1996. Reference to past events in bilingual Italian-Swedish children of school age. *Linguistics* 34:1087–1114.

Wolfram, W. 1985. Variability in tense marking: a case for the obvious. *Language Learning* 35 (2):229–253.

Youseff, V. 1988. The language bioprogram hypothesis revisited. *Journal of Child Language* 15:451–458.

Youseff, V. 1990. On the confirmation of bioprograms. *Journal of Child Language* 17:233–235.

Zagona, K. 1994. Compositionality of aspect: evidence from Spanish aspectual se. In *Aspects of Romance Linguistics: Selected papers from the Linguistic Symposium on Romance Languages XXIV*, edited by C. Parodi, C. Quicoli, M. Saltarelli and M. Zubizarreta. Washington, DC: Georgetown University Press.

Zalewski, J. 1993. Number/person errors in an information-processing perspective: implications for form-focused instruction. *TESOL Quarterly* 27:691–703.

Zayas-Bazán, E., S. Bacon, and José Fernández. 1997. *¡Arriba!: Comunicación y Cultura*. Upper Saddle River, NJ: Prentice Hall.

Name Index

Subject Index

In the series STUDIES IN BILINGUALISM (SiBil) ISSN 0298-1533 the following titles have been published thus far or are scheduled for publication:

1. FASE, Willem, Koen JASPAERT and Sjaak KROON (eds): *Maintenance and Loss of Minority Languages.* 1992.
2. BOT, Kees de, Ralph B. GINSBERG and Claire KRAMSCH (eds): *Foreign Language Research in Cross-Cultural Perspective.* 1991.
3. DÖPKE, Susanne: *One Parent - One Language. An interactional approach.* 1992.
4. PAULSTON, Christina Bratt: *Linguistic Minorities in Multilingual Settings. Implications for language policies.*1994.
5. KLEIN, Wolfgang and Clive PERDUE: *Utterance Structure. Developing grammars again.*
6. SCHREUDER, Robert and Bert WELTENS (eds): *The Bilingual Lexicon.* 1993.
7. DIETRICH, Rainer, Wolfgang KLEIN and Colette NOYAU: *The Acquisition of Temporality in a Second Language.* 1995.
8. DAVIS, Kathryn Anne: *Language Planning in Multilingual Contexts. Policies, communities, and schools in Luxembourg.* Amsterdam/Philadelphia, 1994.
9. FREED, Barbara F. (ed.) *Second Language Acquisition in a Study Abroad Context.* 1995.
10. BAYLEY, Robert and Dennis R. PRESTON (eds): *Second Language Acquisition and Linguistic Variation.* 1996.
11. BECKER, Angelika and Mary CARROLL: *The Acquisition of Spatial Relations in a Second Language.* 1997.
12. HALMARI, Helena: *Government and Codeswitching. Explaining American Finnish.* 1997.
13. HOLLOWAY, Charles E.: *Dialect Death. The case of Brule Spanish.* 1997.
14. YOUNG, Richard and Agnes WEIYUN HE (eds): *Talking and Testing. Discourse approaches to the assessment of oral proficiency.* 1998.
15. PIENEMANN, Manfred: *Language Processing and Second Language Development. Processability theory.* 1998.
16. HUEBNER, Thom and Kathryn A. DAVIS (eds.): *Sociopolitical Perspectives on Language Policy and Planning in the USA.* 1999.
17. ELLIS, Rod: *Learning a Second Language through Interaction.* 1999.
18. PARADIS, Michel: *Neurolinguistic Aspects of Bilingualism.* n.y.p.
19. AMARA, Muhammad Hasan: *Politics and Sociolinguistic Reflexes. Palestinian border villages.* 1999.
20. POULISSE, Nanda: *Slips of the Tongue. Speech errors in first and second language production.* 1999
21. DÖPKE, Susanne (ed.): *Cross-Linguistic Structures in Simultaneous Bilingualism.* 2000
22. SALABERRY, M. Rafael: *The Development of Past Tense Morphology in L2 Spanish.* 2000.